Central Course

These are the different types of pages and symbols used in this book:

Coining it!

This indicates the first page of a mathematical section.

These pages develop mathematical skills, concepts and facts in a wide variety of realistic contexts.

Extended contexts require the use of skills from several different areas of mathematics in a section of work based on a single theme.

39   Detour: Tangram

Detours provide self-contained activities which often require an exploratory, investigative approach, drawing on problem-solving skills.

Reasoning and application pages contain a variety of problems set in different contexts which require the application of knowledge, skills and strategies previously learned.

▶ **Do Worksheet I**

This shows when you need to use a Worksheet.

● **Remember**

This is a reminder of the key information essential for the work of the pages.

▼ **Challenge**

Challenges are more demanding activities designed to stimulate further thought and discussion.

■ **Investigation**

Investigations enhance the work of the page by providing additional opportunities to develop problem-solving skills.

Heinemann

Contents

Toni is head gardener at Kieran House. In the Autumn she spreads compost on the flower beds in the formal garden. She has to know the area and perimeter of each bed.

The square

Perimeter = $s + s + s + s$

$P = 4s$

Area = $s \times s$

$A = s^2$

The rectangle

Perimeter = $l + b + l + b$

$P = 2l + 2b$

Area = $l \times b$

$A = lb$

The triangle

Perimeter = $a + b + c$

$P = a + b + c$

Area = $\frac{1}{2} \times b \times h$

$A = \frac{1}{2}bh$

1 Find the perimeter and area of each flower bed.

(a)
9 m
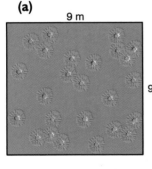
9 m

(b)
6 m
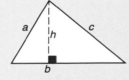
2 m

(d)
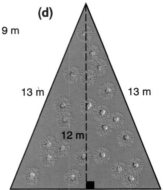
13 m   13 m
12 m
10 m

(c)
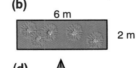
3 m   5 m
4 m

The same markings mean that the sides are of equal length.

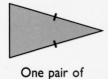

One pair of equal sides.

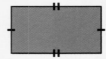

Two pairs of equal sides.

2 Toni is putting a fence around each flower bed. Find the perimeter of each bed.

(a)
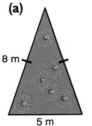
8 m
5 m

(b)
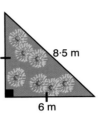
8·5 m
6 m

(c)
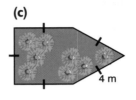
4 m

(d)
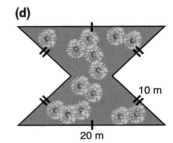
10 m
20 m

3 Toni is making three lawns using different qualities of turf. For each rectangular lawn calculate:

(a) the area   **(b)** the cost of turfing it.

Type of turf	Meadow grass	Rye grass	Lesser timothy
Length of lawn	5 m	3 m	2·8 m
Breadth of lawn	5 m	3·5 m	1·2 m
Price per m²	£1·40	£1·60	£1·75

▼ Challenge

4 (a) A square lawn has area 64 m². What is the perimeter of the lawn?

(b) A rectangular lawn has area 36 m². Find three possible values for its perimeter.

Toni's assistant, Pat, has sketched two of the
flower beds in the garden.

● **Remember**

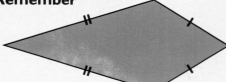

This shape is a kite.
A kite has two pairs of equal sides.

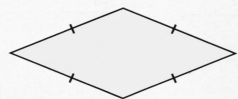

This shape is a rhombus.
A rhombus has four equal sides.

1 (a) Draw this kite on 1 cm squared paper.

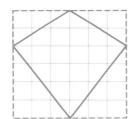

(b) Divide the kite into two triangles and calculate
the area of each.
(c) What is the area of the kite?
(d) Draw the surrounding rectangle for the kite and
calculate its area.
(e) Copy and complete:
The area of the kite is ☐ that of the
surrounding rectangle.

2 Repeat question 1 for this rhombus.

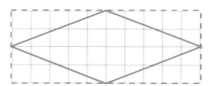

For a **kite** or **rhombus**

Area $= \frac{1}{2} \times l \times b$

$A = \frac{1}{2}lb$

3 Find the area of each flower bed.

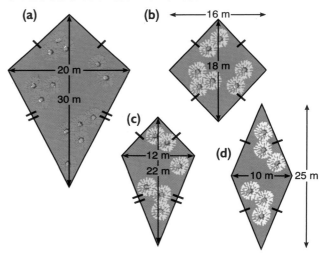

(a) 20 m 30 m

(b) 16 m 18 m

(c) 12 m 22 m

(d) 10 m 25 m

4 Calculate the perimeter of each rose bed.

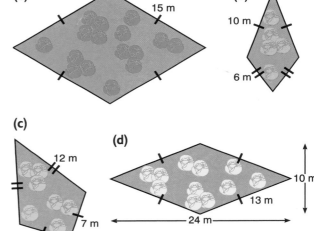

(a) 15 m

(b) 10 m 6 m

(c) 12 m 7 m

(d) 10 m 13 m 24 m

The Walled Garden

Toni is using the winter months to plan next year's fruit and vegetables in the Walled Garden.

She has sketched this strawberry patch.
It is in the shape of a parallelogram.

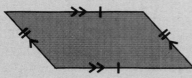

A parallelogram has opposite sides equal and parallel.

You need scissors.

1 (a) Draw this parallelogram on 1 cm squared paper.

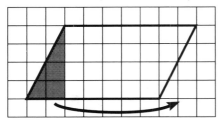

(b) Draw a vertical line as shown and shade in the triangle.
(c) Cut out the triangle and place it on the other side of the parallelogram.
(d) Find the area of the rectangle.

For a **parallelogram**

Area = $b \times h$

$A = bh$

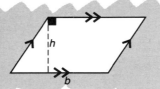

2 Find the area of each strawberry patch.

(a) 3 m, 4 m

(b) 12 m, 16 m

(c) 6 m, 5 m

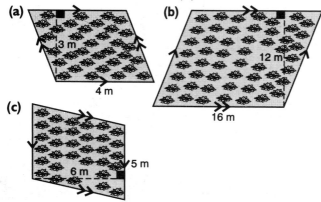

3 Find the perimeter of each vegetable plot.

(a) 3 m, 5 m

(b) 7 m, 4·5 m

(c) 12 m, 15 m

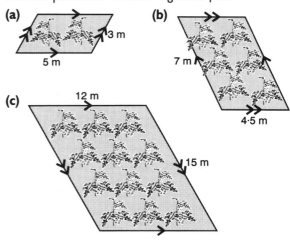

4 Find the area and perimeter of the onion bed.

8 m, 11 m, 14 m

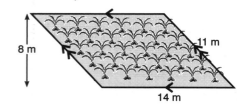

5 From the diagram:
• name two parallelograms
• find the area and perimeter of each.

A, B, C, 10 m, F, E, 12 m, D, 8 m, 20 m

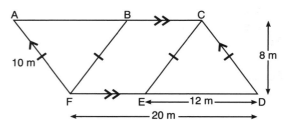

Pat has sketched this cabbage patch.
This shape is a trapezium.
A trapezium has two parallel sides.

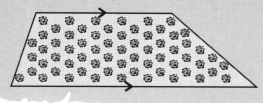

1 (a) On 1 cm squared paper draw this trapezium.

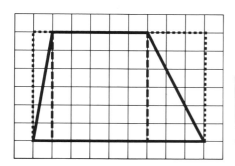

(b) Draw its surrounding rectangle in red and find its area.
(c) Draw its internal rectangle in blue and find its area.
(d) Find the average of the two areas.
(e) Draw the trapezium again.
    Divide it into a rectangle and two triangles.
    Calculate the area of each and add them to find
    the area of the trapezium.
(f) What do you notice?

2 Repeat question 1 for another trapezium.

The area of a **trapezium** is the **average** of the
areas of the internal and surrounding rectangles.

$$A = \tfrac{1}{2}h(a + b)$$

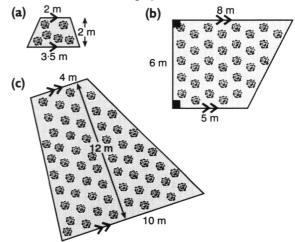

3 Use the internal and surrounding rectangles to find
the area of each cabbage patch.

(a) 2 m, 2 m, 3·5 m

(b) 8 m, 6 m, 5 m

(c) 4 m, 12 m, 10 m

4 Find the perimeter of each herb garden.

(a) 1·6 m, 1·8 m, 0·9 m, 1·5 m

(b) 3·2 m, 4 m, 2·9 m, 3·4 m

(c) 2·1 m, 1·9 m, 1·6 m

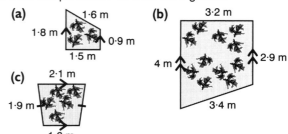

The Old Orchard

In the Spring, Toni needs to apply organic fertiliser to the flower beds in the Old Orchard.

She has to find the area of this flower bed.

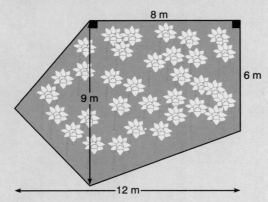

She sketched it and divided it into rectangles and triangles, marking the distances on each.

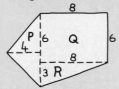

I (a) Find the area of each shape.

(b) What is the total area of the flower bed?

2 Calculate the area of grass in each lawn.

(a)

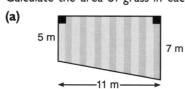

(b)

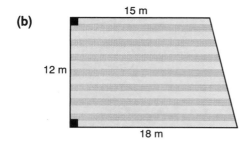

3 Calculate the area of each:
- flower bed
- lawn.

(a)

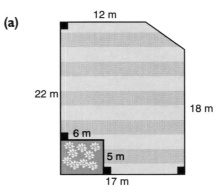

(b)

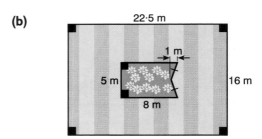

4 Toni is planting low hedges to make this star-shaped flower bed.

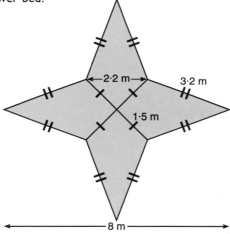

(a) What total length of hedge must she plant?
(b) What is the total area of the bed?
(c) How much fertiliser is used if she puts on 100 g per square metre?

I Name each quadrilateral.

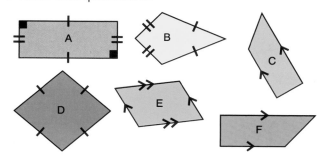

2 For each of the following shapes:
 • plot the points on a coordinate diagram
 • join the points
 • calculate the perimeter
 • calculate the area.

(a) Shape J ($^-$4,2), ($^-$7,2), ($^-$7, 7), ($^-$4,7)
(b) Shape K ($^-$8,$^-$1), ($^-$8,$^-$5), (1,$^-$5), (1,$^-$1)
(c) Shape L (4,$^-$1), (4,$^-$5), (8,$^-$5), (8,$^-$1)

3 Find the area of each shape.

(a) Shape P ($^-$5,2), ($^-$3,6), (3,6), (1,2)
(b) Shape Q ($^-$5,$^-$2), ($^-$3,0), (2,$^-$2), ($^-$3,$^-$4)
(c) Shape R (6,1), (8,5), (6,9), (4,5)
(d) Shape S (1,$^-$3), (7,$^-$2), (7,$^-$5), (1,$^-$8)

4 For each set of coordinates:
 • join the points in order
 • find the perimeter
 • find the area.

(a) Shape G (2,0), (4,0), (4,1), (6,1), (6,3), (2,3)
(b) Shape H ($^-$1,4), (7,4), (7,8), (5,8), (5,6), (2,6), (2,8), ($^-$1,8)

5 Find the area of each shape.

(a) Shape M ($^-$4,2), ($^-$6,4), ($^-$4,6), ($^-$2,5), (0,5), (0,3), ($^-$2,3)
(b) Shape N (4,0), (2,1), (4,3), (3,6), (4,8), (5,6), (4,3), (6,1)

6 The points (2,5) and (8,1) are opposite corners of a rectangle.

(a) Find the coordinates of the remaining corners.
(b) What is the area of the rectangle?

▼ Challenge

7 The points (1,$^-$4) and ($^-$5,5) are opposite corners of a parallelogram. Its area is 42 square units. Find the coordinates of the remaining corners.

Paper trail

Jenny has a local paper round.

I wonder if it's possible to deliver papers to all the houses without having to go along any street twice.

Jenny drew a **network** of her newspaper round to help her.

A network has **nodes** (numbered 1, 2, 3, 4, 5) joined by **arcs** (a, b, c, d, e, f, g).

A network is **traversable** if it can be drawn without lifting your pencil from the paper and without going over any arc more than once.

You can pass through a node as often as you want.

1 (a) Is Jenny's network traversable?
   (b) Can she deliver papers to the houses shown on her map without going along any street twice?

2 Jenny is given another house to deliver to.

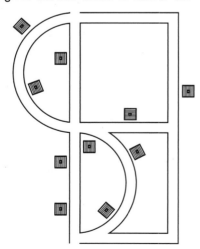

   (a) Draw a new network of her round.
   (b) Is this network traversable?
   (c) Can she deliver to all the houses on this route without going along any road twice?

3 Here are some other networks.

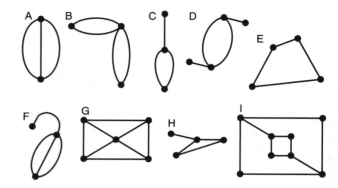

   (a) Copy this table. Complete the Traversable column.

Network	Traversable (Yes/No)	Number of odd nodes	Number of even nodes
A			
B			
C			

   (b) Draw some networks of your own, decide if they are traversable and add them to your table.

An **even node** has an even number of arcs meeting at it.

4 arcs
Even node

An **odd node** has an odd number of arcs meeting at it.

3 arcs
Odd node

4 (a) Complete the last two columns of your table.
   (b) In the eighteenth century Leonhard Euler, a Swiss mathematician, claimed that a network is traversable if it has 0 or 2 odd nodes. Do you agree? Explain.
   (c) Use Euler's rule to decide if networks P, Q and R are traversable. Draw those which are, without lifting your pencil from the paper and without going over any arc twice.

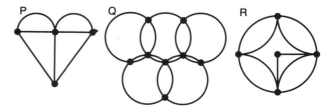

High Jump

Competitor	Best jump
Scott	1 m 17 cm
Bruce	1 m 31 cm
Fergus	1 m 10 cm
Dougal	0 m 98 cm
Angus	1 m 7 cm
Hugh	1 m 3 cm

Throwing the Hammer

Competitor	Best distance
Scott	9 m 97 cm
Hugh	10 m 9 cm
Walter	9 m 98 cm
Blair	9 m 90 cm
Callum	10 m 10 cm
Hamish	9 m 9 cm
Torquil	10 m 0 cm
Lorne	9 m 99 cm

Long Jump

Competitor	Best jump
Angus	3 m 45 cm
Pat	2 m 90 cm
Hugh	3 m 8 cm
Willie	3 m 4 cm
Scott	3 m 27 cm
Fergus	3 m 40 cm

Throwing the Weight

Competitor	Best height
Willie	3 m 35 cm
Ian	2 m 99 cm
Duncan	3 m 8 cm
Colin	2 m 90 cm
Jamie	2 m 89 cm
Corrin	3 m 3 cm
Stewart	3 m 4 cm

1 Look at the results of the high jump competition. Hugh cleared 1 metre and 3 centimetres. This is written as 1·03 metres.
   (a) Write the heights of the other jumps in metres.
   (b) Write the names of the competitors in order, starting with the highest jump.
   (c) Find the difference in height between the highest and lowest jumps.
   (d) Find the average height jumped in the competition in metres and centimetres.

2 Look at the results of the long jump competition.
   (a) Write the length of each jump in metres.
   (b) Write the names of the competitors in order, starting with the longest jump.
   (c) Find the difference in length between the longest and shortest jumps.
   (d) Find the average length jumped in the competition in metres and centimetres.

3 Look at the results of the hammer throwing competition.
   (a) Write the distances of the throws in metres.
   (b) Write the names of the competitors in order, starting with the longest throw.
   (c) Find the difference in distance between the longest and shortest throws.
   (d) Find the average distance thrown in the competition in metres and centimetres.

4 Look at the results of the throwing the weight competition.
   (a) Write the heights of the throws in metres.
   (b) Write the names of the competitors in order, starting with the highest throw.
   (c) Find the difference in height between the highest and lowest throws.
   (d) Find the average height reached in the competition in metres and centimetres.

Inverearn Games

I These are the results of the 100 metres sprint.

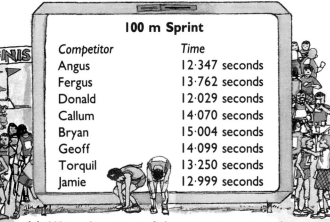

100 m Sprint

Competitor	Time
Angus	12·347 seconds
Fergus	13·762 seconds
Donald	12·029 seconds
Callum	14·070 seconds
Bryan	15·004 seconds
Geoff	14·099 seconds
Torquil	13·250 seconds
Jamie	12·999 seconds

(a) Write the names of the competitors in order, starting with the fastest time.

(b) Find the difference between the fastest and the slowest times.

(c) Find the average time taken to run the 100 metres sprint.

2 These are the results of the 500 m cycle race.

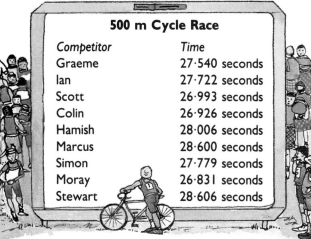

500 m Cycle Race

Competitor	Time
Graeme	27·540 seconds
Ian	27·722 seconds
Scott	26·993 seconds
Colin	26·926 seconds
Hamish	28·006 seconds
Marcus	28·600 seconds
Simon	27·779 seconds
Moray	26·831 seconds
Stewart	28·606 seconds

(a) Write the names of the competitors in order, starting with the fastest time.

(b) Find the difference between the winning time and the slowest time.

(c) Find the average time taken to complete the cycle race.

3 Billy cycles one lap of the 400 metre track in an average time of 23·707 seconds. How long should it take him to cycle:

(a) 15 laps   (b) 19 laps
(c) 4000 metres   (d) 1 km?

At the cake and candy stall Jenny sells home-made sweets. Her trays of toffee each contain ten pieces.
In this tray there are 4 pieces.

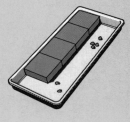

There is $\frac{4}{10}$ of a tray left.

There is 0·4 of a tray left.

$0·4 = \frac{4}{10}$

4 For each tray of toffee, write the amount left:
• as a fraction   • as a decimal fraction
(a)   (b)

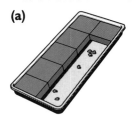   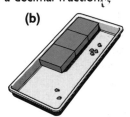

5 When she sells one whole tray of fudge, Jenny makes £6. How much will she make if she sells:

(a) 3 trays   (b) 7 trays   (c) 1·5 trays
(d) 4·4 trays   (e) 2·7 trays   (f) 6·1 trays?

6 How much will Jenny make if she sells:

(a) 0·1 of a tray   (b) 0·5 of a tray
(c) 0·7 of a tray   (d) 0·3 of a tray
(e) 0·9 of a tray   (f) 0·6 of a tray?

7 Copy and complete:
Multiplying £6 by a number greater than one gives an answer ⬚ than £6.
Multiplying £6 by a number less than one gives an answer ⬚ than £6.

• Multiplying by a number greater than one has an increasing effect.
• Multiplying by a number less than one has a decreasing effect.

■ Investigation

8 Investigate the effects of dividing by numbers greater than one and less than one.

Ross, the owner of F. R. Action Ltd, has bought an old cottage which requires renovation.

1 (a) Frank, the plumber, replaces two sections of downpipe. One section is $1\frac{1}{4}$ metres long and the other is $2\frac{1}{2}$ metres long. How much is this altogether?

(b) He bought a length of pipe 4 metres long. How much pipe was left?

2 Find: **(a)** $3\frac{1}{4} + 1\frac{1}{2}$ **(b)** $5\frac{3}{4} + 2\frac{1}{2}$ **(c)** $4\frac{3}{4} + 3\frac{1}{4}$
(d) $4\frac{3}{4} - 1\frac{1}{2}$ **(e)** $3\frac{1}{2} - 3\frac{1}{4}$ **(f)** $2\frac{3}{4} - 1\frac{1}{4}$

Frank has a length of downpipe $3\frac{1}{4}$ m long. He cuts a length $\frac{1}{2}$ m long. How much pipe is left?

$$3\frac{1}{4} - \frac{1}{2}$$

$$= 3\frac{1}{4} - \frac{2}{4} \quad \left[\frac{1}{2} = \frac{2}{4}\right]$$

$$= 2\frac{5}{4} - \frac{2}{4} \quad \left[\begin{array}{l} 3\frac{1}{4} = 2 + 1\frac{1}{4} \\ \quad = 2 + \frac{5}{4} \\ \quad = 2\frac{5}{4} \end{array}\right]$$

$$= 2\frac{3}{4}$$

Frank has $2\frac{3}{4}$ **m** of pipe left.

To add or subtract fractions, the denominators must be the same.

3 The guttering around the roof is badly corroded. Find the length of guttering left if Frank:

(a) cuts a piece $\frac{1}{2}$ m long from a $2\frac{1}{4}$ m length
(b) cuts a piece $\frac{3}{4}$ m long from a $2\frac{1}{2}$ m length
(c) cuts a piece $\frac{3}{4}$ m long from a $1\frac{1}{4}$ m length.

4 Find: **(a)** $4\frac{1}{4} - \frac{1}{2}$ **(b)** $5\frac{1}{4} - \frac{3}{4}$ **(c)** $2\frac{1}{2} - \frac{3}{4}$

Joyce, the joiner, has two pieces of wood. One is $2\frac{3}{8}$ m long and the other is $3\frac{3}{4}$ m long. What length of wood does she have altogether?

$$2\frac{3}{8} + 3\frac{3}{4}$$

$$= 5\frac{3}{8} + \frac{3}{4}$$

$$= 5\frac{3}{8} + \frac{6}{8} \quad \left[\frac{3}{4} = \frac{6}{8}\right]$$

$$= 5\frac{9}{8}$$

$$= 6\frac{1}{8} \quad \left[5 \text{ and } 1\frac{1}{8} = 6\frac{1}{8}\right]$$

The total length of wood is $6\frac{1}{8}$ **metres.**

5 Joyce has two pieces of moulding. One is $1\frac{5}{8}$ m long and the other is $3\frac{1}{4}$ m long. What length of moulding does she have altogether?

6 Two sections of fencing measure $4\frac{3}{8}$ m long and $6\frac{1}{2}$ m long. What is the total length of the sections?

7 Find: **(a)** $2\frac{1}{4} + 3\frac{3}{8}$ **(b)** $1\frac{1}{2} + 4\frac{1}{8}$ **(c)** $7\frac{1}{8} + 4\frac{3}{4}$

8 For the garage roof, Joyce uses two pieces of felt. One is $3\frac{5}{8}$ m long, the other is $4\frac{1}{2}$ m long. What length of felt does she use altogether?

9 Two pieces of facia board measure $3\frac{3}{4}$ m long and $2\frac{7}{8}$ m long. Find the total length of the facia board.

10 Find: **(a)** $3\frac{7}{8} + \frac{3}{8}$ **(b)** $1\frac{3}{8} + 2\frac{5}{8}$ **(c)** $2\frac{3}{8} + 5\frac{3}{4}$
(d) $1\frac{1}{4} + 4\frac{7}{8}$ **(e)** $2\frac{3}{4} + 6\frac{5}{8}$ **(f)** $4\frac{3}{4} + 3\frac{7}{8}$

F. R. Action Ltd

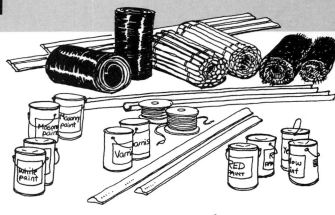

Jackie has two tins of white paint. In one tin there is $1\frac{2}{5}$ litres and the other contains $2\frac{5}{6}$ litres. How much white paint does she have altogether?

$1\frac{2}{5} + 2\frac{5}{6}$

$= 3\frac{2}{5} + \frac{5}{6}$

$= 3\frac{12}{30} + \frac{25}{30}$

$= 3\frac{37}{30}$

$= 4\frac{7}{30}$

$\frac{2}{5} \xrightarrow{\times 6} \frac{12}{30}$ $\frac{5}{6} \xrightarrow{\times 5} \frac{25}{30}$

$\frac{37}{30} = 1\frac{7}{30}$

Jackie has **$4\frac{7}{30}$ litres** of white paint.

1 How much red paint does Jackie have if she has two tins containing $2\frac{1}{6}$ litres and $3\frac{3}{5}$ litres?

2 There are two tins of varnish containing $2\frac{2}{3}$ litres and $3\frac{1}{12}$ litres. How much varnish is there altogether?

3 Two lengths of roofing felt measure $7\frac{4}{9}$ metres and $4\frac{5}{6}$ metres. What is the total length of roofing felt?

4 Find:
(a) $2\frac{5}{6} + 3\frac{2}{3}$ (b) $4\frac{2}{5} + 8\frac{3}{10}$ (c) $6\frac{1}{6} + 4\frac{5}{12}$
(d) $2\frac{1}{8} + 4\frac{5}{9}$ (e) $3\frac{5}{8} + 2\frac{1}{3}$ (f) $7\frac{2}{9} + 3\frac{5}{6}$
(g) $3\frac{1}{7} + 2\frac{2}{3}$ (h) $4\frac{2}{5} + 5\frac{3}{7}$ (i) $6\frac{7}{10} + 5\frac{11}{12}$

Joyce has two lengths of skirting board measuring $3\frac{7}{8}$ metres and $2\frac{2}{5}$ metres. What is the difference in their lengths?

$3\frac{7}{8} - 2\frac{2}{5}$

$= 1\frac{35}{40} - \frac{16}{40}$

$= 1\frac{19}{40}$

$\frac{7}{8} = \frac{35}{40}$ $\frac{2}{5} = \frac{16}{40}$

The difference in length is **$1\frac{19}{40}$ metres**.

5 Sajid has two pieces of electrical cable measuring $3\frac{4}{5}$ metres and $1\frac{3}{8}$ metres. What is the difference in their lengths?

6 Two lengths of coving measure $4\frac{2}{3}$ metres and $3\frac{1}{6}$ metres. What is the difference in their lengths?

7 Two tins of yellow paint contain $2\frac{7}{8}$ litres and $1\frac{5}{6}$ litres. What is the difference between the volume of paint in the two tins?

8 Find:
(a) $4\frac{3}{4} - 2\frac{1}{3}$ (b) $7\frac{4}{5} - 5\frac{1}{4}$ (c) $6\frac{4}{9} - 3\frac{1}{6}$
(d) $8\frac{7}{8} - 6\frac{2}{5}$ (e) $7\frac{6}{7} - 4\frac{2}{3}$ (f) $4\frac{9}{10} - 2\frac{7}{12}$

Dave lays two rolls of garden turf measuring $4\frac{2}{5}$ metres and $1\frac{3}{4}$ metres. What is the difference in their lengths?

$4\frac{2}{5} - 1\frac{3}{4}$

$= 3\frac{8}{20} - \frac{15}{20}$

$= 2\frac{28}{20} - \frac{15}{20}$

$= 2\frac{13}{20}$

$\frac{2}{5} = \frac{8}{20}$ $\frac{3}{4} = \frac{15}{20}$

$3\frac{8}{20} = 2 + 1\frac{8}{20}$

$= 2 + \frac{28}{20}$

$= 2\frac{28}{20}$

The difference in length is **$2\frac{13}{20}$ metres**.

9 In the shed Jackie has two tins of masonry paint containing $4\frac{1}{4}$ litres and $2\frac{4}{5}$ litres. What is the difference between the volume of paint in the two tins?

10 Find:
(a) $4\frac{1}{3} - 2\frac{1}{2}$ (b) $5\frac{2}{5} - 2\frac{3}{4}$ (c) $3\frac{1}{6} - 1\frac{3}{5}$
(d) $7\frac{2}{9} - 4\frac{3}{8}$ (e) $6\frac{4}{7} - 3\frac{9}{10}$ (f) $5\frac{3}{10} - 4\frac{7}{8}$

11 For each pair of fractions find:
• the total • the difference.
(a) $2\frac{1}{2}$ and $1\frac{1}{3}$ (b) $3\frac{4}{5}$ and $2\frac{2}{3}$ (c) $5\frac{5}{6}$ and $4\frac{3}{8}$
(d) $3\frac{2}{7}$ and $1\frac{3}{5}$ (e) $4\frac{7}{10}$ and $2\frac{4}{9}$ (f) $7\frac{11}{12}$ and $3\frac{9}{10}$

Frank spends 50 minutes replacing a section of guttering. Write this as a fraction of an hour in its simplest form.

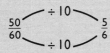

$$\frac{50}{60} \quad \begin{matrix} \div 10 \\ \div 10 \end{matrix} \quad \frac{5}{6}$$

50 minutes is $\frac{5}{6}$ **of an hour** in its simplest form.

1 Write each time as a fraction of an hour in its simplest form.

(a) 30 minutes (b) 15 minutes (c) 45 minutes
(d) 10 minutes (e) 40 minutes (f) 20 minutes
(g) 25 minutes (h) 35 minutes (i) 48 minutes
(j) 24 minutes (k) 21 minutes (l) 51 minutes

2 Write each fraction in its simplest form.

(a) $\frac{15}{25}$ (b) $\frac{8}{20}$ (c) $\frac{14}{16}$ (d) $\frac{9}{21}$
(e) $\frac{12}{30}$ (f) $\frac{24}{36}$ (g) $\frac{28}{42}$ (h) $\frac{49}{56}$

How much will Frank be paid for replacing the guttering if he is paid at the rate of £7·80 per hour?

He worked $\frac{5}{6}$ of an hour.

$$\frac{1}{6} \text{ of } £7·80 = £7·80 \div 6 = £1·20$$

So $\frac{5}{6}$ of £7·80 = £1·20 × 5 = £6·00

Frank was paid **£6·00** for replacing the guttering.

3 Find the amount Ross pays each person.

Name	Pay per hour	Time worked
Sajid	£7·20	30 minutes
Frank	£7·80	30 minutes
Joyce	£6·60	45 minutes
Jackie	£6·00	40 minutes
Dave	£5·10	55 minutes

How much will Frank be paid if he works 3 hours 35 minutes?

$$35 \text{ minutes} = \frac{7}{12} \text{ of an hour}$$

$$\frac{1}{12} \text{ of } £7·80 = £7·80 \div 12 = £0·65$$

So $\frac{7}{12}$ of £7·80 = £0·65 × 7 = £4·55

3 hours at £7·80 per hour = £23·40

Frank will be paid £4·55 + £23·40 = **£27·95**.

4 Calculate how much each person will be paid.
(a) Joyce works 7 hours 15 minutes.
(b) Sajid works 2 hours 40 minutes.
(c) Jackie works 5 hours 50 minutes.

Jackie paints 4 doors. Each door needs $\frac{5}{6}$ of a litre of undercoat. How much undercoat will she need?

$$4 \times \frac{5}{6} = \frac{20}{6}$$

$$= 3\frac{1}{3} \longleftarrow \boxed{\frac{20}{6} = 3\frac{2}{6} = 3\frac{1}{3}}$$

Jackie will need **$3\frac{1}{3}$ litres** of undercoat.

5 How much gloss paint will Jackie need for the four doors if each door needs $\frac{3}{8}$ of a litre?

6 Jackie has to paint eight window frames. Each frame needs $\frac{2}{5}$ of a litre of undercoat and $\frac{2}{9}$ of a litre of gloss paint. How many litres will she need of:
(a) undercoat (b) gloss paint?

7 Dave has to lay 3 rows of slabs in the drive. Each row of slabs needs $\frac{5}{6}$ of a bag of sand as a foundation. How much sand does he need altogether?

Oatfield College Farm

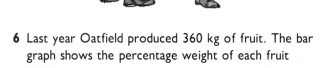

Oatfield is an agricultural college which provides farming courses for 120 students.

The farm covers an area of 700 acres of which $56\frac{1}{2}$% is used to grow crops.

To find $56\frac{1}{2}$% of 700

Enter **700.** Press ✕ **5** **6** **.** **5** **%**

to give **395.5**

$56\frac{1}{2}$% = $\frac{56\cdot5}{100}$

= $0\cdot565$

or

Enter **0.565** Press ✕ **7** **0** **0** **=**

to give **395.5**

An area of **395·5 acres** is used for crops.

1 Find the area of land used for:
   (a) buildings 12%   **(b)** animals 21%
   (c) greenhouses 8%   **(d)** recreation $2\frac{1}{2}$%.

2 Of the 120 students find the number who:
   (a) are male 65%   **(b)** are female
   (c) are left-handed 7·5%   **(d)** are right-handed
   (e) wear glasses $32\frac{1}{2}$%   **(f)** do not wear glasses
   (g) have a driving licence $47\frac{1}{2}$%
   (h) do not have a driving licence.

3 Write the **percentage** of students who:
   (a) are female
   (b) are right-handed
   (c) do not wear glasses
   (d) do not have a driving licence.

4 There are 400 animals on the farm.
   (a) Find the number of:
      • cows 18·75%   • sheep $44\frac{1}{4}$%
      • goats $7\frac{1}{2}$%   • pigs $6\frac{3}{4}$%.
   (b) The rest are hens. Find:
      • the number of hens • the percentage of hens.

5 There are 395·5 acres of crops. Find, to the nearest 0·1 acre, the area of:
   (a) wheat 32%   **(b)** oats 28%
   (c) barley 13·5%   **(d)** potatoes $14\frac{1}{4}$%
   (e) carrots $6\frac{3}{4}$%   **(f)** fruit $5\frac{1}{2}$%

6 Last year Oatfield produced 360 kg of fruit. The bar graph shows the percentage weight of each fruit grown.

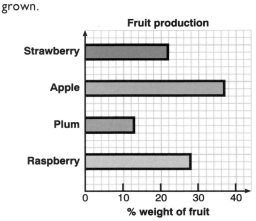

Fruit production

% weight of fruit

Find the weight of:
   (a) strawberries   **(b)** raspberries
   (c) apples   **(d)** plums.

7 Greenhouses cover an area of 56 acres. The pie chart shows the area used for each crop.

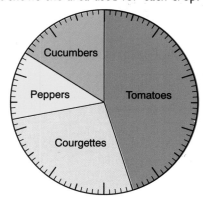

What area is used for:
   (a) tomatoes   **(b)** peppers
   (c) courgettes   **(d)** cucumbers?

This year there are 120 students in the college. Next year the college plans to increase the number of students by $22\frac{1}{2}\%$.

$$22\frac{1}{2}\% \text{ of } 120 = 27$$

$$120 + 27 = 147$$

100% + $22\frac{1}{2}\%$

= $122\frac{1}{2}\%$

or

$122\frac{1}{2}\%$ of 120 = 147

There will be **147 students** next year.

The college shop is holding an end of term sale. All goods are reduced by 15%. Find the sale price of a college scarf originally costing £18·65.

$$15\% \text{ of } £18·65 = £2·80 \text{ to the nearest 1p}$$
$$£18·65 - £2·80 = £15·85$$

or

$$85\% \text{ of } £18·65 = £15·85$$

100% − 15%
= 85%

The sale price of the scarf is **£15·85**.

1 There are 15 lecturers at the college. How many lecturers will there be if the number is increased by 20%?

2 The college farm covers an area of 700 acres. Land is bought to increase the area by 16%.
(a) Find the increase in the area.
(b) Find the new area of the farm.

3 The college wage bill for lecturers was £345 000. They received an increase of $5\frac{1}{2}\%$.
(a) Find the increase in the lecturers' wage bill.
(b) Find the new wage bill.

4 At present 56 acres are under glass. It is planned to extend the area by $8\frac{3}{4}\%$. Find the new area to be under glass.

5 The farm is to increase its production of fruit from 360 kg by 7·8%. Find, to the nearest kg, the weight of fruit to be produced.

6 Find the sale price of each item.
(a) track suit   (b) stationery set
(c) sweat shirt   (d) A4 folder
(e) A4 note pad   (f) jogging trousers
(g) pen and pencil set   (h) note book

7 At present students spend 14 hours a week learning practical farming jobs. Next term it is planned to reduce this by $12\frac{1}{2}\%$. How much time will students spend learning practical farming jobs next term?

8 Last year 4·2 tonnes of fertiliser was used. This amount is to be reduced by 6·8%. How much fertiliser, to the nearest 0·1 tonne, is to be used?

9 The volume of pesticide sprayed on the fruit trees is to be reduced from 260 litres by $8\frac{3}{4}\%$. How much pesticide, to the nearest litre, will be used?

Oatfield statistics

The college staff are planning a new farm layout. They plan to use 420 acres for crops of which 120 acres will be used to grow wheat.

The fraction to be used for wheat is

$$\frac{120}{420} = \frac{12}{42} = \frac{2}{7}$$

To find the percentage to be used for wheat:

Enter **120.** Press **÷ 4 2 0 =**

to give **0.2857142**   0·2857142 is 28·57142%

or

Enter **120.** Press **÷ 4 2 0 %**

to give **28.571429**

28·571429 is **28·6 to the nearest tenth**.

About **28·6%** will be used to grow wheat.

1 The table shows how the remainder of the 420 acres will be used for crops. For each crop find:
(a) the fraction
(b) the percentage of the area to be used.

oats	105 acres
fruit	50 acres
potatoes	40 acres
carrots	35 acres
barley	70 acres

2 The new total farm area is 812 acres. Forty acres is to be used for the study of wildlife. Find:
(a) the fraction
(b) the percentage of the farm to be used.

3 Out of a 32 hour week, students spend 10 hours in lectures.
(a) What fraction of their time is spent in lectures?
(b) What percentage of their time is spent in lectures?

4 The college decided to build a new sports and recreation centre. 75 students completed a questionnaire about the recreation centre. The number of students who made each choice is shown below. For each question find the percentage who made each choice.

(a) Which of the following indoor sports would you like to have available in the centre?

table tennis	20	snooker	16
badminton	11	squash	28

(b) Which of the following outdoor sports would you like to have available at the centre?

football	32	hockey	15
running	9	tennis	19

(c) Which of the following flavours of drink would you like to have on sale?

cola	38	orange	12
lemon	5	blackcurrant	20

(d) Which of the following flavours of crisps would you like to have on sale?

salted	12	bacon	17
cheese	24	prawn	22

5 The college decided to provide everything that at least $\frac{1}{5}$ of the students voted for. Write a report with your recommendations, based on these figures.

Tracy and Shirin are building solids using 1 cm cubes.

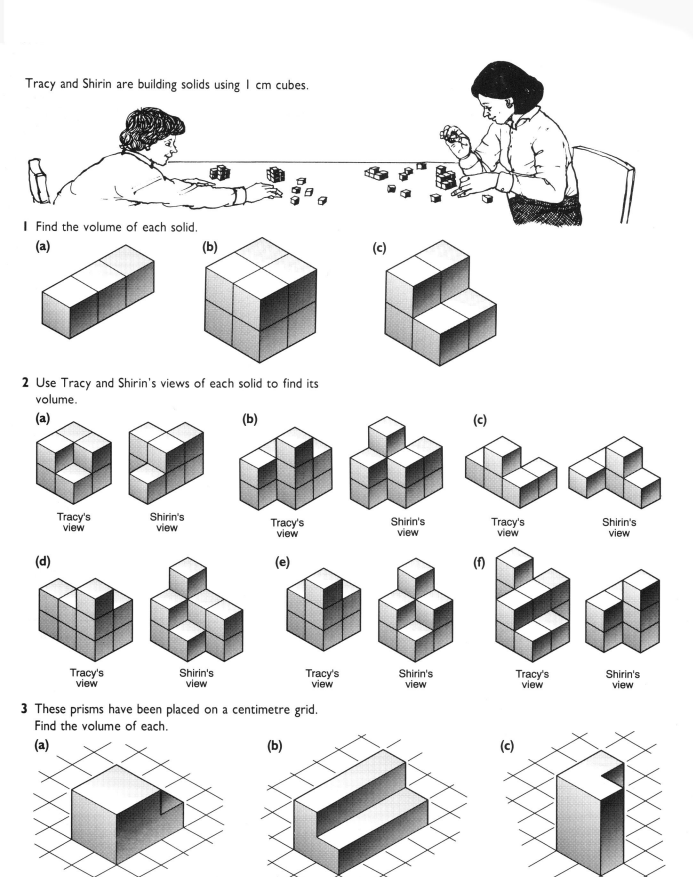

1 Find the volume of each solid.

(a)

(b)

(c)

2 Use Tracy and Shirin's views of each solid to find its volume.

(a)

Tracy's view   Shirin's view

(b)

Tracy's view   Shirin's view

(c)

Tracy's view   Shirin's view

(d)

Tracy's view   Shirin's view

(e)

Tracy's view   Shirin's view

(f)

Tracy's view   Shirin's view

3 These prisms have been placed on a centimetre grid.
Find the volume of each.

(a)

(b)

(c)

Dot-to-dot

Tracy sketches her solids on isometric dot paper.

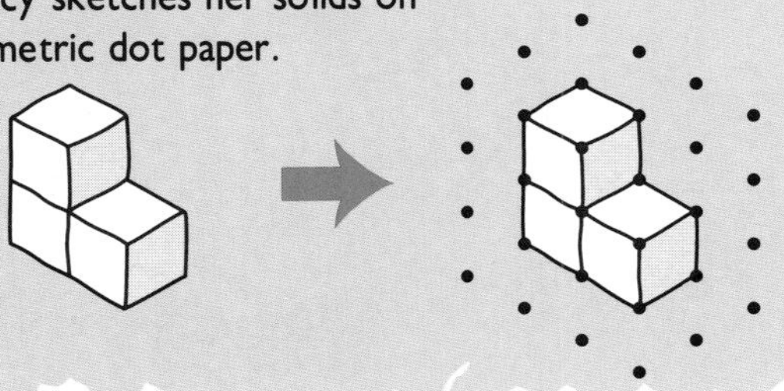

You need isometric dot paper.

1 Sketch each solid on isometric dot paper.

(a)

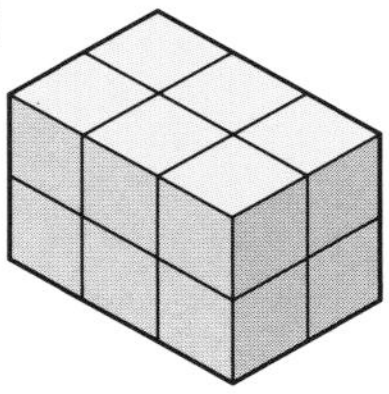

(b)

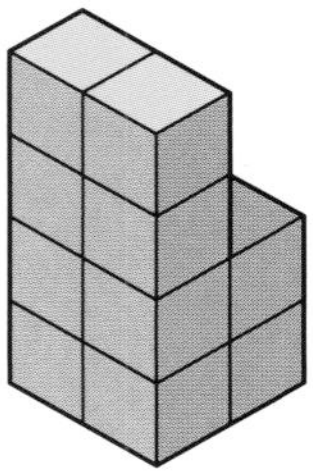

(c)

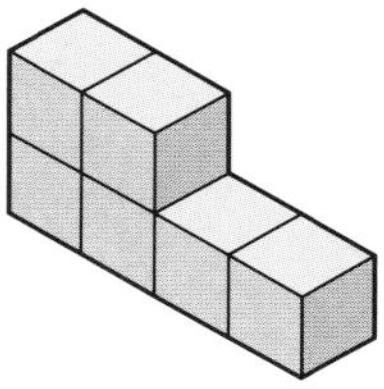

(d)

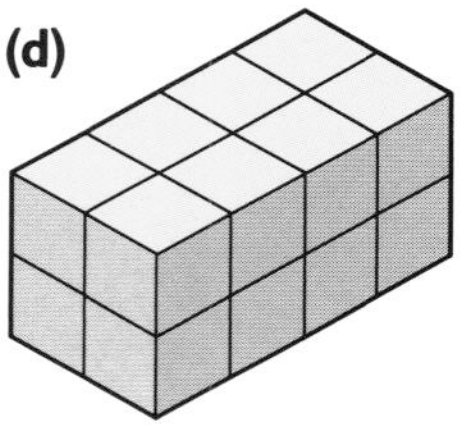

(e)

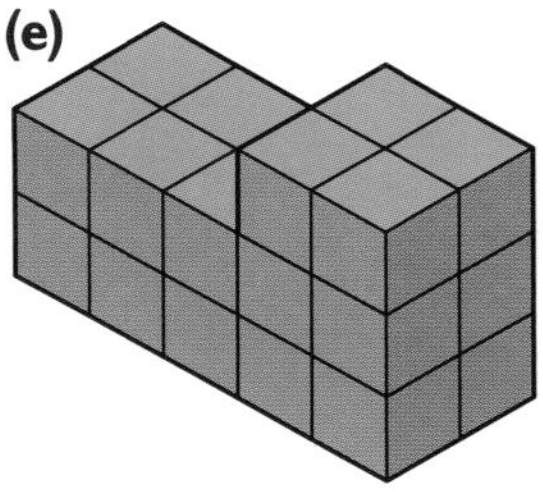

(f)

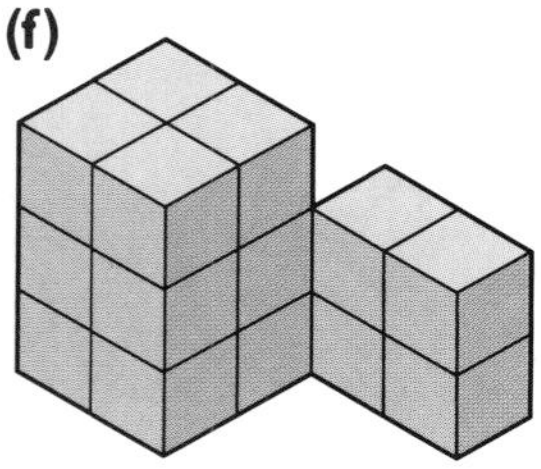

(g)

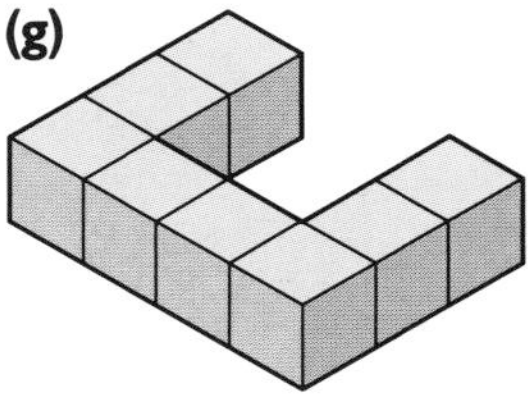

(h)

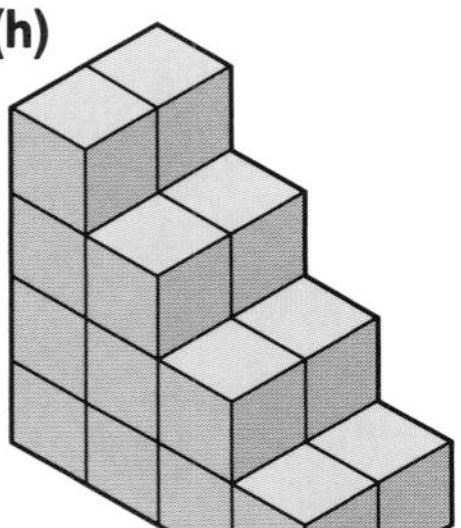

2 Each net folds to make a cuboid.
Draw each cuboid on isometric dot paper.

(a)

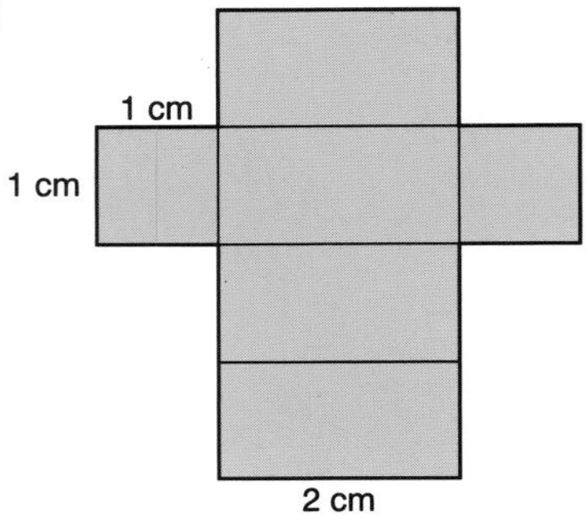

(b)

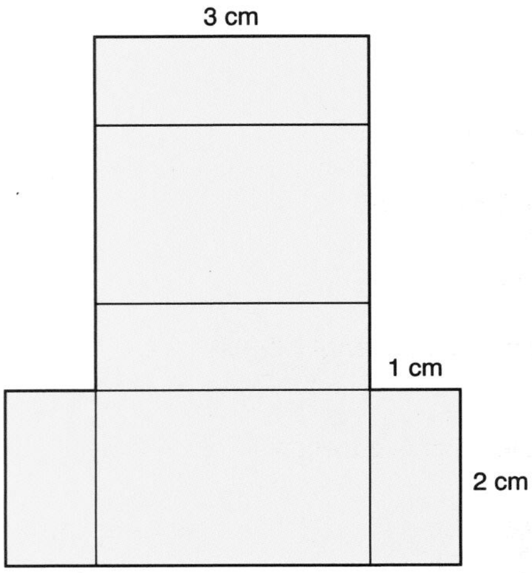

3 This solid is made from five 1 cm cubes.

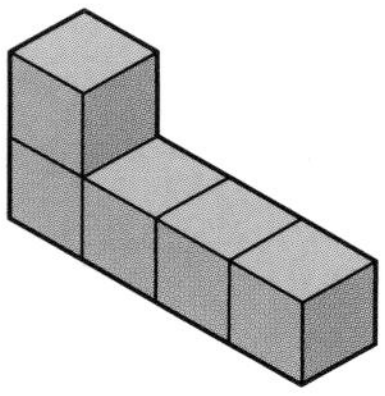

How many **different** solids can be made from five 1 cm cubes?
Sketch each solid.

Challenge

4 How many **different** solids with volume 6 cm^3 can be made using 1 cm cubes?
Sketch each solid.

Joe is making rabbit runs.
How much wood has he used for the frame of this run?

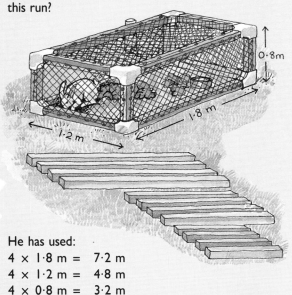

0·8 m
1·8 m
1·2 m

He has used:
4 × 1·8 m = 7·2 m
4 × 1·2 m = 4·8 m
4 × 0·8 m = 3·2 m
Total = 15·2 m

The **total edge length** of the run is **15·2 m**.

1 Find the total edge length of each run.

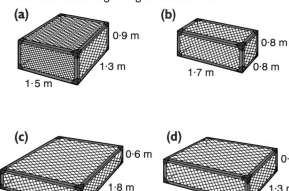

(a) 0·9 m, 1·3 m, 1·5 m

(b) 0·8 m, 0·8 m, 1·7 m

(c) 0·6 m, 1·8 m, 2 m

(d) 0·7 m, 1·3 m, 2·2 m

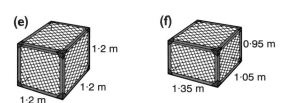

(e) 1·2 m, 1·2 m, 1·2 m

(f) 0·95 m, 1·05 m, 1·35 m

2 Joe has covered the edges of these pet boxes with plastic strips.
Find the total length of plastic strip in each.

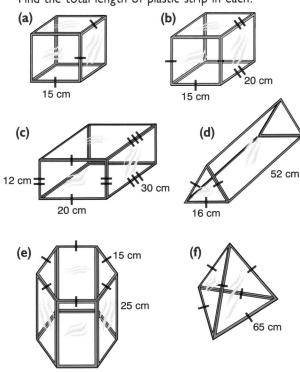

(a) 15 cm

(b) 20 cm, 15 cm

(c) 12 cm, 20 cm, 30 cm

(d) 52 cm, 16 cm

(e) 15 cm, 25 cm

(f) 65 cm

3 Calculate the total edge length of each designer pet box.

Slumbapet ©
THE BEST FOR YOUR PET!

a. HAMSTER
square based pyramid
base edge 50cm
sloping edge 30cm

b. RABBIT
equilateral triangular prism
length 45cm
sloping edge 35cm

c. CAT
regular hexagonal prism.
length 80cm
other edges 25cm

NEW BROCHURE

NEW

Made to measure

Sue makes glass display boxes.
For each box she needs to know:
- the total edge length
- the volume
- the total surface area, that is, the area of glass.

For this box:
- *Total edge length*
  - 4 × 40 = 160 cm
  - 4 × 30 = 120 cm
  - 4 × 60 = 240 cm
  - Total edge length is **520 cm**

- *Volume*
  - 40 × 30 × 60 = 72 000 cm³
  - Volume is **72 000 cm³**

- *Total surface area*
  - 2 × (40 × 30) = 2400 cm²
  - 2 × (30 × 60) = 3600 cm²
  - 2 × (40 × 60) = 4800 cm²
  - Total surface area is **10 800 cm²**

1 Find the total edge length, volume and total surface area of each display box.

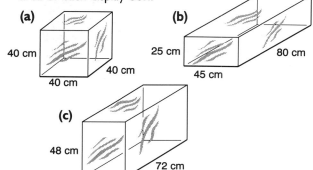

(a) 40 cm, 40 cm, 40 cm

(b) 25 cm, 45 cm, 80 cm

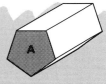

(c) 48 cm, 72 cm, 36 cm

● **Remember**

Volume of a prism = Area of base × height
$$V = A \times h$$
$$V = Ah$$

2 Some of Sue's display boxes are prisms.
Find the volume of each box.

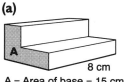

(a) 8 cm
A = Area of base = 15 cm²

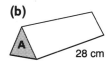

(b) 28 cm
A = Area of base = 30 cm²

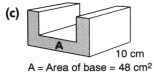

(c) 10 cm
A = Area of base = 48 cm²

3 For each of these boxes find: • the area of the base
 • the volume.

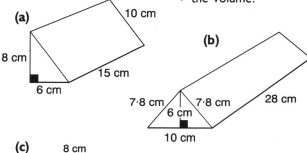

(a) 10 cm, 8 cm, 15 cm, 6 cm

(b) 7·8 cm, 7·8 cm, 6 cm, 28 cm, 10 cm

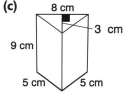

(c) 8 cm, 3 cm, 9 cm, 5 cm, 5 cm

4 Find the total edge length and total surface area of each prism in question **3**.

▼ **Challenge**

5 This cuboid is made from four triangular prisms.
For each different triangular prism, find:
- **(a)** the total edge length
- **(b)** the volume.

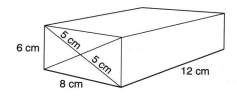

6 cm, 5 cm, 5 cm, 8 cm, 12 cm

1 Derek sells ice cream in boxes which hold multiples of $\frac{1}{4}$ litre.

(a) Find the volume of this ice cream box.

(b) How many litres of ice cream is it designed to hold?

2 Calculate the volume of water in each fish tank.

(a)

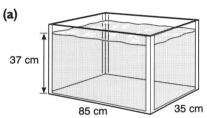

(b)

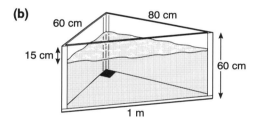

3 If 60 000 cm³ of sand is spread evenly to a depth of 20 cm, what area of ground will it cover?

4 Find: (a) the length of wood
         (b) the area of mesh
required to build this rabbit run.

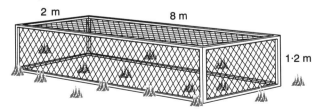

5 Find the weight of the monument.

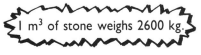

I m³ of stone weighs 2600 kg.

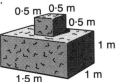

● **Remember**

We measure:
● length in units: mm, cm, m, km.
● area in square units: mm², cm², m², km².
● volume in cubic units: mm³, cm³, m³, km³.

6 Sarah has calculated the total edge length, total surface area and volume of this gift box.
What is: (a) the total surface area
         (b) the total edge length
         (c) the volume of the box?

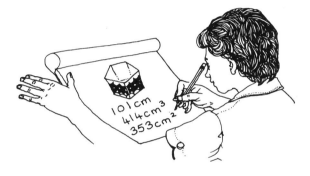

▼ **Challenge**

7 Sarah has designed a gift box for John.

John's gift box
7200 cm²
36 000 cm³
440 cm

(a) What is the volume of the box?
(b) The gift box is a cuboid.
    Find the dimensions of the box.

La Patisserie

La Patisserie
PRICE LIST

Croissant   c pence
Éclair   e pence
Pastry   p pence
Large éclair 2e pence

Look at the price list. The cost in pence of:
- four croissants is
$c + c + c + c = 4 \times c = 4c$
- five large éclairs is
$2e + 2e + 2e + 2e + 2e = 5 \times 2e = 10e$

1 Find:

(a) $e + e + e$ (b) $p + p + p + p + p$
(c) $d + d$ (d) $m + m + m + m$
(e) $6 \times t$ (f) $3 \times r$
(g) $8 \times f$ (h) $12 \times s$
(i) $z + z$ (j) $b + b + b + b + b + b$
(k) $c \times 7$ (l) $24 \times n$
(m) $16 \times q$ (n) $c \times 22$
(o) $32 \times y$ (p) $15 \times k$

2 Find:

(a) $3a + 3a$ (b) $4d + 4d + 4d$
(c) $5f + 5f$ (d) $6t + 6t + 6t + 6t$
(e) $5 \times 8u$ (f) $7 \times 5r$
(g) $11 \times 11k$ (h) $20 \times 3n$

Sue buys 8 croissants and Alan buys 5 croissants.
- The total cost in pence is $8c + 5c = 13c$
- The difference in cost is $8c - 5c = 3c$

$7e - e = 6e$ $9n - 8n = n$
$3r + 6r - 2r = 7r$

3 Find each total:

(a) $3p + 8p$ (b) $7k + 3k$
(c) $5t + 8t$ (d) $5s + 3s + 6s$
(e) $8d + 7d + 5d$ (f) $11m + 9m + 3m$
(g) $8q + q + 7q$ (h) $n + 9n + 2n$
(i) $8x + 4x + 2x$ (j) $5t + t + t$
(k) $2w + 8w + w$ (l) $15r + 5r + 11r$

4 Find each difference:

(a) $8g - 3g$ (b) $3f - 2f$ (c) $6m - 4m$
(d) $12t - t$ (e) $24d - 11d$ (f) $16r - 9r$
(g) $22h - 21h$ (h) $50s - 25s$ (i) $19y - 7y$
(j) $11x - 3x$ (k) $10b - b$ (l) $8p - 6p$
(m) $14k - 9k$ (n) $19d - 11d$ (o) $31w - 19w$
(p) $9a - 9a$ (q) $12d - 3d$ (r) $4f - 4f$

5 Find:

(a) $3e + 5e + e$ (b) $6t + 2t - 5t$
(c) $5s - 2s + 8s$ (d) $15m - 6m + 4m$
(e) $19d + 2d - 20d$ (f) $b + b + b - b$
(g) $11x + x - 9x$ (h) $30p - 2p + 4p$
(i) $17u - 9u - u$ (j) $9r - 2r + 5r + 3r$
(k) $8t + 4t - t + 3t$ (l) $18y + 2y - 5y$
(m) $13w - 2w + 9w$ (n) $21a - 3a + 8a$
(o) $4m - 2m - m$ (p) $6r - 2r - 4r$

You can simplify expressions like this:

$$6t + 5s + 2t - 3s$$
$$= 6t + 2t + 5s - 3s$$
$$= 8t \quad + \quad 2s$$

$$3x + 6 + 4x + 9$$
$$= 3x + 4x + 6 + 9$$
$$= 7x \quad + \quad 15$$

$$11g + 9h - 6g + 5h + 3g$$
$$= 11g - 6g + 3g + 9h + 5h$$
$$= 8g \quad + \quad 14h$$

The Patisserie sells boxes of cakes.
The total cost in pence of these two boxes is

$$5e + 2p + 2e + 3p$$
$$= 5e + 2e + 2p + 3p$$
$$= 7e \quad + \quad 5p$$

> 5e and 2e are like terms.
> 2p and 3p are like terms.
> You can add and subtract like terms.
> This is called simplifying.

1 Simplify:
 (a) $4c + 5e + 7c + 8e$
 (b) $9p + 3c + 8p + 2c$
 (c) $5t + 3s + 8t + 8s$
 (d) $4x + 7y + 10x + 8y$
 (e) $8u + 6v + 3u + 4v$
 (f) $10m + 2n + m + 6n$
 (g) $5a + 9b + a + b$
 (h) $12w + 9z + 3w + 11z$
 (i) $3d + 7f + 8d + f$

2 Simplify:
 (a) $4s + 7t - 2s + 3t$
 (b) $6y + 9x - 4y + 2x$
 (c) $8q + 7r + 3q - 5r$
 (d) $2w + 9v + 8w - 6v$
 (e) $5m + 3n - m + 6n$
 (f) $2t + 10y - t + 8y$
 (g) $12a + 11b - 2a - 5b$
 (h) $3d + 5c - d + c + 4d$
 (i) $3k + 7b + 2k - 5b - k$
 (j) $8u + 9v + 7w + 2u + 6v - 4w$
 (k) $11a + 9b + 8c - a - 3b + 7c$

3 Simplify:
 (a) $7w + 8 + 4w + 1$
 (b) $6j + 12 + 3j - 9$
 (c) $8p + 19 - 3p + 5$
 (d) $6x + 8 - 2x - 7$
 (e) $12r + 2 + r - 2$
 (f) $18f + 21 - 9f - 5$
 (g) $9m + 16 - m + 5$
 (h) $3h + 7 + 5h + 7$
 (i) $5t + 8 - 4t - 7$
 (j) $4a + 7b + 8a + 3b - 2a + 7b$
 (k) $8x + 9y + 10x - y - 3x + 15y$
 (l) $12k + 10e + 15k - e - 9k - 9e$
 (m) $17u + 20v + u - 9v + 3u - v$
 (n) $4s + 7t + 6 - s + 2t + 3$
 (o) $8p + 6q + 11 - 2p - q - 5$
 (p) $4g + 6h + 2g + 7 - 4 - 3h$
 (q) $a + 16 + 4b + 9a + 2b + 6$

La Patisserie

The cost in pence of three boxes like this is:

$$2e + 3p + 2e + 3p + 2e + 3p$$
$$= 2e + 2e + 2e + 3p + 3p + 3p$$
$$= \quad 6e \quad + \quad 9p$$

or

$$3(2e + 3p)$$
$$= 3 \times 2e + 3 \times 3p$$
$$= \quad 6e \quad + \quad 9p$$

1 Multiply out:

(a) $2(5r + 4s)$ (b) $5(6y + 2x)$
(c) $8(5f + 2g)$ (d) $4(4m + 3n)$
(e) $7(4h + 5j)$ (f) $10(6u + v)$
(g) $6(8a + 3b)$ (h) $11(4x + 2z)$
(i) $8(10s + 5t)$ (j) $20(2w + 5v)$
(k) $7(7p + 3q)$ (l) $8(11a + 12b)$

A presentation box of cakes costs 10 pence extra for wrapping. The cost in pence of five presentation boxes is:

$$5(6e + 5p + 10)$$
$$= 5 \times 6e + 5 \times 5p + 5 \times 10$$
$$= \quad 30e \quad + \quad 25p \quad + \quad 50$$

2 Multiply out:

(a) $4(3a + 5b + 7)$ (b) $6(5r + 7s + 3)$
(c) $8(9x + 3y + 1)$ (d) $3(8u + v + 11)$
(e) $8(6d + 5f + 4)$ (f) $10(3w + 4z + 10)$
(g) $7(2m + 5n + 7)$ (h) $5(11x + 12y + 15)$
(i) $20(6g + 5h + 20)$ (j) $9(2p + 7q + 8)$

You can multiply out brackets like this.

$$4(6a + 5b - 3)$$
$$= 4 \times 6a + 4 \times 5b - 4 \times 3$$
$$= \quad 24a \quad + \quad 20b \quad - \quad 12$$

$$8(3j - 4k + 7)$$
$$= 8 \times 3j - 8 \times 4k + 8 \times 7$$
$$= \quad 24j \quad - \quad 32k \quad + \quad 56$$

3 Multiply out:

(a) $5(2a - 3b)$ (b) $6(7x - 3y)$
(c) $4(9m - n)$ (d) $10(4f + 3g)$
(e) $6(7r + 8s - 4)$ (f) $5(9t - 3s + 2)$
(g) $9(10x - 11y - 9)$ (h) $10(5h - g + 7)$
(i) $3(8d + 9e - 8)$ (j) $11(2u - 7v - 11)$

You can multiply out brackets and simplify like this:

$$2(2e + 3c) + 3(4e + 5c)$$
$$= \quad 4e + 6c + 12e + 15c$$
$$= \quad 4e + 12e + 6c + 15c$$
$$= \quad 16e \quad + \quad 21c$$

$$3(2a + 3b + 10) + 5(6a + b - 4)$$
$$= \quad 6a + 9b + 30 + 30a + 5b - 20$$
$$= \quad 6a + 30a + 9b + 5b + 30 - 20$$
$$= \quad 36a \quad + \quad 14b \quad + \quad 10$$

4 Multiply out and simplify:

(a) $2(3a + 4b) + 5(3a + 5b)$
(b) $4(6s + 5t) + 6(2s + 3t)$
(c) $8(2x + y) + 7(3x + 4y)$
(d) $10(6f + 2g) + 8(5f + 5g)$
(e) $3(5u + 4v) + 6(2u - v)$
(f) $6(8m + 5n) + 2(10m - 8n)$
(g) $11(4h + 3j) + 10(5h - 2j)$
(h) $3(6c + d) + 5(c + 11d)$

5 Multiply out and simplify:

(a) $4(2x + 3y + 4) + 3(3x + 2y + 7)$
(b) $5(4x + 6y + 8) + 7(3x + 2y - 4)$
(c) $5(5p + 8q + 6) + 6(2p - 3q + 8)$
(d) $7(4m + 7n + 9) + 4(5m - 6n - 11)$
(e) $10(6r + 7s + 10) + 4(5r - 10s - 8)$
(f) $3(8f + 9g + 11) + 2(12f - 7g + 5)$

Julie and Salma are playing a game on the computer. They have to put +, − , × or ÷ between the dice to eliminate one of the numbers in the panel.

Their teacher Mrs Gupta settles the argument:

Always multiply or divide BEFORE you add or subtract.

So 5 + 2 × 4
= 5 + 8
= 13

1 Which number would be eliminated in each of the following?

(a) **(b)**

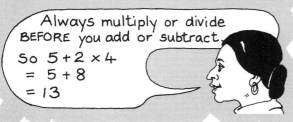

(c) **(d)**

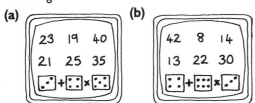

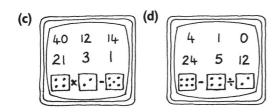

2 Find:
(a) 8 + 2 × 4   **(b)** 20 − 4 × 3
(c) 10 × 3 + 5   **(d)** 16 ÷ 2 + 5
(e) 15 − 14 ÷ 7   **(f)** 3 + 2^2
(g) 4^2 + 3   **(h)** 20 − 2^3

3 Copy and complete by inserting signs:
(a) 5   2   2 = 1   **(b)** 6   3   1 = 9
(c) 4   10   2 = 38   **(d)** 5   3   2 = 11

4 Use the numbers: ☐1 ☐2 ☐3 ☐4

and the signs   ☐+ ☐− ☐× ☐÷
to make the numbers 1 to 10, using these rules:

Rules
- all the numbers **must** be used
- a number can only be used once
- signs can be used more than once
- not all the signs need be used.

For example, 4 × 3 ÷ 2 + 1 = 7

To settle another argument Mrs Gupta tells them:

Always evaluate brackets first.

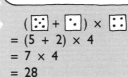
= (5 + 2) × 4
= 7 × 4
= 28

5 Use the bracket rule to find:
(a) (☐ + ☐) × ☐   **(b)** (☐ + ☐) × ☐
(c) (☐ − ☐) × ☐   **(d)** ☐ × (☐ + ☐)
(e) ☐ × (☐ − ☐)   **(f)** (☐ + ☐) ÷ ☐
(g) ☐ × (☐ − ☐)   **(h)** ☐ × (☐ − ☐)

6 Evaluate:
(a) 10 + (5 × 3)   **(b)** (8 − 4) × 15
(c) 12 + (24 ÷ 8)   **(d)** (14 + 6) × 7
(e) (3 + 1) × (2 + 8)   **(f)** 2^3 + (6 × 3)
(g) (17 − 12) × 5^2 **(h)** (9 − 4) × (12 + 6)

7 Evaluate:
(a) $(3 + 4)^2$ **(b)** 3 + 4^2
(c) $(50 ÷ 5)^2$ **(d)** 50 ÷ 5^2
(e) $(27 ÷ 3)^2$ **(f)** 27 ÷ 3^2

▼ Challenge

8 Copy and complete by inserting signs and brackets:
(a) 3   2   4 = 18   **(b)** 6   2   7 = 28
(c) 12   8   5 = 20   **(d)** 8   4   3 = 4

Iain McGael is a television weather forecaster.

Gale force winds of up to 80km/h or 50 mph are expected to hit the south coast of England tonight and may cause structural damage...

...whilst in Scotland subtropical breezes have brought heatwave conditions of 30°c or 86°F.

To change speeds from kilometres per hour, km/h, to miles per hour, mph, he uses the formula:

m = 0·625 k   where m is the speed in mph and k is the speed in km/h.

To change 80 km/h to mph $m = 0.625\,k$
$m = 0.625 \times 80$
$m = 50$

The wind speed is **50 mph**.

1 The table shows part of the Beaufort scale which describes the strength of winds. Re-write the table giving the speeds in mph.

Beaufort Scale	Description	Average speed at 10 m above ground level
0	Calm	0 km/h
1	Light air	3 km/h
2	Light breeze	9 km/h
3	Gentle breeze	17 km/h
4	Moderate breeze	24 km/h
5	Fresh breeze	35 km/h
6	Strong breeze	44 km/h
7	Near gale	56 km/h
8	Gale	69 km/h
9	Strong gale	82 km/h
10	Storm	94 km/h

To change from degrees Celsius, C, to degrees Fahrenheit, F, he uses the formula:

F = 1·8C + 32   To change 30°C:
$F = 1.8C + 32$
$F = 1.8 \times 30 + 32$
$F = 86$

The temperature is **86°F**.

2 Change each temperature to degrees Fahrenheit.
 (a) 10°C **(b)** 20°C **(c)** 5°C **(d)** 19°C
 (e) 0°C **(f)** 1·5°C **(g)** 33·5°C **(h)** 68·5°C

To change from degrees Fahrenheit, F, to degrees Celsius, C, he uses the formula:

$$C = \frac{5(F-32)}{9}$$ To change 212°F:

$$C = \frac{5(F-32)}{9}$$

$$C = \frac{5 \times (212-32)}{9}$$

$$C = \frac{5 \times 180}{9}$$

$$C = 100$$

The temperature is **100°C**.

3 Change each temperature to degrees Celsius.
 (a) 122°F **(b)** 86°F **(c)** 32°F
 (d) 158·9°F **(e)** 97·7°F **(f)** 32·9°F

I These formulae are used in different areas of Science. Evaluate each formula.

(a)

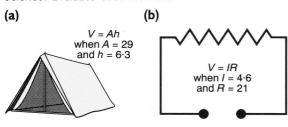

$V = Ah$
when $A = 29$
and $h = 6·3$

(b)

$V = IR$
when $I = 4·6$
and $R = 21$

(c)

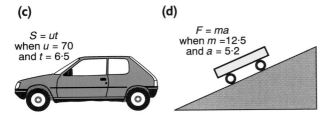

$S = ut$
when $u = 70$
and $t = 6·5$

(d)

$F = ma$
when $m = 12·5$
and $a = 5·2$

(e)

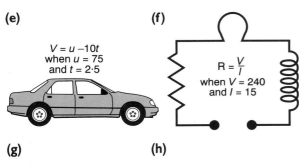

$V = u - 10t$
when $u = 75$
and $t = 2·5$

(f)

$R = \frac{V}{I}$
when $V = 240$
and $I = 15$

(g)

$W = \frac{mv}{10}$
when $m = 25$
and $v = 5$

(h)

$d = f\lambda$
when $f = 10·2$
and $\lambda = 0·34$

The formula for calculating distances, given an initial speed, u, acceleration, a, and time, t, is:

$s = ut + \frac{1}{2}at^2$

What is the distance, s, if $u = 10$, $t = 5$ and $a = 9·8$?

$s = ut + \frac{1}{2}at^2$

$s = 10 \times 5 + \frac{1}{2} \times 9·8 \times 5^2$

$s = 50 + 122·5$

$s = 172·5$

2 Use $s = ut + \frac{1}{2}at^2$ to find s when:
  (a) $u = 5$, $t = 4$ and $a = 10$
  (b) $u = 8$, $t = 3$ and $a = 6$
  (c) $u = 2·5$, $t = 1·5$ and $a = 8$.

3 Evaluate these formulae used in science.
  (a) $s = 0·5 at^2$ when $a = 9·8$ and $t = 2·5$
  (b) $P = I^2R$ when $I = 13$ and $R = 6·3$
  (c) $K = \frac{1}{2}mv^2$ when $m = 25$ and $v = 12$
  (d) $q = u^2 + 2as$ when $u = 2·5$, $s = 1·6$ and $a = 3·2$
  (e) $d = (a - b)^2$ when $a = 2·1$ and $b = 1·2$
  (f) $u = a + (n - 1)d$ when $a = 5·5$, $n = 10$ and $d = 0·4$
  (g) $a = \frac{(v - u)}{t}$ when $v = 3·2$, $u = 1·4$ and $t = 0·9$
  (h) $R = \frac{(r_1 + r_2)}{r_1 r_2}$ when $r_1 = 20$ and $r_2 = 40$

Some formulae are often written in words rather than symbols.

4 When cooking a chicken the cooking time is 20 minutes per lb weight of the chicken then add 20 minutes. How long should it take to cook a chicken weighing:
  (a) 3 lb   **(b)** 5·25 lb   **(c)** 2·5 lb?

5 Lisa is a hillwalker. She uses this formula to estimate the time taken for a walk.

Naismith's Rule

Allow 12 minutes for every kilometre on the map, then add 10 minutes for every 100 metres climbed.

Use Naismith's Rule to estimate the time taken for each of the following walks.
  (a) Map distance of 10 km with 900 m of climbing.
  (b) Map distance of 20 km with 400 m of climbing.
  (c) Map distance of 15 km with 890 m of climbing.
  (d) Map distance of 12 km with 1010 m of climbing.

Ismael conducted a survey of the different types of articles in newspapers. Although the articles were spread throughout the paper, she estimated the equivalent number of pages for each type of article.

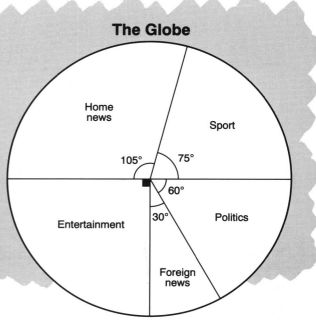

The Globe

The Globe had 24 pages.
The pie chart shows Ismael's results.
How many pages of sport were there?

The sector representing sport has an angle of 75°.

This represents $\frac{75}{360}$ of the whole paper.

Number of sports pages = $\frac{75}{360}$ of 24

Enter **24.** Press **÷** **3** **6** **0** **×** **7** **5** **=**

to give **5.**

There are the equivalent of **5 pages** of sport in *The Globe*.

1 (a) For *The Globe* find the equivalent number of pages of:
   - home news
   - entertainment
   - politics
   - foreign news.
(b) Check that the pages for all five types of article add up to 24.

You need a protractor.

2 *The Banner* had 30 pages. The articles Ismael found in *The Banner* are represented in the pie chart.
(a) Use your protractor to measure the angle of each sector.
(b) Of the 30 pages, how many were devoted to:
   - home news
   - foreign news
   - sport
   - entertainment
   - politics?
(c) Check that your answers add up to 30.

The Banner

3 The *Weekly Journal* contained 90 pages. How many pages were devoted to each type of article?

The Weekly Journal

The Post has the following pages:

Article	Foreign news	Home news	Sport	Entertainment	Politics	TOTAL
Number of pages	7	8	4	6	5	30

To display the information in a pie chart Ismael calculated the angle for foreign news like this.

The fraction of the paper which is foreign news is $\frac{7}{30}$.

Angle size = $\frac{7}{30}$ of 360°.

Enter **360** Press **÷** **3** **0** **×** **7** **=**

to give **84.**

The angle size for foreign news is 84°.

Ismael drew a circle and a radius. She then measured an angle of 84°, drew another radius and labelled the sector.

The Post

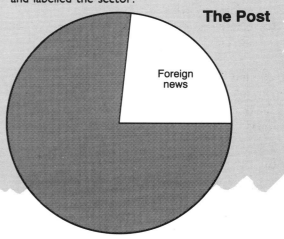

You need compasses.

4 Using a radius of 5 cm, draw a pie chart to show the information for *The Post*.

5 Ismael counted the number of equivalent pages devoted to each feature in *The Standard*.
- Sport, 4   • Home news, 3   • Entertainment, 6
- Politics, 2   • Foreign news, 3.
Display the information in a pie chart.

■ Investigation

6 Work in a group.
Choose a newspaper and estimate the number of pages devoted to each kind of article. Display the information in a pie chart.

Going for Gold

Pauline and Dave carried out a survey at the Target Sports Centre. They asked athletes to take part in a number of sports.

1 Pauline recorded the weights of ten men and the distances they threw the shot.

(a) How many men weighed 75 kg?
(b) Who threw the shot 17 m?
(c) How far did Jim throw the shot?
(d) Who threw the shot furthest?
(e) How many men threw the shot over 15 m?
(f) Who weighed least?
(g) What can you say about Bob?
(h) What distance did the heaviest man throw?
(i) What distance did the lightest man throw?

2 Look carefully at the graph.
There is a relationship or **correlation** between weight and distance thrown.
Copy and complete:
As the men's weights **increased** the distance the shot was thrown ☐.

3 Dave recorded the heights of ten women who took part in the high jump.

	Height (m)	Jump (m)
Eve	1·64	1·04
Ann	1·58	0·98
Jill	1·60 ·	1·00
Kate	1·70	1·20
Una	1·65	1·10
Dot	1·59	1·02
Fay	1·67	1·18
Sue	1·74	1·24
Cath	1·73	1·28
Jen	1·62	1·02

(a) Show this information on a graph.

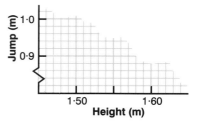

(b) Who was the tallest?
(c) Who jumped the highest?
(d) Who was the smallest?
(e) Whose jump was lowest?
(f) Look at your graph. Copy and complete this statement about the correlation.
As the women's height increased the distance they jumped ☐.

4 Dave recorded the weights of ten men and the number of laps of the track they ran in 40 minutes.

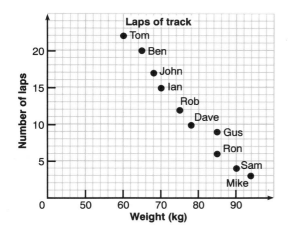

(a) How many men weighed 85 kg?
(b) Who weighed the most?
(c) Who completed the smallest number of laps?
(d) How many laps did the lightest man complete?
(e) Look at the graph. Copy and complete:
As the men's weights increased the number
of laps they ran ▢.

5 Pauline recorded the weights of eight men and their times for the 400 m hurdles.

	Weight (kg)	Time (s)
Rob	74	180
John	70	156
Ali	82	218
Sam	78	198
Ben	84	234
Ross	80	210
Ken	72	172
Said	76	192

(a) Show this information
on a graph.
(b) Look at your graph.
Make a statement
about the correlation
between the men's
weights and their
times for the hurdles.

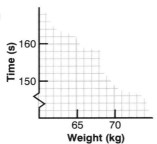

6 Pauline recorded the heights of eight women and their times for the 100 m freestyle.

	Height (m)	Time (s)
Sue	1·64	84
Jen	1·62	88
Lou	1·72	68
Kate	1·70	72
Lucy	1·66	80
Tina	1·60	87
Gail	1·68	78
Eve	1·76	64

(a) Show this
information
on a graph.

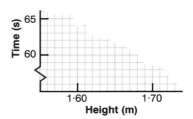

(b) Make a statement about the correlation
between the women's heights and their swim
times.

Going for Gold

7 Dave recorded the weights of ten women and the distances they threw the javelin.

	Weight (kg)	Distance (m)
Eve	62	25
Ann	70	34
Jill	66	28
Kate	72	36
Una	60	24
Dot	58	21
Fay	74	38
Sue	56	20
Cath	68	33
Jen	64	26

(a) Show this information on a graph.
(b) Make a statement about the correlation between the women's weights and the distances they threw the javelin.

8 Pauline recorded the heights of ten men who took part in the long jump.

	Height (m)	Jump (m)
Ken	1·78	4·2
Bill	1·90	5·0
Joe	1·62	3·0
Ron	1·84	4·4
Drew	1·76	4·0
Tom	1·68	3·4
Ali	1·88	4·8
Pete	1·70	3·6
Sam	1·64	3·2
Bob	1·74	3·8

Draw a graph and make a statement about the correlation between the men's heights and their jumps.

9 Dave recorded the heights of ten women and their times for the sprint.

	Height (m)	Time (s)
Jen	1·64	38
Lou	1·70	32
Jill	1·58	44
Pam	1·62	40
Ella	1·74	30
Sue	1·68	33
Kay	1·76	33
Eve	1·60	41
Amy	1·72	31
Sara	1·66	35

Draw a graph and make a statement about the correlation between the women's heights and their times for the sprint.

▶ Challenge

10 Pauline recorded the weights of ten men and their maximum snooker breaks.

	Weight (kg)	Break
Ian	68	50
Rob	74	32
John	76	44
Tom	70	46
Jim	78	30
Ross	72	34
Said	74	38
Ihab	68	32
Ali	82	48
Ken	80	36

Make a statement about the correlation between the men's weights and their maximum snooker breaks.

Anna drops a ball from different heights and measures the height of the bounce.

Drop height (m)	0	1	2	3	4	5	6
Bounce height (m)	0	0·6	1·3	1·7	2·4	2·9	3·7

Anna draws a graph from the results. She cannot draw a straight line through all the points. She draws a line which **seems** to fit best. It is the **line of best fit**.

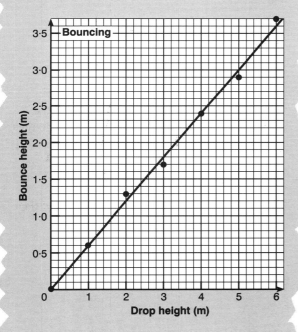

In Ihab's experiment different weights are hung on a spring. He measures the distance the spring stretches.

Weight (g)	0	10	20	30	40	50	60
Stretch (mm)	0	8	14	24	34	41	47

Ihab draws a graph from the results.

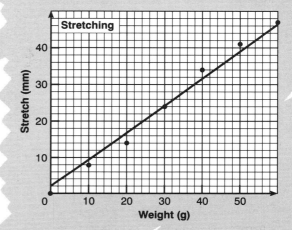

5 What does one small interval represent on:
(a) the weight axis   (b) the stretch axis?

6 Use Ihab's graph. Estimate the distance the spring is stretched by weights of:
(a) 14 g   (b) 38 g   (c) 55 g

7 Use the graph to estimate the weight needed to stretch the spring.
(a) 20 mm   (b) 35 mm   (c) 42 mm

8 ▶ **Do Worksheet 1, question 2.**

9 Freda is measuring the amount of water lost from a dripping tap.

Time (min)	0	1	2	3	4	5	6	7
Water (cm³)	0	12	22	35	50	60	71	86

(a) Show her data on a graph and draw the line of best fit.
(b) Use your graph to estimate the volume of water lost in: • 1·5 min   • 6·5 min.

1 What does one small interval represent on:
(a) the drop axis   (b) the bounce axis?

2 Use Anna's graph.
Estimate the bounce height for drops of:
(a) 2·4 m   (b) 3·5 m   (c) 5·6 m

3 Use the graph to estimate the drop height if the bounce height is:
(a) 1 m   (b) 2·5 m   (c) 3·5 m

4 ▶ **Do Worksheet 1, question 1.**

Trevor and Clare are playing the balancing game.
They put numbers and letters on the scales and
solve the equation to find the number which will
balance the letter.

"To solve an equation you always do the opposite operation."

$$2y + 6 = 14$$

Subtract 6 from each side.

$$2y = 8$$

Divide each side by 2.

$$y = \frac{8}{2}$$
$$y = 4$$

1 Copy and complete to solve each equation.

(a) $3x + 5 = 11$

(b) $2 + 4y = 22$

(c) $41 = 5c + 6$

(d) $8 + 2f = 8$

2 Solve each equation.

(a) $6t + 4 = 70$ **(b)** $7 + 3w = 16$
(c) $20 = 2t + 4$ **(d)** $9 = 3 + 3r$
(e) $10y + 3 = 43$ **(f)** $6 + 4p = 66$
(g) $65 = 30 + 7c$ **(h)** $28 = 4 + 8a$

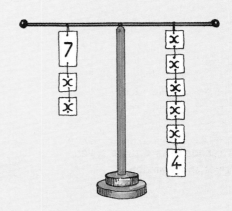

$$2x + 7 = 5x + 4$$

Subtract 2x from each side.

$$7 = 3x + 4$$

Subtract 4 from each side.

$$3 = 3x$$

Divide each side by 3.

$$\frac{3}{3} = x$$

$1 = x$ is the same as $x = 1$.　$\longrightarrow$　$x = 1$

3 Copy and complete to solve each equation.

(a) $3v + 4 = 2v + 7$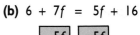

(b) $6 + 7f = 5f + 16$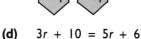

(c) $10w = w + 9$

(d) $3r + 10 = 5r + 6$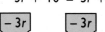

(e) $6t + 10 = 7t$

(f) $8 + 2y = 4y + 2$

4 Solve each equation.

(a) $4t + 6 = 2t + 30$ **(b)** $4k + 13 = 6k + 1$
(c) $8x = 5x + 15$ **(d)** $18 + 7d = 10d + 12$
(e) $6p + 30 = 30 + 10p$ **(f)** $9n + 6 = 10n$

Remember

< means *is less than*
≤ means *is less than or equal to*
> means *is greater than*
≥ means *is greater than or equal to*

Clare cannot balance these scales.
This gives an inequation.

> You solve an inequation the same way as an equation.

$$2p + 3 > 9$$

Subtract 3 from each side. -3 -3

$$2p \quad > 6$$

Divide each side by 2. $p \quad > \frac{6}{2}$

$$p \quad > 3$$

1 Copy and complete to solve each inequation.

(a) $5d + 7 \geqslant 22$ (b) $6 + 4v < 30$
   -7 -7 -6 -6

(c) $24 \geqslant 3k + 12$ (d) $20 > 8w + 4$
   -12 -12 -4 -4

2 Find the solution to each inequation.

(a) $2x + 5 \leqslant 25$ (b) $2 + 5f \geqslant 32$
(c) $24 > 4r + 8$ (d) $7 + 4c \leqslant 55$
(e) $3g + 4 \geqslant 10$ (f) $3 + 7b > 59$
(g) $28 < 3 + 5p$ (h) $9 + 5n \geqslant 14$

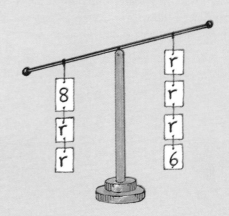

$$8 + 2r > 3r + 6$$

Subtract $2r$ from
each side. $-2r$ $-2r$

$$8 \quad > r + 6$$

Subtract 6 from each
side. -6 -6

$$2 \quad > r$$

> $2 > r$ is the same as $r < 2$.

$$r < 2$$

3 Copy and complete to solve each inequation.

(a) $4t + 4 \leqslant t + 13$
   $-t$ $-t$

(b) $7 + 2w \geqslant 2 + 3w$
   $-2w$ $-2w$

(c) $2r + 7 > 3r$
   $-2r$ $-2r$

(d) $9p < 3p + 6$
   $-3p$ $-3p$

4 Solve:

(a) $6k + 2 \geqslant 3k + 32$ (b) $10 + 5y \leqslant 6y + 3$
(c) $8v < 3v + 15$ (d) $20 + 5w \geqslant 9w$
(e) $7r + 10 > 10 + 4r$ (f) $3h + 14 \leqslant 5 + 4h$

Equations:
$ax \pm b = cx \pm d$
$ax \pm b > cx \pm d$

The Sweet Tooth

Clare works in *The Sweet Tooth* after school.
A full packet of these sweets weighs p grams.
Each sweet weighs one gram.

Clare balances these scales
by removing 4 sweets.

$2p - 4 = 100$

Add 4 to each side.

$2p = 104$

$p = 52$

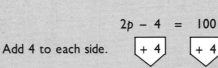

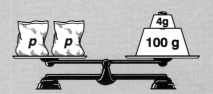

Each full packet weighs **52 grams**.

1 Copy and complete to solve each equation or inequation.

(a) $6p - 5 = 13$

(b) $1 = 4w - 3$

(c) $5w - 1 \leqslant 24$

(d) $3 < 2k - 7$

(e) $12 - 2m = 4m$

(f) $50 - 3a = 2a$

(g) $3x < 49 - 4x$

(h) $60 - 7x \geqslant 8x$

(i) $35 - 2r = 5r$

(j) $15x - 20 \leqslant 5x$

(k) $14 - 2f > 5f$

(l) $8p - 12 < 6p$

2 Solve:

(a) $3d - 4 = 11$ **(b)** $5 = 2x - 7$
(c) $4t - 7 > 29$ **(d)** $47 < 7m - 30$
(e) $3c = 35 - 4c$ **(f)** $5a = 7a - 60$
(g) $4b - 26 < 2b$ **(h)** $80 - 3y > 7y$
(i) $8 < 6p - 10$ **(j)** $80 < 9k - 1$

$5a - 6 = 3a + 4$

$-3a \qquad -3a$

$2a - 6 = 4$

$+6 \qquad +6$

$2a = 10$

$a = 5$

3 Solve:

(a) $4v - 20 = 2v + 6$ **(b)** $5r + 2 \geqslant 8r - 10$
(c) $6f - 3 = 2f + 5$ **(d)** $14 + v \leqslant 2v - 4$
(e) $3 + 10y > 3 + 8y$ **(f)** $4t - 5 = 2t + 11$

Trevor and Clare are finding the weight of sweets, b grams, in this gift tray.

Trevor weighs one bag.

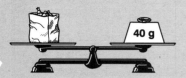

$\frac{1}{5}b = 40$

$b = 40 \times 5$

$b = 200$

Multiply each side by 5.

Clare weighs 2 bags.

$\frac{2}{5}b = 80$

$2b = 80 \times 5$

$2b = 400$

$b = 200$

The tray has **200 grams** of sweets.

$\frac{1}{3}b$ can be written as $\frac{b}{3}$ $\frac{2}{7}c$ can be written as $\frac{2c}{7}$

1 Solve each equation.

(a) $\frac{1}{2}x = 3$ **(b)** $\frac{k}{3} = 9$

(c) $10 = \frac{1}{4}p$ **(d)** $16 = \frac{1}{8}w$

(e) $5 = \frac{n}{7}$ **(f)** $\frac{m}{9} = 12$

(g) $\frac{2}{3}y = 6$ **(h)** $9 = \frac{3}{4}a$

(i) $\frac{2r}{9} = 8$ **(j)** $80 = \frac{5b}{6}$

(k) $\frac{4f}{5} = 16$ **(l)** $\frac{4}{11}n = 4$

(m) $50 = \frac{5w}{7}$ **(n)** $\frac{7c}{20} = 14$

(o) $\frac{7}{10}y = 56$ **(p)** $105 = \frac{3v}{8}$

(q) $\frac{5d}{12} = 100$ **(r)** $\frac{8}{15}x = 64$

(s) $\frac{6y}{25} = 12$ **(t)** $18 = \frac{3p}{50}$

(u) $\frac{9a}{7} = 18$ **(v)** $\frac{3}{5}b = 48$

(w) $40 = \frac{8r}{3}$ **(x)** $\frac{9}{5}k = 63$

$\frac{x}{2} - 3 = 9$ $\frac{3y}{7} + 4 = 10$

$+3 \quad +3$ $-4 \quad -4$

$\frac{x}{2} = 12$ $\frac{3y}{7} = 6$

$x = 12 \times 2$ $3y = 6 \times 7$

$x = 24$ $3y = 42$

$y = 14$

2 Solve each equation.

(a) $\frac{y}{3} - 6 = 4$ **(b)** $\frac{p}{5} + 2 = 7$

(c) $40 = \frac{1}{8}x - 2$ **(d)** $16 = \frac{b}{10} + 3$

(e) $3 + \frac{1}{8}y = 25$ **(f)** $\frac{2a}{3} + 10 = 30$

(g) $\frac{4}{5}b - 9 = 35$ **(h)** $21 = \frac{3}{8}v - 6$

(i) $68 = 12 + \frac{7}{10}m$ **(j)** $20 + \frac{3}{4}w = 47$

▶ **Challenge**

3 Find the solution to each equation.

(a) $\frac{15}{x} = 3$ **(b)** $\frac{25}{t} = 5$

(c) $\frac{147}{p} = 7$ **(d)** $\frac{56}{v} = 8$

Sweet secrets

The cost in pence of a tray of sweets is t.
For an extra 20 pence the trays can be put in a gift box.

The cost of this box is $2t + 20$.

Mrs Reed has ordered
3 of these boxes.

Clare works out the cost like this.

$$3(2t + 20)$$
$$= 6t + 60$$

1 Four people have placed special orders.
For each person find:
- the cost of one box
- the total cost.

(a) Jill

(b) David

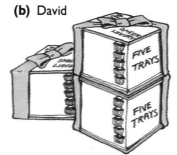

(c) Margaret

(d) Niall

2 Find:
- **(a)** $3(2c + 4)$
- **(b)** $4(5y + 3)$
- **(c)** $6(2 + 7p)$
- **(d)** $10(2 + t)$
- **(e)** $5(3d - 8)$
- **(f)** $7(5k - 1)$
- **(g)** $9(4 - 5w)$
- **(h)** $12(6 - 10m)$
- **(i)** $2(5 + 8y)$
- **(j)** $7(9 - 3r)$
- **(k)** $4(5f + 10)$
- **(l)** $6(7b + 3)$

Clare has charged Fiona £5·20 for these boxes.

You can find the cost of one tray like this.

$$\begin{aligned} 2(3t + 20) &= 520 \\ 6t + 40 &= 520 \\ 6t &= 480 \\ t &= 80 \end{aligned}$$

One tray costs **80 pence**.

3 Find the cost, in pence, of one tray in each set of boxes.

(a)

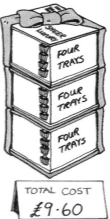

TOTAL COST
£9·60

(b)

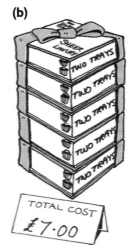

TOTAL COST
£7·00

4 Solve each equation.
- **(a)** $3(5k + 2) = 96$
- **(b)** $9(4 + 2p) = 90$
- **(c)** $66 = 2(3 + 6y)$
- **(d)** $245 = 7(5 + 3n)$
- **(e)** $6(8r - 1) = 42$
- **(f)** $8(40 - 4m) = 128$
- **(g)** $50 = 5(40 - 3w)$
- **(h)** $24 = 2(5r - 8)$
- **(i)** $4(1 + 5x) = 404$
- **(j)** $10(2v + 6) = 300$
- **(k)** $96 = 8(50 - a)$
- **(l)** $80 = 2(3b - 5)$

For this bag of mints:
• the bag weighs 5 grams when empty
• the average weight of a mint is 15 grams.
How many mints are in the bag?

We can write this formula:

$W = 15n + 5$
where W is the weight of the full bag
and n is the number of mints.

For this bag of mints, $W = 455$

$455 = 15n + 5$
$450 = 15n$
$n = 30$

There are **30 mints** in the bag.

1 Use the formula $W = 15n + 5$ to find the number of mints in a bag which weighs:

(a) 380 grams   (b) 755 grams
(c) 845 grams   (d) 995 grams.

2 Use each formula to find the number of sweets in each bag.

(a)   (b)

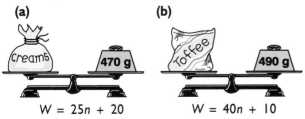

$W = 25n + 20$ $W = 40n + 10$

(c)

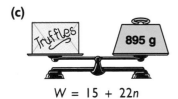

$W = 15 + 22n$

3 Clare's pay, P pounds, can be calculated from the formula
$P = 5 + 2h$
where h is the number of hours worked.

Pay	
Friday	£9
Saturday	£21
Sunday	£15

For each day in the table, use the formula to make an equation and solve it to find the number of hours Clare worked.

4 Trevor uses the formula $T = 2(l + b)$ to find the length of tape, T metres, needed to edge a board of length l metres and breadth b metres.

Find the breadth of a board when:
(a) $l = 3$ and $T = 8$ (b) $l = 5$ and $T = 18$.

5 At the ice-cream counter the takings, P pounds, can be calculated using the formula:

$P = 3l + 2s$
where l is the number of large tubs sold
and s is the number of small tubs sold.

(a) Find the number of small tubs sold:
• when the number of large tubs sold is 8 and the takings are £48
• when the number of large tubs sold is 10 and the takings are £62.
(b) Find l when $P = 85$ and $s = 20$
(c) Find s when $P = 61$ and $l = 19$.

Pieces of seven

The seven piece tangram is made from a square partitioned as shown.
Make an accurate copy on card and cut out the seven pieces.

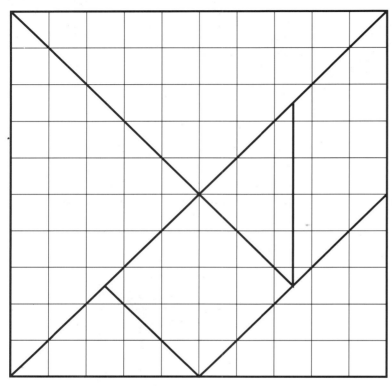

Using the pieces you can make triangles, squares, rectangles, parallelograms and trapezia.

1 Follow these steps to see if it is possible to make each shape with each of 1, 2, 3, 4, 5, 6 or 7 pieces.

Step 1 Copy the table.

	Number of pieces						
	1	2	3	4	5	6	7
Triangle							
Square							✓
Rectangle							
Parallelogram							
Trapezium							

Step 2 Try to make each shape with each number of pieces.
Record your answers by:
• drawing round them.
• marking off the space in the table.

2 Which ones, if any, are impossible?

1 Paul sells kitchens in the *A la Carte* showroom. His salary each month is calculated using the formula:

$$S = 1000 + 4\% K$$

where S is his salary in £ and
K is the value of kitchens he has sold in £.

(a) Find his salary in a month in which he sells £35 000 worth of kitchens.

(b) In one month he earned £1800. What was the value of the kitchens he sold?

2 The profit, P, on each kitchen depends on its cost price, c, and selling price, s.

(a) Find the profit on each kitchen.

Style	Cost price (c)	Selling price (s)
Nevis	£4 250	£4 720
Lomond	£5 225	£6 350
Ochil	£7 785	£9 875
Pentland	£14 675	£16 665

(b) Write a formula for the profit, P, when you know the cost price, c, and the selling price, s.

3 Before he sells a kitchen Paul has to work out the cost of each unit. A unit contains 1 shelf, 3 drawers and 2 doors. The cost of these is given by the expression $(s + 3r + 2d)$
where s is the cost of a shelf
r is the cost of a drawer and
d is the cost of a door.

(a) The kitchen designed for Mrs Thornton uses 7 units.
Multiply out $7(s + 3r + 2d)$ to find an expression for the cost of the shelves, drawers and doors.

(b) A kitchen design costs $4s + 12r + 8d$. How many units are used in the design?

4 Base units are cuboid in shape and measure 60 cm by 90 cm by 60 cm.

(a) Find the volume of a base unit.

(b) Strips of polystyrene are used to protect all edges during transport.
What is the total length of polystyrene needed for each unit?

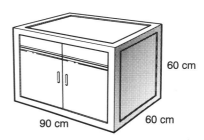

5 The showroom also sells pine mirrors. Each mirror is rectangular and has a pine frame. The cost depends on the area of the mirror and the length of wood used in the frame.

(a)   **(b)**

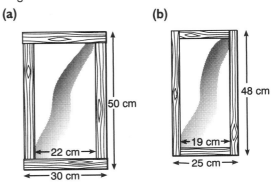

For each pine mirror find:

• the area of the mirror

• the length of the frame

• the total cost if the mirror costs 20 pence per cm² and the frame costs £1·50 per metre.

1 (a) Copy and complete the table of petrol costs.

No of litres	5	10	15	20	25
Cost (£)	2·40	4·80			

(b) Use the information in your table to draw a graph **on 2 mm squared paper**.

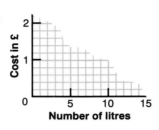

● **Remember**

The number of litres and the cost are in **direct proportion**. The graph is a straight line passing through the origin.

2 Use your graph.

(a) How much would it cost to buy:
- 30 litres
- 22 litres
- 33 litres of petrol?

(b) How many litres of petrol can be bought for:
- £16·80
- £8·40
- £10·00
- £15·00?

Sarah bought 5 gallons of petrol. Approximately how many litres is this? She could use a **conversion graph** to change from gallons to litres.

1 gallon is about $4\frac{1}{2}$ litres.

5 gallons is about $22\frac{1}{2}$ litres.

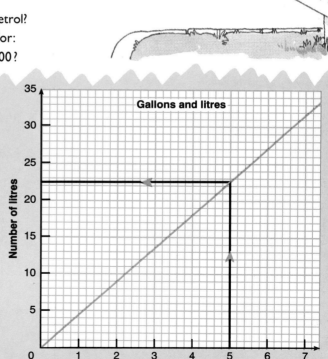

3 Use the graph to convert to litres:

(a) 2 gallons **(b)** 4 gallons **(c)** 5·2 gallons
(d) 0·4 gallons **(e)** 6·8 gallons **(f)** 4·5 gallons

4 Use the graph to convert to gallons:

(a) 9 litres **(b)** 11 litres **(c)** 18 litres
(d) 15 litres **(e)** 21 litres **(f)** 29 litres

Tony is taking his car into the garage to be serviced. If the service takes 3 hours the labour cost will be £43·44. How much will the labour cost be if the service takes 5 hours?

Time (hours)	Cost (£)
3	43·44
1	43·44 ÷ 3
5	43·44 ÷ 3 × 5 = 72·4

The labour costs will be **£72·40** if it takes 5 hours.

5 How much will the labour cost be if it takes:

(a) 4 hours   **(b)** 7 hours

(c) $\frac{1}{2}$ hour   **(d)** $4\frac{1}{2}$ hours?

6 Jim is working on Ronnie's car.
It takes him 32 minutes to fit brake shoes to all four wheels. How long will it take him to fit brake shoes to 3 wheels?

7 The cost of Luboil is directly proportional to its volume. Fifteen litres cost £19·50.

(a) How much does it cost for:
- 5 litres   • 10 litres
- 20 litres   • 25 litres?

(b) On 2 mm squared paper, draw a graph to show the cost of Luboil.

(c) From your graph find the cost of:
- 12 litres   • 18 litres
- 21 litres of Luboil.

(d) How much would 55 litres of Luboil cost?

8 Robbie is working in the tyre bay.
It takes her 24 minutes to change 4 tyres.

(a) How long will it take her to change:
- 6 tyres   • 8 tyres
- 2 tyres   • 3 tyres?

(b) How many tyres can she change in:
- 54 minutes   • $\frac{1}{2}$ hour   • $1\frac{1}{2}$ hours?

9 Afzal is making the weekly petrol delivery in his tanker. He delivers 5000 litres of petrol in 40 minutes.

(a) How many litres of petrol can he deliver in:
- one hour   • 20 minutes
- $1\frac{1}{2}$ hours   • 2 hours and 15 minutes?

(b) How long will it take Afzal to deliver:
- 20 000 litres   • 17 500 litres
- 3000 litres   • 750 litres?

Road up!

1 A new drainage pipe is to be laid along 120 metres of motorway. The pipe is available in sections of different lengths.

(a) Copy and complete the table.

Section length (m)	1	2	3	4	5	6	8	10
No of sections	120		40			20		

(b) What happens to the number of sections needed when the length of each section is doubled?

(c) Copy and complete the graph.

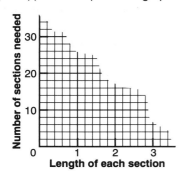

2 A crash barrier is to be fitted along a 180 metre stretch of motorway.

(a) Copy and complete the table.

Section length (m)	1	2	3	4	5	6	10	12
No of sections	180		60			30		

(b) What happens to the number of sections needed when the length of each section is doubled?

(c) Draw a graph to show the information in the table.

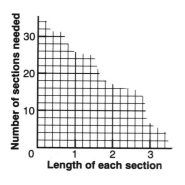

3 New kerb-stones are to be laid along one side of a 200 metre stretch of motorway. The stones are available in three different lengths.

(a) Copy and complete the table.

Length of stone (m)	0·5	1·0	2·0
Number of stones		200	

(b) What happens to the number of stones needed when the length of each stone is halved?

4 A crane can lift 2880 kg. How many kerb stones can it lift when each stone weighs:

(a) 20 kg **(b)** 40 kg **(c)** 80 kg?

These are examples of **inverse proportion**.

5 Copy and complete these statements about inverse proportion.

(a) When one quantity is **doubled**, the other is ☐.

(b) When one quantity is **halved**, the other is ☐.

(c) The graph of two quantities in inverse proportion is ☐ a straight line.

6 One machine can tar a stretch of road in 3 hours. How long will it take 2 machines to do the job?

7 Two road rollers can roll a stretch of road in 30 minutes. How long will the rolling take when:

(a) one road roller is used

(b) four road rollers are used?

8 A car travelling at 30 mph takes 40 seconds to pass the roadworks. How long will it take for a car travelling at:

(a) 60 mph   (b) 15 mph?

9 White lines have to be painted along a stretch of road using a line painting machine. Copy and complete the table.

Speed of the machine in mph	0·5	1	2	
Time taken in minutes		24		6

10 A worker has to move 48 cones to another part of the roadworks. If he moves one cone at a time he will have to make 48 trips.

(a) Copy and complete the table.

Number of cones on each trip	1	2	3		6	8		
Number of trips	48			12			4	3

(b) When the number of cones per trip is **trebled**, what happens to the number of trips needed?

11 Three dumper trucks will take 6 hours to remove a pile of rubble.

(a) How long will it take if only one truck is used?

(b) How many trucks would be needed to do the job in:

• 3 hours   • 2 hours?

12 Copy and complete these statements about **inverse proportion**.

(a) When one quantity is **trebled**, the other is ☐.

(b) When one quantity is **divided by 3**, the other is ☐.

Pumped dry

Three pumps will take 8 days to empty a pond. With one pump it will take three times as long.

Number of pumps	Number of days
3	8
1	8 × 3 = 24

3 pumps take 8 days
1 pump takes 8 × 3 = **24 days**.

1 How long will it take **one** pump to empty each of these ponds?

(a)

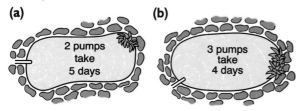

2 pumps take 5 days

(b)

3 pumps take 4 days

(c)

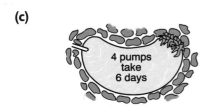

4 pumps take 6 days

2 Three pumps can empty a swimming pool in 5 hours. How long will it take if one pump is used?

An engineer calculates that two pumps will take 30 hours to clear the water from a mine shaft. Another pump becomes available.

Number of pumps	Number of hours
2	30
1	30 × 2 = 60
3	60 ÷ 3 = 20

2 pumps take 30 hours
1 pump takes 30 × 2 = 60 hours
3 pumps takes 60 ÷ 3 = **20 hours**.

3 How long would it have taken to clear the mine shaft with:

(a) 4 pumps   (b) 5 pumps
(c) 6 pumps   (d) 8 pumps?

4 Three pumps can remove the water from a flooded basement in 12 hours. How long would it have taken:

(a) 2 pumps   (b) 4 pumps
(c) 6 pumps   (d) 8 pumps?

5 Two lorries can "in-fill" a pond in sixty hours.

(a) How long will it take three lorries?
(b) How many lorries will be needed to do the job in 20 hours?
(c) How many lorries will be needed to do the job in 25 hours?

Before you answer questions **1** to **5** decide whether each question involves either:
- direct proportion
- inverse proportion

or if the quantities are not in proportion.

Helen, Ted, Ihab and Sabrina work in Chunk's Chocolate Factory.

1 In 5 minutes Ted's machine produces 70 chocolate biscuits. How many biscuits will his machine produce in:

(a) 8 minutes   (b) 12 minutes

(c) half an hour   (d) 2 hours?

2 Sabrina's machine packs 24 boxes of chocolate biscuits in 15 minutes. How many boxes of biscuits will her machine pack in:

(a) 10 minutes   (b) 25 minutes

(c) 55 minutes   (d) $1\frac{1}{2}$ hours?

3 Ihab is in charge of chocolate making. Three machines produce 10 tonnes of chocolate in 4 hours. To produce the same amount how long would it take:

(a) 1 machine   (b) 5 machines   (c) 8 machines?

4 Helen is in charge of stores. It takes 8 men 6 hours to move one load of biscuits into the warehouse. How long would it take:

(a) 1 man   (b) 6 men   (c) 16 men?

5 Helen takes 20 minutes to travel to work each day and earns £180 per week. Ihab earns £216 per week. How long does it take him to travel to work?

6 The price of a Chunky Bar is directly proportional to its weight. A 60 gram bar costs 24p.

(a) Copy and complete the table.

Weight of bar (g)	Cost of bar (p)
20	
40	
60	24
80	
100	

(b) Draw a graph to show the information in the table.

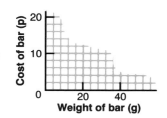

(c) How much will the following bars cost?
- 50 g
- 95 g
- 165 g

▼ Challenge

7 The table shows the cost of different sizes of Corky Bars.

Weight of bar (g)	Cost of bar (p)
30	18
50	30
80	45
130	70
200	105

Is the cost of a Corky Bar directly proportional to its weight? Explain your answer.

Trying triangles

In this triangle each number is found by adding the two numbers underneath it.

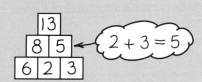

2 + 3 = 5

1 Copy and complete each of these triangles.

(a)

(b)

(c)

(d)

2 Find the value of *n* in each of these triangles.

(a)

(b)

(c)

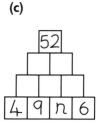

(d)

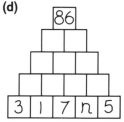

3 Copy and complete each of these triangles.

(a)

(b)

(c)

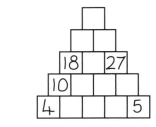

4 (a) Copy and complete each of these triangles.

(b) Make another triangle with 3 consecutive numbers along the bottom. What do you notice about the middle consecutive number and the number at the top?

(c) Test that this works for another 3 consecutive numbers.

5 This triangle can be completed in four different ways using whole numbers only. Find all four different ways.

6 Find all the ways this triangle can be completed using whole numbers only.

This diagram shows some of the dimensions of a car from a brochure. The scale is 1 : 60.

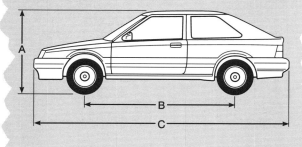

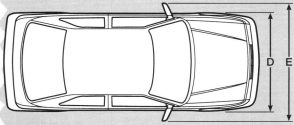

Scale 1 : 60

What is the true height, A, of the car?

Height on plan = 2·3 cm
True height = 2·3 cm × 60
= 138 cm
= **1·38 m**

1 Find the true sizes of:
- the wheelbase, B
- the length, C
- the width, D (excluding door mirrors)
- the width, E (including door mirrors).

2 This is the engineer's drawing for Peak Flow pumping station.

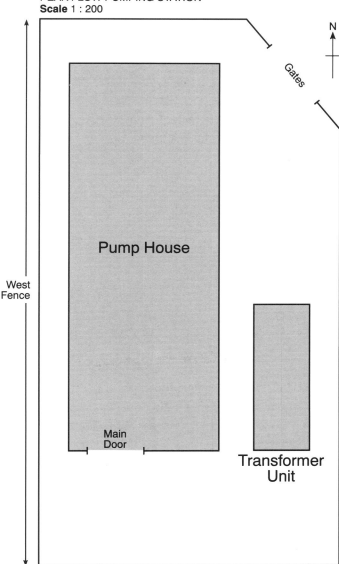

PEAK FLOW PUMPING STATION
Scale 1 : 200

(a) What is the scale of the drawing?
(b) Find the true size of:
- the length of the Pump House
- the width of the Pump House
- the width of the Transformer Unit.

(c) Will a truck 3·5 m wide be able to drive through the gates? Explain.
(d) There are posts erected every 3 metres along the West Fence. How many posts are there?

Mapping it out

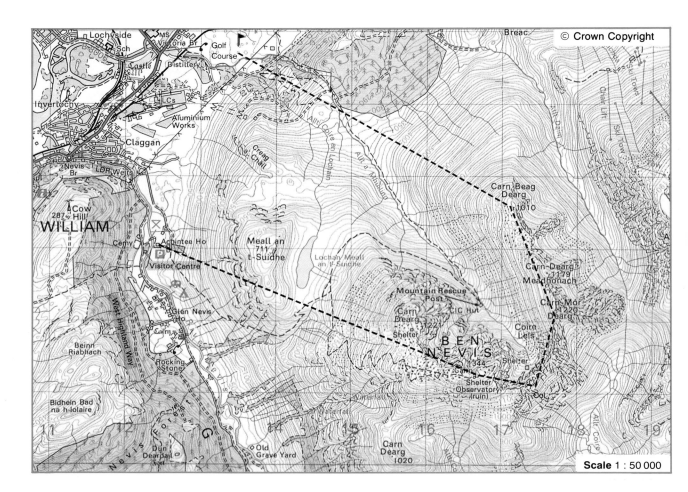

Scale 1 : 50 000

Mountaineers often use Ordnance Survey maps when planning routes. This map shows the Ben Nevis area in Scotland.

The scale of a map or plan is often called a **representative fraction**.

The scale, or representative fraction, of this map is 1 : 50 000.

> Doug and Clare have planned the route shown on the map. What is the true distance from the Golf Course to Carn Beag Dearg?
>
> Length on map = 8·4 cm
> True length = 8·4 cm × 50 000
> = 420 000 cm
> = 4200 m = **4·2 km**

1 Copy and complete the following table for each part of the route.

From	To	Map distance	True distance
Golf Course	Carn Beag Dearg	8·4 cm	4·2 km
Carn Beag Dearg	Carn Mor Dearg		
Carn Mor Dearg	Col		
Col	Ben Nevis △		
Ben Nevis △	Achintee House		

2 Clare is planning a climbing trip to Chamonix. The representative fraction of her map is 1 : 25 000. The map distance from Aiguille du Midi to Mont Blanc is 21·6 centimetres. What is the true distance?

3 Doug needs a more detailed map for following a route called *The Walker Spur*. He uses a map with a scale of 1 : 10 000. The map distance of *The Walker Spur* is 7·5 centimetres. What is the true distance?

● **Remember**

Bearings are angles which give directions.
3-figure bearings are measured clockwise from North.

The bearing of **North is 000°**, **East is 090°** and **South-West is 225°**

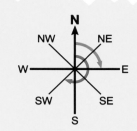

1 Write each of these directions as bearings.
(a) NE (b) SE (c) S (d) NW

2 Colin is taking part in an orienteering competition. This map shows his course.
(a) Copy this table.

Stage	Bearing
Start → 1	
1 → 2	
2 → 3	
3 → 4	
4 → 5	
5 → Finish	

(b) Measure the bearing for each stage and enter your results in the table.

3 Draw each of these bearings on separate diagrams.
(a) 060° (b) 095° (c) 175°
(d) 260° (e) 315° (f) 243°

4 The table shows the bearings of the mountains Gordon can see from the summit of Ben Macdui. Copy and complete the diagram to show this information.

Mountain	Bearing
Cairn Gorm	019°
Carn Etchachan	036°
Beinn a'Bhuird	080°
Carn a'Mhaim	172°
Cairn Toul	238°
Braeriach	285°

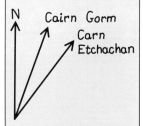

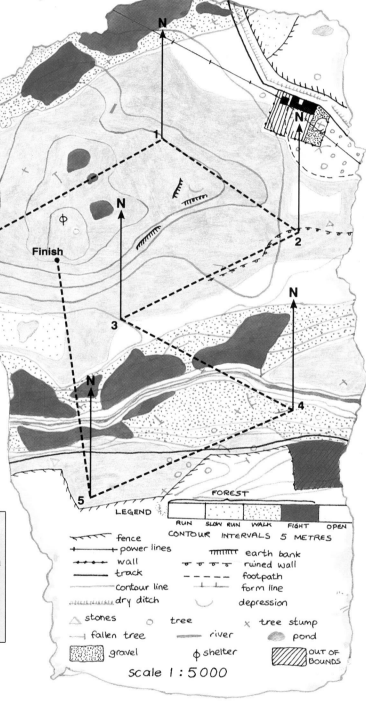

LEGEND
CONTOUR INTERVALS 5 METRES

RUN SLOW RUN WALK FIGHT OPEN

fence
power lines
wall
track
contour line
dry ditch
stones
fallen tree
gravel

earth bank
ruined wall
footpath
form line
depression
tree
river
shelter
tree stump
pond
OUT OF BOUNDS

scale 1 : 5000

Getting to the point

Some pipelines run along the seafloor out to sea from factories on land. The end of each pipeline is usually marked with a buoy. The position of a buoy can be found by taking bearings from two points on the coast.

From point A the buoy is on a bearing of 060°.

From point B the buoy is on a bearing of 315°.

The position of the buoy is where the two lines cross.

1 ▶ You need Worksheet 2.

Use the information in the table to show the position of each buoy on the Worksheet.

Buoy	Bearing from point A	Bearing from point B
1	055°	295°
2	125°	225°
3	165°	030°
4	220°	325°
5	086°	334°
6	043°	281°

2 The Coastguard station at Bennet Head is 8 kilometres due West of Tower Point. The bearing of a ship is 145° from Bennet Head and 215° from Tower Point.

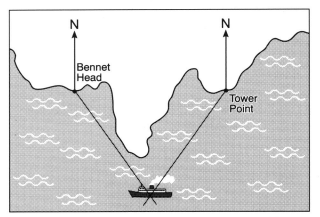

(a) Using a scale of 1 cm to represent 1 km, make a scale drawing to show the position of the ship.

(b) How far is the the ship from:
- Bennet Head
- Tower Point?

(c) What is the bearing of Bennet Head from the ship?

3 Air traffic controllers use bearings to locate planes in flight. Control Centre Alpha is 60 kilometres due North of Control Centre Beta. A plane is on a bearing of 165° from Control Centre Alpha and on a bearing of 110° from Control Centre Beta.

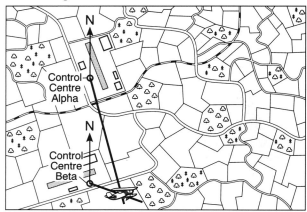

(a) Using a scale of 1 cm to represent 10 km, make a scale drawing to show the position of the plane.

(b) How far is the plane from:
- Control Centre Alpha
- Control Centre Beta?

You can find the height of a building by making scale drawings.

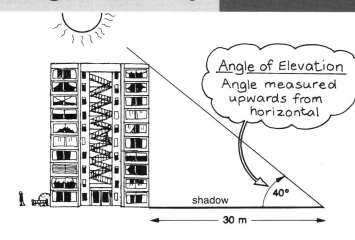

Angle of Elevation
Angle measured upwards from horizontal

shadow   40°

30 m

1 David wants to find the height of this block of flats.
The angle of elevation of the sun is 40°.
The shadow of the flats is 30 m long.

   (a) Make a scale drawing using a scale of
   1 cm to 5 m.

   (b) What is the height of the building?

2 Using the scales given, make scale drawings to find
the height of each of these buildings.

   (a) Statue of Liberty

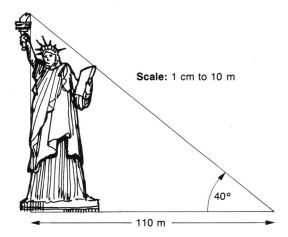

Scale: 1 cm to 10 m

40°

110 m

   (b) Telecom Tower

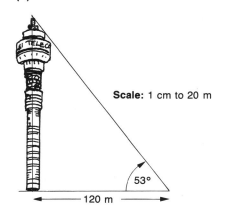

Scale: 1 cm to 20 m

53°

120 m

   (c) Eiffel Tower

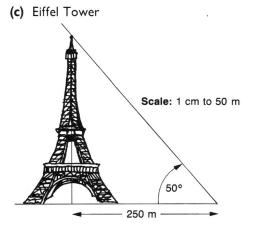

Scale: 1 cm to 50 m

50°

250 m

   (d) Empire State Building

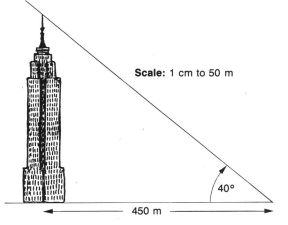

Scale: 1 cm to 50 m

40°

450 m

3 A building casts a shadow 25 m long when the angle
of elevation of the sun is 43°.

   (a) Using a suitable scale, make a scale drawing.
   (b) Find the height of the building.
   (c) Find the length of the shadow when the
   elevation of the sun is 28°.

▼ Challenge

4 Sylvia is watering her roof garden on a building
which is 76 m high. She is 60 m away from a second
building. The angle of elevation from Sylvia to the
top of this building is 19°. How high is the second
building?

1 Kathy and Joanna are standing on Tor Cliff, 60 metres above sea level. They see a yacht out to sea. The angle of depression is 47°. Make a scale drawing to find how far the yacht is from the base of the cliff.

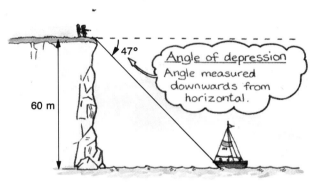

2 Joanna also sees a dinghy in the distance. The angle of depression of the dinghy is 31°. How far is the dinghy from the base of the cliff?

3 The lighthouse at Tor Cliff casts a shadow 35 m long when the angle of elevation of the sun is 43°. What is the height of the lighthouse?

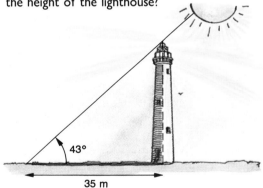

4 From the top of the cliff, Kathy sees a fishing boat sailing towards them. The angle of depression is 28°. Fifteen minutes later the angle of depression of the fishing boat is 39°. How far has the boat sailed in that time?

5 A search-and-rescue helicopter is flying at a height of 400 m. It is 900 m from the dinghy.

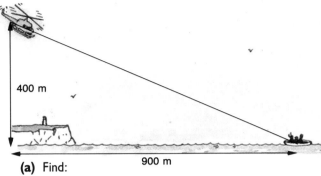

(a) Find:
  • the angle of elevation of the helicopter from the dinghy
  • the angle of depression of the dinghy from the helicopter.

(b) What do you notice about the two angles?

6 A speedboat is towing a paraglider at the end of a 25 m rope. The angle of elevation of the rope is 34°.

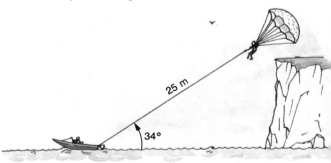

(a) What is the height of the paraglider above sea-level?

(b) The paraglider loses height. The rope is now inclined at an angle of 27° to the horizontal. How much height has the paraglider lost?

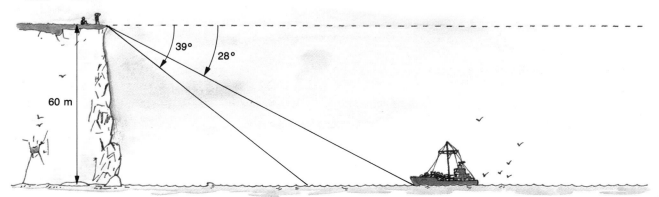

The Redhill and Hilltop radio transmitters are 30 km apart. The Redhill transmitter has a range of 15 km and the Hilltop transmitter has a range of 20 km.

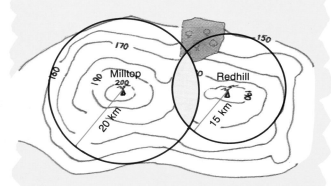

The shaded area shows where both signals can be picked up.

1 The Hawsforth and Westgarth transmitters are 60 km apart. The Hawsforth transmitter has a range of 45 km and the Westgarth transmitter has a range of 30 km. Make a scale drawing using a scale of 1 cm to 10 km to show where both signals can be picked up.

2 ▶ **You need Worksheet 3.**

(a) The island of Luandata has four transmitters. Show the range of each of these transmitters on the Worksheet.

Transmitter	Range in km
Malu	50
Hapil	70
Merta	45
Fallou	30

(b) Which towns are within range of the Malu transmitter?
(c) Which towns are within range of the Hapil and Merta transmitters?
(d) Which town can pick up transmissions from all four transmitters?
(e) Which town is outside the range of any transmitter?

3 A goat is tied to a post in the centre of a rectangular field. The length of the rope is 10 metres.

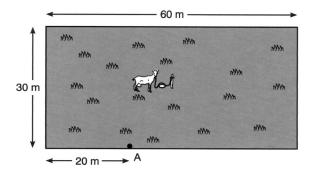

(a) Make a scale drawing of the field.
(b) Accurately mark the centre of the field.
(c) Show where the goat can graze.
(d) A second goat is tied to a post at point A using a rope 15 metres long. Show where both goats can graze.

4 Bowser, the guard dog, is tied to the corner of his owner's garage by a 3 metre long chain.

(a) Using a scale of 1 cm to 1 m make a scale drawing to show the area in which Bowser can walk.
(b) Make another scale drawing to show where Bowser can walk if his chain is 5 metres long.

The scale of the problem . . .

1 Tom is cutting down a diseased poplar tree in his garden. From a point 5 metres away the angle of elevation of the top of the tree is 65°. Tom's house is 10 metres from the foot of the tree. Will the tree hit his house if it falls in that direction?

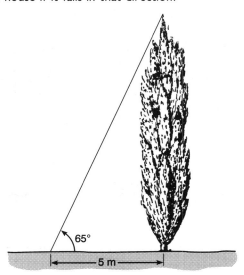

2 Mike has a rectangular lawn. He uses two types of garden sprinkler. The first is a rotating sprinkler which waters within a radius of 3 metres. The second is a hose 10 metres long which waters 2 metres on either side.

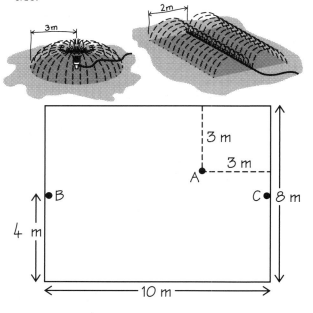

He placed the rotating sprinkler at A and laid the hose sprinkler from B to C. Make a scale drawing of Mike's lawn to show the area he watered.

3 The *Pride of the Firth* is sailing due North. At 3 pm the ship is 20 kilometres from a Coastguard station on a bearing of 120°. An hour later the bearing of the ship from the Coastguard station is 050°.

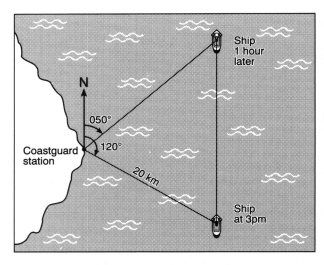

(a) How far was the ship from the Coastguard station at 4 pm?

(b) How far did the ship travel between 3 pm and 4 pm?

(c) What was the average speed of the ship?

(d) If the *Pride of the Firth* continues to sail North at this speed, what will be its bearing from the Coastguard station at 5 pm?

4 Hitop Hill lies 25 km due West of Blacktop Hill. Viewforth Hill has a bearing of 075° from the top of Hitop Hill and a bearing of 320° from the top of Blacktop Hill.
How far is Viewforth Hill from:
• Hitop Hill
• Blacktop Hill?

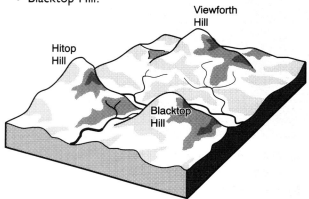

5 Point B is 2 kilometres due south of point A.
A pipeline, 2000 metres long, reaches out to sea
from point A on a bearing of 055°. What is the
bearing and the distance of the end of the pipeline
from point B?

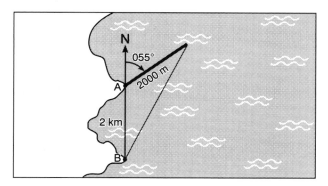

6 Alan, a surveyor, measures the bearing of point R
from point Q as 325°. If point P is 60 metres due
North of point Q and point R is 80 metres from
point Q, how far is point R from point P?

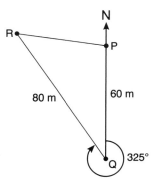

7 Janie has designed this windsurfing course for a
competition.

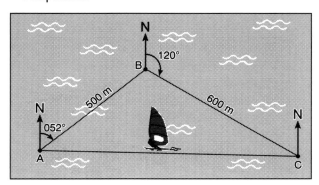

(a) Make an accurate scale drawing of Janie's
course.
(b) What is the bearing of A from C?
(c) Find the total distance of the course.

8 An aircraft takes off at an angle of 24°.
(a) When the aircraft is directly above a point on
the ground which is 3 kilometres from the
airport, what is the height of the aircraft?
(b) How far is the aircraft from the airport when it
reaches a height of 2 kilometres?

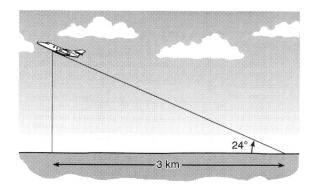

9 This table shows the distances and bearings of places of
interest from the viewpoint in Craglea Country Park.

Landmark	Bearing	Distance
Picnic Park	065°	2 km
Golf Club	125°	5 km
Castle	272°	3 km
Shooting Range	317°	6 km

Alison, one of the countryside rangers, is producing
a diagram of this information for a guide book.

Copy and complete her diagram.

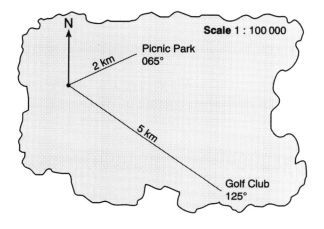

1 At the marina the boats are moored between pontoons arranged in sections.

Section

Size 1

Size 2

Size 3

Size 4

(a) Copy and complete:

Section size (s)	1	2	3	4
Number of pontoons (p)	3			

(b) The increase in the number of pontoons each time is ☐.

(c) Write a formula for the number of pontoons:
   • in words   • in letters.

(d) Use your formula to find the number of pontoons for size 5.

(e) Continue the table to check your answer.

(f) Use your formula to find the number of pontoons in 10 sections.

The increase in the number of pontoons each time is 2. This is called the **first difference**.

2 Robert wants to hire a power boat. The costs are given in the table:

Number of hours (h)	1	2	3	4	5
Hire cost in £ (c)	8	13	18	23	28

(a) Find the first difference from the table.

(b) Write the formula for the hire cost:
   • in words   • in letters.

(c) Use the formula to find how much it will cost Robert to hire the boat for 6 hours. Continue the table to check your answer.

(d) Use the formula to find the hire cost for 12 hours.

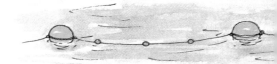

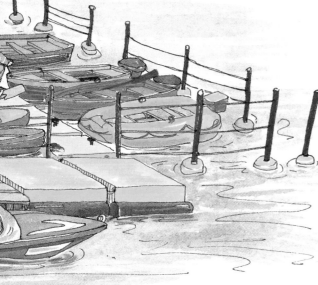

4 The small dinghies are moored in an enclosure marked by buoys and ropes.

(a) Copy and complete:

Number of buoys (b)	1	2	3	4	5
Number of ropes (r)	0	3			

(b) Find the first difference from the table.
(c) Write the formula for the number of ropes.
(d) Check the formula for 6 buoys.
(e) Use the formula to find the number of ropes in an enclosure with 30 buoys.

5 Part of Ocean Park has been designed as a play area. A number of rafts have been joined using cables.

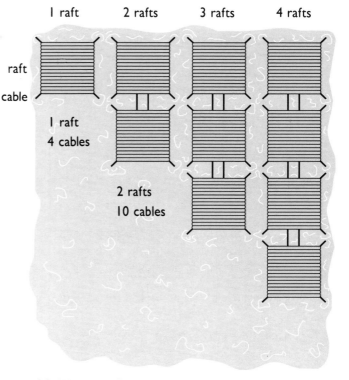

1 raft   2 rafts   3 rafts   4 rafts

raft

cable

1 raft
4 cables

2 rafts
10 cables

3 Ocean Park has organised a sailing display with yachts and dinghies. Each line of yachts will have a dinghy at the front and back.
Each yacht will have a dinghy on either side.

(a) Copy and complete:

Number of yachts (y)	1	2	3	4	5
Number of dinghies (d)			8		

(b) Find the first difference from the table.
(c) Write the formula for the number of dinghies.
(d) Check the formula for 6 yachts.
(e) Use the formula to find the number of dinghies for 15 yachts.

(a) Write the formula for the number of cables.
(b) Check the formula for 5 rafts.
(c) Use the formula to find the number of cables for 15 rafts.

Mosaic patterns

1 ▶ **Do Worksheets 4 and 5**.

2 Here is a new pattern Fatima is working on. It starts at size 2.

Size 2   Size 3   Size 4

Size 5   Size 6

(a) Copy and complete:

Size (s)	2	3	4	5	6
Number of tiles (n)	3	8			

(b) Make a difference table to find the second difference.

(c) Copy and complete:
The second difference is [   ] so the formula begins with [   ].

(d) Copy and complete:

Size^2 (s^2)	4	9	16		
Number of tiles (n)	3	8			

(e) Copy and complete:
Number of tiles = Size^2 – [   ]

or $n = s^2 -$ [   ]

(f) How many tiles will be needed for size 10?

3 For each pattern:
- make a table and find the second difference
- make a table using s^2
- write the formula for the number of tiles
- use the formula to find the number of tiles for size 7, then check by drawing.

(a)
Size 2   Size 3   Size 4

Size 5   Size 6

(b)
Size 2   Size 3   Size 4

Size 5   Size 6

A list of numbers like this is called a **sequence**.
1, 3, 5, 7, 9, 11, 13, 15, . . .

Each number in the sequence is called a **term**.
The 4th term is 7.

The term-link for this sequence is *add 2*.
1 + 2 = 3,   3 + 2 = 5,   5 + 2 = 7, . . .

For the sequence 2, 6, 18, 54, 162, 486, . . .
the term-link is *multiply by 3*.
2 × 3 = 6,   6 × 3 = 18,   18 × 3 = 54, . . .

The dots at the end of the sequence mean
"and so on".

1 In the sequence 1, 3, 5, 7, 9, 11, 13, 15, . . . write:
  (a) the 6th term   **(b)** the 8th term
  (c) the 1st term   **(d)** the 7th term.

2 Write the term-link for each sequence.
  (a) 4, 7, 10, 13, 16, 19, 22, 25, . . .
  (b) 5, 12, 19, 26, 33, 40, 47, 54, . . .
  (c) 38, 34, 30, 26, 22, 18, 14, 10, . . .
  (d) 85, 73, 61, 49, 37, 25, 13, 1, . . .
  (e) 1, 3, 9, 27, 81, 243, 729, 2187, . . .
  (f) 64, 32, 16, 8, 4, 2, 1, $\frac{1}{2}$, . . .

In a sequence the 1st term is 58 and the term-link
is *subtract 4*.

The sequence is 58
             58 − 4 = 54
             54 − 4 = 50 . . .

to give 58, 54, 50, 46, 42, 38, 34, 30, . . .

3 Write the first **eight** terms in each sequence.
  (a) The 1st term is 3.
       The term-link is add 5.
  (b) The 1st term is 8.
       The term-link is add 9.
  (c) The 1st term is 50.
       The term-link is subtract 6.
  (d) The 1st term is 92.
       The term-link is subtract 11.

4 Write the first **six** terms in each sequence.
  (a) The 1st term is 2.
       The term-link is multiply by 2.
  (b) The 1st term is 729.
       The term-link is divide by 3.
  (c) The 1st term is 1.
       The term-link is add 8.
  (d) The 1st term is 120.
       The term-link is subtract 15.
  (e) The 1st term is 1.
       The term-link is multiply by 10.
  (f) The 1st term is 42.
       The term-link is subtract 5.

In the sequence 3, 6, 9, 12, 15, . . .
the 4th term is 12
or the term number 4 is 12.

5 For each sequence write:
  • term number 1
  • term number 6
  • term number 7.
  (a) 5, 11, 17, 23, 29, 35, . . .
  (b) 13, 16, 19, 22, 25, 28, . . .
  (c) 56, 51, 46, 41, 36, 31, . . .
  (d) 2, 3, 5, 9, 17, 33, . . .
  (e) 3, 6, 12, 24, 48, 96, 192, 384, . . .
  (f) 1, 5, 25, 125, 625, . . .
  (g) 10 000, 1000, 100, 10, 1, $\frac{1}{10}$, . . .

6 Here is a table for the sequence 3, 6, 9, 12, 15, . . .

Term number	Term
1	3
2	6
3	9
4	12
5	15
6	18

Write the:
  (a) 2nd term   **(b)** 5th term
  (c) 6th term   **(d)** 7th term
  (e) 8th term   **(f)** 10th term.

Number sequences

Using a table a **sequence rule** can be found, which connects the term number to its term.

Term number	Term
1	3
2	6
3	9
4	12
5	15

The term-link is *add 3*.

The sequence rule is *multiply by 3*.

Term number	Term
1	$1 \times 3 = 3$
2	$2 \times 3 = 6$
3	$3 \times 3 = 9$
4	$4 \times 3 = 12$
5	$5 \times 3 = 15$

The number you add in the term-link is the number you multiply by in the sequence rule.

1 Draw a table for the first eight terms in each sequence with sequence rule:

(a) multiply by 2
(b) multiply by 5
(c) multiply by 6 then add 5
(d) multiply by 7 then subtract 3
(e) square the number
(f) square the number then add 3.

2 Find the sequence rule for:

(a) 4, 8, 12, 16, 20, . . .
(b) 7, 14, 21, 28, 35, 42, . . .
(c) 6, 12, 18, 24, 30, . . .
(d) 10, 20, 30, 40, 50, . . .
(e) 4, 7, 10, 13, 16, . . .
(f) 7, 11, 15, 19, 23, . . .
(g) 4, 9, 14, 19, 24, . . .
(h) 5, 13, 21, 29, 37, . . .

The sequence rule of a sequence is *multiply by 5 then add 4*.

Term number	Term
1	$1 \times 5 + 4 = 9$
2	$2 \times 5 + 4 = 14$
3	$3 \times 5 + 4 = 19$
n	$n \times 5 + 4 = 5n + 4$

The nth term of sequence U is written U_n. For this sequence $U_n = 5n + 4$

3 For each sequence, U:

• make a table   • write the nth term, U_n.

(a) 2, 4, 6, 8, . . . (b) 2, 6, 10, 14, . . .
(c) 2, 5, 8, 11, . . . (d) 1, 4, 9, 16, . . .
(e) 3, 6, 11, 18, . . . (f) 0, 3, 8, 15, . . .

The nth term of sequence P is $P_n = n^2 + 5$.

Term number	Term
1	$1^2 + 5 = 6$
2	$2^2 + 5 = 9$
3	$3^2 + 5 = 14$
4	$4^2 + 5 = 21$

Sequence P is 6, 9, 14, 21, . . .

4 Write the first five terms in each sequence:

• in a table   • as a list.

(a) $A_n = n + 1$ (b) $B_n = 3n + 5$
(c) $F_n = 2n - 1$ (d) $U_n = \frac{1}{2}n + 3$
(e) $W_n = n^2$ (f) $S_n = n^2 + 7$

▼ Challenge

5 For each sequence, U:

• make a table   • write the nth term.

(a) $1, \frac{1}{2}, \frac{1}{3}, \frac{1}{4}, \ldots$ (b) $\frac{1}{2}, \frac{1}{3}, \frac{1}{4}, \frac{1}{5}, \ldots$
(c) $1, \frac{1}{4}, \frac{1}{9}, \frac{1}{16}, \ldots$ (d) $\frac{1}{2}, \frac{2}{3}, \frac{3}{4}, \frac{4}{5}, \ldots$

Johnny Chung is a designer for Fly-High Kites. He designs kites of many different shapes. Some of them are triangles.

● **Remember**

A triangle is a flat shape with 3 straight sides. The angles of a triangle add up to 180°.

Type of triangle	Properties
Isosceles	Two equal sides. Two equal angles.
Equilateral	All sides are equal. All angles are 60°.
Right-angled	One angle is 90°.
Acute-angled	Each angle is less than 90°.
Obtuse-angled	One angle is greater than 90°.
Scalene	All sides are different lengths.

1 Johnny has designed these triangular shaped kites. For each triangle:
- calculate the sizes of the marked sides and angles
- describe the type of triangle it is.
  Some triangles may be more than one type.

(a)

90 cm   *b*   90 cm
40°   *a*
138 cm

(b)

y
60°   60°
1·3 m   *x*
a

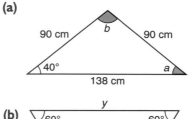

(c)

72°
1·7 m   1·7 m
a   *b*
2 m

(d)

75 cm   *b*   75 cm
a   45°
106 cm

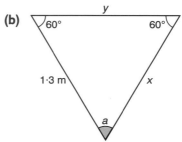

(e)

x   *a*   50 cm
50°   50°
64 cm

(f)

1 m   *c*
a   1 m
1 m   *b*

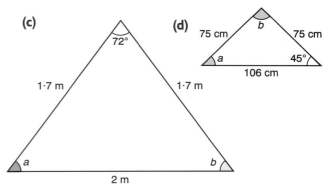

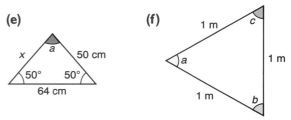

Flying high

● **Remember**

A **quadrilateral** is a flat shape with 4 straight sides. The angles of a quadrilateral add up to 360°.

Type of quadrilateral	Properties
Parallelogram	Opposite sides are equal. Opposite sides are parallel. Opposite angles are equal. Diagonals bisect each other.
Rectangle	Opposite sides are equal. Opposite sides are parallel. All angles are right angles. Diagonals are equal. Diagonals bisect each other.
Square	All sides are equal. Opposite sides are parallel. All angles are right angles. Diagonals are equal. Diagonals bisect each other. Diagonals meet at 90°.
Rhombus	All sides are equal. Opposite sides are parallel. Opposite angles are equal. Diagonals bisect each other. Diagonals meet at 90°.
Kite / *V-Kite*	Two pairs of adjacent sides are equal. One pair of opposite angles is equal. One diagonal is bisected by the other one. Diagonals meet at right angles.

I Johnny also designs kites which are quadrilaterals. Which type of quadrilateral best describes each kite?

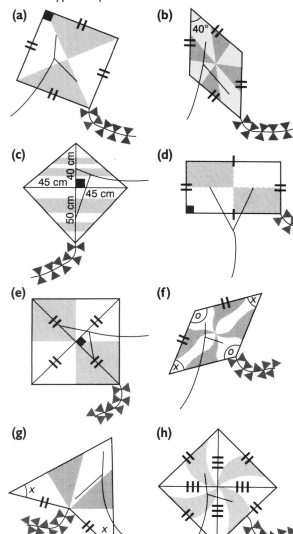

(a)

(b) 40°

(c) 45 cm 40 cm 45 cm 50 cm

(d)

(e)

(f) x o o x

(g) x x

(h)

2 Calculate the sizes of the marked lengths and angles.

(a)

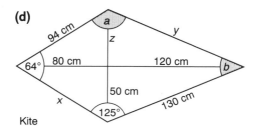

1·2 m

z

1·5 m

x

0·9 m

y

Rectangle

(b)

50°

2·4 m

b

x

a

y

22°

1·4 m

V-Kite

(c)

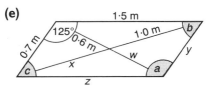

0·6 m

0·5 m

74°

y

v

a

d

c

0·8 m

z

x

w

b

Rhombus

(d)

94 cm

a

z

y

64°

80 cm

120 cm

b

x

50 cm

125°

130 cm

Kite

(e)

1·5 m

125°

0·6 m

1·0 m

b

0·7 m

w

y

c

x

a

z

Parallelogram

3 ABCD is a quadrilateral with A (4,5), B (1,2) and C (4,⁻1).

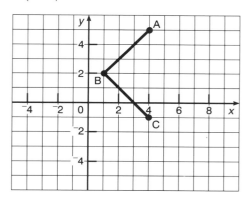

Draw separate diagrams to find the coordinates of D when ABCD is:

(a) a square

(b) a kite with one diagonal 8 units long

(c) a kite with one diagonal 4 units long

(d) a V-kite with one diagonal 2 units long.

4 Here are some clues about quadrilaterals. What type(s) could each be? You may find that drawing sketches will help.

(a) The sides are equal and meet at 90°.

(b) The diagonals are different lengths and do not meet at 90°.

(c) The opposite sides are not equal but the diagonals meet at 90°.

(d) The sides are equal and the diagonals meet at right angles.

(e) All the sides are the same length.

(f) The diagonals are not equal.

(g) The opposite sides are parallel.

Lines and points

● **Remember**

Each of these shapes has at least one line or axis of symmetry.

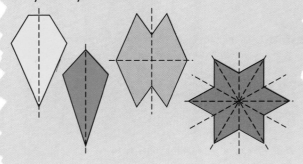

I All of Johnny's kites must have an axis of symmetry. Explain why a kite must have an axis of symmetry if it is to fly properly.

2 ▶ **Do Worksheet 6.**

If a shape fits onto its own outline more than once in one full turn it has **rotational symmetry**.

The **order** of rotational symmetry is the number of times a shape fits onto its outline in one full turn.

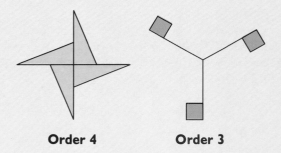

Order 4   Order 3

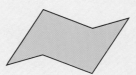

Order 2   Half-turn

A shape with symmetry of order 2 is said to have **half-turn symmetry**.

When designing the covers for his kites, Johnny often uses shapes which have rotational symmetry.

3 Find the order of rotational symmetry of these shapes. You may find it helpful to trace each shape.

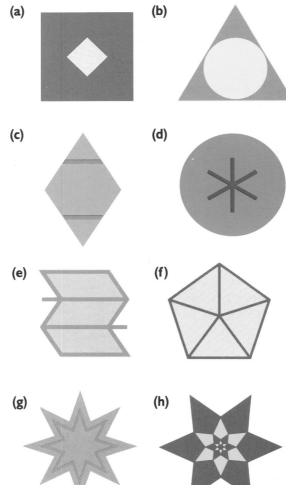

(a)   (b)

(c)   (d)

(e)   (f)

(g)   (h)

4 ▶ **Do Worksheet 7.**

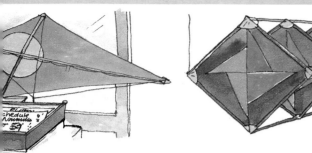
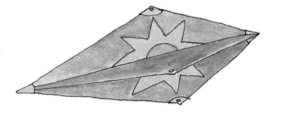

For some kite designs Johnny has to draw quadrilaterals.

1 Follow these steps to draw a rhombus with sides 8 cm long meeting at angles of 40° and 140°.

Step 1

Make a rough sketch and mark the lengths of sides and sizes of angles.

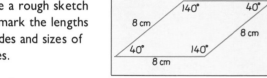

Step 2

Draw a line 8 cm long. Draw an angle of 40° at one end.

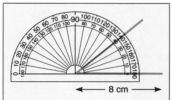

Step 3

Draw an angle of 140° at the other end of the line.

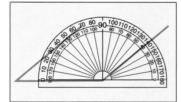

Step 4

Measure 8 cm along each sloping side and join the ends.

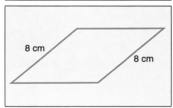

2 Draw each of these shapes accurately using ruler and protractor.
  (a) A square of side 6 cm.
  (b) A rectangle with sides 5 cm and 7 cm.
  (c) A rhombus with sides 5 cm meeting at angles of 50° and 130°.
  (d) A square with diagonals 6 cm.
  (e) A rhombus with diagonals 8 cm and 6 cm.
  (f) A rectangle with diagonals 10 cm meeting at an angle of 50°.

3 Follow these steps to draw a rhombus with sides 6 cm and one of its diagonals 10 cm.

Step 1

Make a rough sketch and mark all lengths.

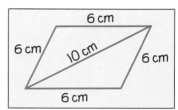

Step 2

Draw a line 10 cm long. Set compasses to 6 cm.
Draw arcs above and below the line.

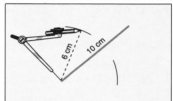

Step 3

Draw arcs 6 cm from the other end of the line.

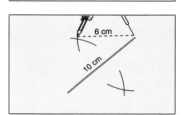

Step 4

Join the intersections of the arcs to the ends of the line.

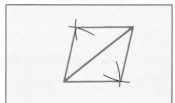

4 Draw each of these shapes accurately using ruler and compasses.
  (a) A rhombus with sides 3 cm and one diagonal 5 cm.
  (b) A rhombus with sides 5 cm and one diagonal 6 cm.
  (c) A kite with sides 3 cm and 5 cm and one diagonal 7 cm.
  (d) A kite with sides 4·5 cm and 10 cm and one diagonal 7 cm.
  (e) A parallelogram with sides 5 cm and 8 cm and one diagonal 10 cm.

What's the angle?

● **Remember**

Angles which make a straight line add up to 180°.

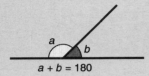

$a + b = 180$

Parallel lines are shown using arrows like this.

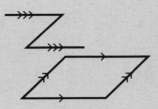

Vertically opposite angles are equal

Corresponding angles are equal

Alternate angles are equal

1 Sang Won and Jin Woo put together the frames for Johnny's designs. These are parts of some of the kites. Calculate the sizes of the marked angles.

(a)

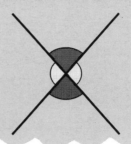

40°, a

(b)

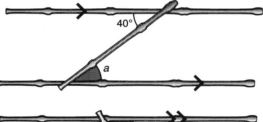

a, 65°

(c)

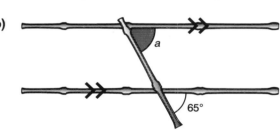

a, b, 37°, 58°

(d)

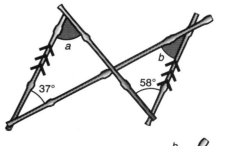

b, 50°, a

(e)

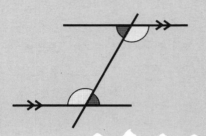

100°, c, d, b, a

(f)

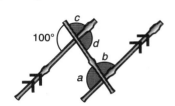

a, c, d, 34° b, 124°

(g)

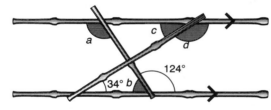

28°, 130°, b, a, c, d

(h)

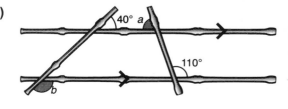

40° a, 110°, b

2 Calculate the sizes of the marked angles.

(a)

(b)
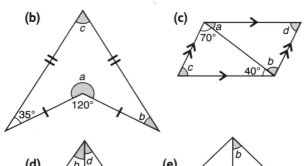

(c)

(d)
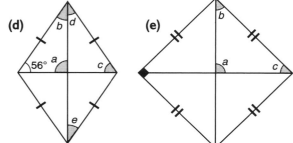

(e)

(f)
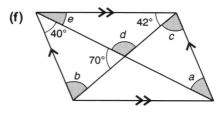

(g)

(h)
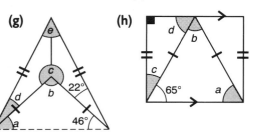

(i)
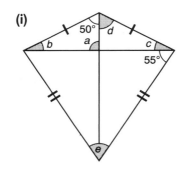

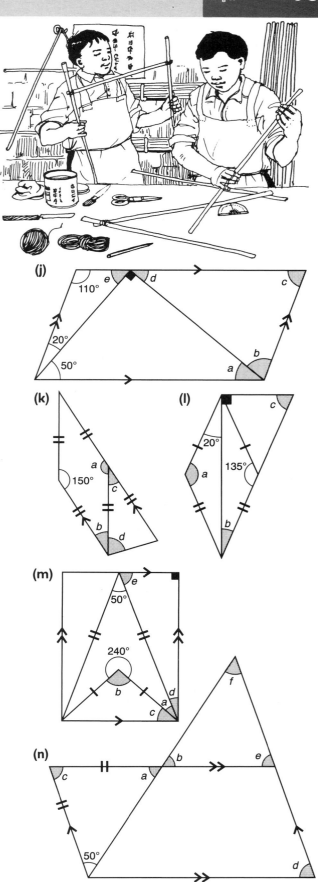

The Fly-High catalogue

A **polygon** is a flat shape with straight sides.

A **regular** polygon has all its sides equal and all its angles equal.

Number of sides	Geometric name	Shape	Regular shape
5	Pentagon		
6	Hexagon		
8	Octagon		

1 What are the common names for:
 (a) a regular quadrilateral
 (b) a regular triangle?

2 Winnie Tam produces catalogues for Fly-High kites. Make a list of the kites she has drawn and give the geometric name for each.

Fly-High Kites

Sanjo Rokkaku
Li Special
Bermudan
Barndoor
Diagonal Three-stick
V-Form Three-stick
Bow Three-stick
Levitor
Diagonal Four Stick

A regular hexagon can be divided into six **congruent** (identical) triangles.

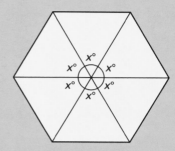

The sum of the six marked angles is 360°.

The size of each marked angle is
360° ÷ 6 = **60°**

For some kite designs Johnny has to draw regular hexagons.

1 Follow these steps to draw a regular hexagon.

Step 1

Draw a circle with a radius of 5 cm and mark its centre.

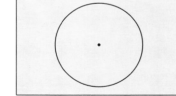

Step 2

Draw two radii making an angle of 60°.

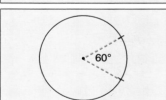

Step 3

Draw four more angles of 60°. Check that the remaining angle is also 60°.

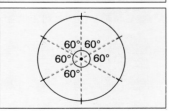

Step 4

Join the ends of the radii to form a regular hexagon. Rub out the radii and circle.

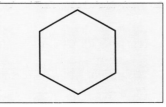

2 For each of these shapes:
  - calculate the angle to be drawn at the centre of the circle
  - draw the shape.
  (a) a regular octagon   **(b)** a regular pentagon
  (c) a square   **(d)** an equilateral triangle.

▼ **Challenge**

3 (a) Calculate the size of the angle at each **vertex** of:
  - a regular hexagon
  - a regular pentagon
  - a regular octagon.
  (b) Check your calculations by measuring the angles of the shapes which you drew in questions **1** and **2**.

Some of Johnny's kite designs are in the shape of stars. These shapes can be drawn in a similar way to that for regular polygons.

4 Follow these steps to draw a 6-pointed star.

Step 1

Carry out Steps 1 – 3 for a regular hexagon.

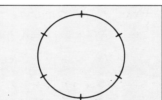

Step 2

Join a point to the one next to its neighbour.

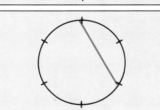

Step 3

Repeat step 2 for the other points.

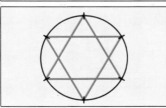

5 Draw star polygons based on:
  (a) a regular octagon
  (b) a regular pentagon.

Decimal places is often written as **dp**

● Remember

The number of **decimal places** is the number of digits after the decimal point.
18·790 has **3 decimal places**.
The number of decimal places indicates the **accuracy** of a number or measurement.

1 How many decimal places does each number have?
(a) 2·13   (b) 189·0   (c) 3·04
(d) 98·261   (e) 0·26   (f) 0·008

2 Write the numbers marked by the arrows.

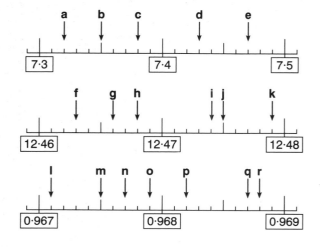

3 (a) Draw a number line and mark:
• 8·3   • 7·9   • 1·6
(b) Draw a number line and mark:
• 86·13   • 5·78   • 0·22
(c) Draw a number line and mark:
• 6·014   • 9·978   • 0·825

4·78 lies between
4·7 and 4·8
but is closer to 4·8.

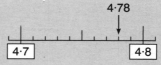

4·78 rounded to **1 dp is 4·8**.

8·5737 lies between
8·57 and 8·58
but is closer to 8·57.

8·5737 rounded to **2 dp** is **8·57**.

Rounding is always carried out so that the smallest possible error is introduced into a number.

4 Round:
(a) 2·36 to 1 dp   (b) 13·32 to 1 dp
(c) 8·238 to 2 dp   (d) 10·401 to 2 dp
(e) 5·3572 to 3 dp   (f) 6·7146 to 2 dp
(g) 93·143769 to 3 dp   (h) 0·176195 to 1 dp
(i) 13·973 to 1 dp   (j) 0·9973 to 2 dp.

6·285 is mid-way between 6·28 and 6·29.

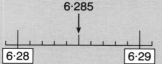

6·285 rounded to 2 dp is either **6·28 or 6·29**.

5 Round:
(a) 6·75 to 1 dp   (b) 9·315 to 2 dp
(c) 18·8205 to 3 dp   (d) 189·45 to 1 dp
(e) 78·95 to 1 dp   (f) 5·495 to 2 dp
(g) 7·6758 to 2 dp   (h) 10·8995 to 3 dp
(i) 1·10651 to 3 dp   (j) 4·99503 to 2 dp.

Astronomers have to work with large numbers.

The radius of the Earth is 6378 km.

> This is the highest place value

This distance is 6000 km to **1 significant figure**
6400 km to **2 significant figures**
6380 km to **3 significant figures**.
The number of significant figures can be used to express the accuracy of a number or measurement.

> For numbers > 1
> • to round to **1** significant figure - round to the **highest place** value.
> • to round to **2** significant figures - round to the **second highest** place value.

1 The mean distances from the sun to the planets are given in the table.

Planet	Mean distance from Sun (km)
Mercury	57 900 000
Venus	108 208 000
Jupiter	778 298 400
Uranus	2 875 039 000

Round each distance to:
(a) 1 sig fig
(b) 2 sig fig
(c) 3 sig fig.

> Significant figures is often written as sig fig

The time taken for a radio signal to travel from

the Earth to Saturn is 1·185 hours.

> This is the highest place value

This time is 1 hour to **1 sig fig**
1·2 hours to **2 sig fig**
1·18 or 1·19 hours to **3 sig fig**.

2 These are the times taken for radio signals to travel from the Earth to other planets.

Radio signals from Earth	
Planet	Time
Mars	4·3333 min
Jupiter	34·91667 min
Uranus	2·52028 h
Neptune	4·02778 h

Round each to:
(a) 1 sig fig **(b)** 2 sig fig **(c)** 3 sig fig.

3 The length of one year on the planet Mars is 1·8808 Earth years. Round this time to:
(a) 1 sig fig **(b)** 2 sig fig **(c)** 3 sig fig.

4 Repeat question 3 for each planet.
• Jupiter – 11·8617 Earth years
• Saturn – 29·473 Earth years
• Uranus – 84·0189 Earth years
• Pluto – 248·552 Earth years

Beetling about

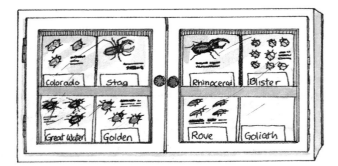

Dr Cheung is an entomologist. She is measuring the lengths of her favourite creatures – beetles. The instrument she is using can measure lengths very accurately but, when she writes about the beetles in scientific journals, she often uses rounded lengths.

> For numbers < 1
> - to round to **1** sig fig – round to the **highest non-zero** place value.
> - to round to **2** sig fig – round to the **next highest** place value.

A Goliath beetle has a length of 0·1087 m.

> This is the highest non-zero place value

This is • **0·1 m to 1 significant figure**
• **0·11 m to 2 significant figures.**

A Chafer beetle has a length of 0·0183 m.

> This is the highest non-zero place value

This is • **0·02 m to 1 significant figure**
• **0·018 m to 2 significant figures.**

1 Give the lengths of these beetles correct to:
(a) 1 sig fig (b) 2 sig fig.

Beetle	Length (m)
Blister	0·0148
Colorado	0·0253
Golden	0·0267
Great Water	0·0314
Rhinoceros	0·0901
Rove	0·0235
Stag	0·0752

2 A Ladybird is 0·0066 m long. Write this length correct to 1 sig fig.

3 Round the length of each Weevil beetle to 1 sig fig.

Weevil	Length (m)
A	0·0032
B	0·0028
C	0·0057
D	0·0065
E	0·0044
F	0·0045

4 Round the length of each Hercules beetle to:
(a) 1 sig fig (b) 2 sig fig (c) 3 sig fig.

Hercules beetle	Length (m)
U	0·1528
V	0·1699
W	0·1467
X	0·1853
Y	0·1350
Z	0·1235

5 How many Rhinoceros beetles placed end to end would fit the perimeter of your classroom?

Simon could find an **approximate** answer mentally by first rounding each number to 1 significant figure.

£27·99 ≃ £30   £8·49 ≃ £8
£30 + £8 = £38

His answer should be approximately £38, so £112·89 cannot be correct.

1 For each calculation:
- round each number to 1 sig fig
- find an approximate answer
- calculate the exact answer.

(a) 17 + 41   (b) 258 + 794
(c) 7·28 + 12·7   (d) 0·51 + 0·26
(e) 508 − 177   (f) 7·39 − 2·5
(g) 19·15 − 3·295   (h) 1287 − 462
(i) 2·14 × 3·41   (j) 17 × 3·76
(k) 0·39 × 0·21   (l) 0·058 × 0·92
(m) 18·3 ÷ 5·41   (n) 164 ÷ 75
(o) 7·95 ÷ 0·183   (p) 0·13 ÷ 10·29

2 For this calculation:
- estimate the answer
- carry out the calculation exactly.

The infield in baseball is a square of side 27·4 m with a base at each corner. How far does a player have to run in a Home run? (That is, once round the square.)

3 For each calculation:
- estimate the answer
- carry out the calculation exactly.

(a) An American football pitch is 109 m long by 49 m broad. What is the area?

(b) An Australian rules football pitch is elliptical in shape. What is the area of a pitch if it can be calculated as 3·14 × 68·6 × 91·4 m²?

(c) A doubles tennis court has an area of 261·8 m² and is 10·97 m wide. What is its length?

Often, when you look at an answer, your common sense tells you that it cannot be correct. Try to **estimate** what a reasonable answer would be.

4 Select which of the four given measures is most appropriate.

(a) The weight of a building brick.
    A 1 g   B 100 g
    C 1 kg   D 10 kg

(b) The time to fly from Manchester direct to Florida.
    A 1 hour   B 10 hours
    C 20 hours   D 1 day

(c) The height of a one-storey house.
    A 1 m   B 5 m
    C 10 m   D 100 m

(d) The volume of a bucket.
    A 1 litre   B 10 litre
    C 100 litre   D 1000 litre

(e) The running speed of a boy.
    A 1 km/h   B 10 km/h
    C 100 km/h   D 1000 km/h

Unavoidable errors

Ken is a quality control engineer in a factory which makes car engines. His job is to ensure that the engines work satisfactorily before they are sent to car manufacturers.

One of Ken's jobs is to check the sizes of various parts of the engines.

1 **(a)** He has to measure this valve. What would he say its length is if he used a ruler with only cm markings?

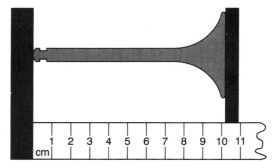

What would Ken record as the length of the same valve if he used measuring instruments with these scales?

(b)   **(c)**

   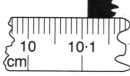

(d) These measurements are all of the **same** valve.
- Are any of them exact? Explain.
- How many significant figures does each have?
- Which is the most accurate measurement?

It is impossible to measure anything exactly.
All measurements are approximate and their accuracy depends on the measuring instrument used.
The more significant figures used, the more accurate a measurement is.

When Ken makes a measurement he records it in his notebook.

He notes that the valve-stem diameter is 6·9 mm. When writing a report later, he will know that this is not exact and that the actual diameter is bigger than 6·85 but smaller than 6·95.

The **lower bound** is 6·85 mm.
The **upper bound** is 6·95 mm.

2 These measurements are taken from Ken's notebook. Copy and complete the table.

	Measure-ment	Lower bound	Upper bound
Bore	72 mm		72·5 mm
Stroke	61 mm		
Capacity	993 cm^3		
Power output	3·3 kW	3·25 kW	
Valve seat width	1·4 mm		
Camshaft endfloat	0·3 mm		
Valve spring length	24·0 mm		
Oil capacity	2·25 *l*	2·245 *l*	
Valve guide diameter	7·03 mm		
Piston diameter	78·87 mm		
Main bearing play	0·023 mm		
Bearing diameter	40·968 mm		

Ken checks the sizes of parts supplied to the factory by other manufacturers.

Since you cannot measure exactly, a range of acceptable sizes is often given.

± means *plus or minus*

(15 ± 0.2) mm means that
• the lower bound = $15 - 0.2 = 14.8$ mm
• the upper bound = $15 + 0.2 = 15.2$ mm
• the tolerance = $15.2 - 14.8$
    = 0.4 mm

The tolerance is the difference between the upper and lower bounds

1 For these measurements find:
• the lower and upper bounds
• the tolerance.

(a) (18 ± 0.1) mm (b) (5.7 ± 0.2) cm
(c) (3 ± 0.25) kg (d) (135 ± 1.5) kg
(e) (0.5 ± 0.01) litre (f) (5.24 ± 0.002) litre
(g) (0.14 ± 0.003) m (h) (0.014 ± 0.0001) m

2 (a) Ken checked a consignment of bolts with lengths specified as (6.5 ± 0.3) cm. Which bolt lengths meet the specification?
• 6·52 cm • 6·31 cm • 6·15 cm
• 6·78 cm • 6·84 cm • 6·07 cm

(b) The diameter of these bolts was specified as (1.20 ± 0.002) cm. On checking, Ken found bolts with the following diameters. Which of them are acceptable?
• 1·213 cm • 1·201 cm • 1·194 cm
• 1·198 cm • 1·203 cm • 1·199 cm

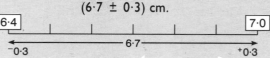

The range 6·4 cm to 7·0 cm can be written as (6.7 ± 0.3) cm.

3 Write each range of measurements in the same way.
(a) 4 cm to 6 cm (b) 17 mm to 18 mm
(c) 5·2 kg to 5·6 kg (d) 135·4 kg to 136·0 kg
(e) 4·0 m to 4·5 m (f) 1350 cm³ to 1400 cm³
(g) 0·124 m to 0·126 m (h) 0·080 l to 0·086 l

4 Carry out each calculation by first rounding the answer to each bracket to the specified accuracy.
(a) $(3.14 \times 6.2) + (8.2 \times 3.3)$ to 2 sig fig
(b) $(12.18 \times 0.20) - (8.4 \div 5.6)$ to 2 sig fig
(c) $\dfrac{(3.374 \times 9.175) - (5.182 \times 3.296)}{(3.17 \times 1.925)}$ to 3 sig fig

Ken often has to carry out calculations in which he has to decide how accurately to give his answers. He uses these rules:
• round only the final answer
• do not have more significant figures in the answer than there are in the **least** accurate measurement in the calculation.

Least accurate number has 1 sig fig

For example $2.4 \times 1.83 + 0.7$
so $2.4 \times 1.83 + 0.7 = 5.092$
    = **5 to 1 sig fig**

5 Carry out each calculation in question **4** again but **rounding only the final answer** to the specified accuracy.

6 Compare your answers to questions **4** and **5**. What do you notice?

7 Ken is doing calculations using measurements he has made on an engine. Carry out each of his calculations to an appropriate degree of accuracy.
(a) The volume swept out by a piston is $3.14 \times 6.1 \times 7.2 \times 7.2$ cm³.
(b) The play on three bearings in the engine is 0·032 mm, 0·01 mm and 0·002 mm. Calculate the mean play.

Many problems can be solved by first considering a simpler problem.

1 The diagrams show a network of one-way cycle paths.

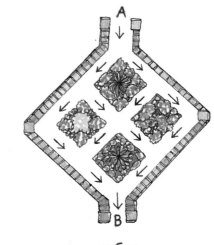

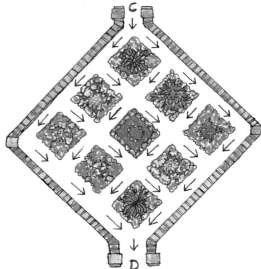

(a) How many different routes can Ishmail take from A to B?

(b) How many different routes can Sheila take from C to D?

2 You need one red counter, at least seven yellow counters and squared paper.

(a) Draw a 2 × 2 grid and place the counters as shown. Follow these rules:

- The red counter always starts in the bottom left hand square. The top right hand square always starts empty.
- A counter can move one square horizontally or vertically, but not diagonally.
- A counter can only move into an empty square.

Find the least number of moves to position the red counter in the top right hand square.

(b) Repeat for a 3 × 3 grid.
(c) Record your results in a table.
(d) Find the least number of moves to position the red counter in the top right hand square of a 10 × 10 grid.

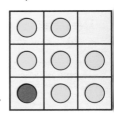

3 (a) How many cubes are needed to make this symmetrical model five layers high?

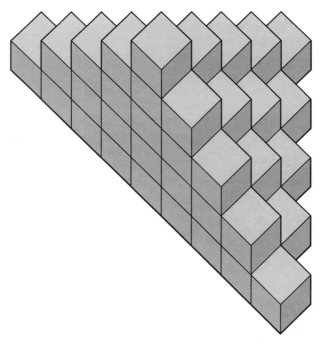

(b) How many cubes are needed to make a similar model ten layers high?

You need a die and a counter.

Hexagon Game

▶ **You need Worksheet 8.**
Place the counter in
the centre of the board on **S**.
Roll the die.
Move the counter
one space in the
direction shown
according to the
number on the die.

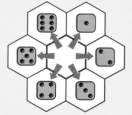

The game finishes after five moves.

1 **(a)** Play the Hexagon Game. Did you win or lose?
  (b) Copy the table and extend it for ten games.

Game number	Win	Lose
1		
2		
3		

(c) Play ten games. Record with a tick in the table
  when you win or lose each game.
(d) A game is fair when there is an equal chance of
  winning or losing. Is this game fair?
(e) Make a conjecture about where the boundary
  line should be to make the game fair.
(f) Test your conjecture by playing the game ten
  times.
(g) Does your conjecture hold? If not alter your
  conjecture and test it.

Square Game

▶ **You need Worksheet 9.**
This is played in
a similar way.
The moves are
shown here.

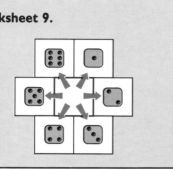

The game finishes
after 5 moves.

2 **(a)** Make a conjecture about where the boundary
  line should be to make the game as fair as
  possible.
  (b) Test your conjecture by playing ten games.
  (c) Record your results in a table.
  (d) Does your conjecture hold?
  (e) If necessary, alter your conjecture and test it by
  playing more games.

Triangle Game

▶ **You need Worksheet 10.**
For this game, if the die:

• shows **one** or **six**, move the counter one space
  to the **right**
• shows **three** or **four**, move it one space to the
  left
• shows **two** or **five**, move it one space **up or
  down** according to the direction of the triangle.

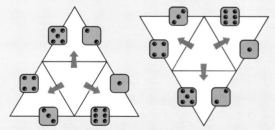

The game finishes after 5 moves.

3 **(a)** Make a conjecture about where the boundary
  line should be to make the Triangle Game fair.
  (b) Test your conjecture by playing ten games.
  (c) Record your results in a table.
  (d) If necessary, alter your conjecture and test it by
  playing more games.

Sunningdale

▶ **You need Worksheet 11.**

1 At the Sunningdale campsite caravans are parked on the grass beside the roads. Each caravan is allocated an 8 m by 8 m area of pitch.

(a) Using the scale 1 cm to 10 m mark on the map all pitches suitable for caravans.

(b) A caravan pitch earns £1500 per annum on average. How much money would be earned for your number of pitches?

2 The rest of the site is used for tents. Each tent is allocated a 5 m by 10 m pitch.

(a) How many tents can you fit on the site?

(b) Tent pitches earn £1100 per annum on average. How much money would be earned for your number of pitches?

3 Three power points are to be installed on the site, to supply electricity to tents. Each point will provide electricity within a radius of 30 m but not across a road.

(a) Select positions for the three power points to supply the maximum number of tents.

(b) Shade the area supplied by each point.

4 There are five drinking water taps on the site at C9, H13, L9, J1 and R8.

(a) Mark the positions of the taps on the map.

(b) What is the longest distance to a tap from any point on the site?

5 The takings for one night in May were £195. How many tents and how many caravans were on site that night?

6 There are five permanent caravans for hire at Sunningdale. Complete the booking chart to find which family cannot be accommodated.

September Holiday Weekend Requested Bookings			
Name	Number in party	Arriving	Departing
Clark	4	Friday	Monday
Jones	2	Sunday	Monday
Ford	3	Saturday	Tuesday
Pennel	5	Monday	Wednesday
Dalton	5	Friday	Monday
Farren	6	Friday	Monday
Simpson	4	Sunday	Tuesday
Burke	3	Friday	Sunday

7 Each month in the summer there is a swimming race at the camp pool. In July there were six contestants, Joan, Paul, Helen, Sheila, Ann and Maurice. Use the clues to find the order of finishing.

Maurice beat Joan and Helen

Ann was immediately behind Sheila

Paul was last

Helen was slower than Joan

Ann swam faster than Maurice

8 Strangehill School used the campsite pool for a sponsored swim.

   (a) What is the length of the pool in metres?
   (b) Find the missing values in these sponsor forms.

Number of lengths	Total distance	Amount per metre	Total
8	p	q	£24
r	360 m	5p	s
t	510 m	u	£35·70

9 The camp shop sells three kinds of rolls, brown, white and granary, and four kinds of cold meat, ham, lamb, pork and beef.

   (a) How many different kinds of meat rolls can be made?
   (b) If mustard is added as a possible ingredient how many kinds would there be?

Problems, problems . . .

1 (a) Andrew is using a computer robot to draw the rhombus ABCD.

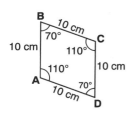

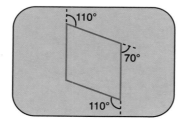

The robot started at A pointing up the screen. Andrew entered these commands:

FORWARD 10
RIGHT 110
FORWARD 10
RIGHT 70
FORWARD 10

The robot is now at D pointing **down** the screen. Which two commands would Andrew have to give the robot to complete the rhombus?

(b) Andrew clears the computer screen. List the commands needed to draw the kite PQRS when the robot starts at P pointing up the screen.

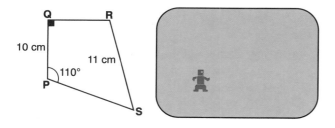

2 The 36 members of the Triple Star Club are planning their ten day camp. Jo buys their food.

(a) Jo knows that 5 lb of potatoes is enough to feed 4 people for a day. What weight of potatoes will she need:

• each day

• for the duration of the camp?

(b) After Jo has bought all the provisions, 6 members find they cannot go to the camp. If everyone attending were given the original potato ration, how long should Jo's stock of potatoes last?

3 This series of chemical compounds is made from carbon (C) and hydrogen (H) atoms.

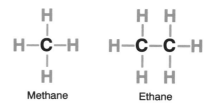

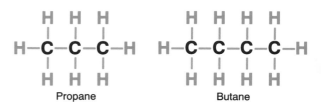

(a) Draw the next two compounds, pentane and hexane, in this series.

(b) Octane is the member of this series with 8 carbon atoms. How many hydrogen atoms does it have?

(c) Another compound in this series has 34 hydrogen atoms. How many carbon atoms will it have?

(d) Write down a formula for the number of hydrogen atoms, h, if there are c carbon atoms.

4 This is a flat aluminium casting.

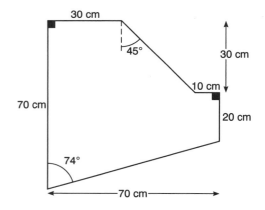

(a) Find the length of the perimeter of the casting. Give your answer correct to 2 sig fig.

(b) The casting is to be edged with a steel band. If the cost of material for this band is £15 per metre, how much will it cost?

5 From this rectangular piece of card four equal squares of side t cm are cut from the corners to make the net of a cuboid without a lid.

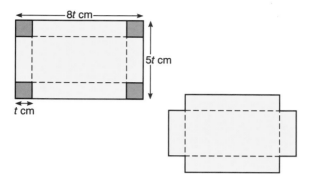

(a) Write the perimeter of the net in terms of t.
(b) If the perimeter of the net is 65 cm find the value of t.

6 Kelly is packing cylindrical tins each containing $1\frac{1}{2}$ litres of paint into a container. Each tin has diameter 12 cm and height 14 cm. The container is 37 cm long, 25 cm broad and 28 cm high.

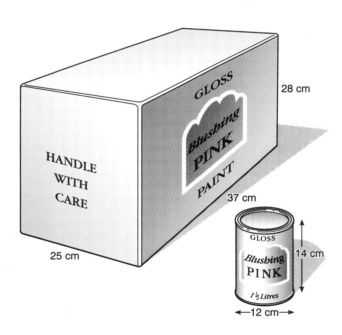

(a) Find the maximum number of paint tins which Kelly can fit inside the container.
(b) Trish considers what would happen if instead of packing the tins she poured the same volume of paint into the container. How far up the sides, to the nearest cm, would the paint reach?

7 The design for a multi-storey car park has each floor above the first supported by 8 pillars. The diagram shows a car park with 3 floors but the design can be used with many floors.

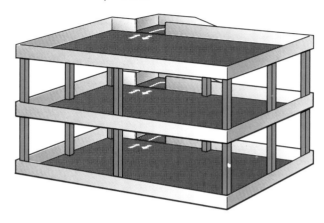

(a) How many pillars are needed for three floors?
(b) Copy and complete the table to show the number of pillars needed for different numbers of floors.

Number of floors	1	2	3	4	5	6
Number of pillars	0					

(c) Write a formula to find the number of pillars, P, needed for x floors.
(d) A new car park is to be built with 9 floors. Use your formula to find the number of pillars needed.

8 At Christmas Grandma gave £50 to be shared among her three grandchildren Rachel, Morven and Alasdair. The money was divided according to age with Rachel, the eldest, being given the most and Alasdair, the youngest, being given least.

(a) Suggest one possible way the money could have been divided.
(b) In fact Rachel was given £11 more than Morven, and Alasdair was given £6 less than Morven. How much did each child receive?

Rona is playing Zap, the new adventure game. The scores are shown on the screen.

```
10
 9
 8
 7
 6
 5
 4
 3
 2
 1
 0
⁻1
⁻2
⁻3
⁻4
⁻5
⁻6
⁻7
⁻8
⁻9
⁻10
⁻11
⁻12
⁻13
⁻14
⁻15
```

1 Find Rona's score for an attack when she shoots:

(a) a fireball and a missile
(b) a fireball and a robot
(c) a fireball and a dragon
(d) a missile and a robot
(e) a missile and a dragon
(f) a robot and a dragon
(g) a fireball, a robot and a dragon
(h) a dragon, a robot and a missile.

● **Remember**

Adding a negative number is the same as subtracting the positive number.

$$5 + {}^-1 \qquad {}^-7 + {}^-2 \qquad 3 + {}^-10$$
$$= 5 - 1 \qquad = {}^-7 - 2 \qquad = 3 - 10$$
$$= 4 \qquad = {}^-9 \qquad = {}^-7$$

2 Find:

(a) ⁻3 + 5
(b) ⁻8 + 4
(c) 2 − 7
(d) 10 − 5
(e) ⁻4 − 9
(f) ⁻6 − 10
(g) 5 + ⁻3
(h) ⁻4 + ⁻8
(i) 7 + ⁻7
(j) 9 + ⁻18
(k) 4 + ⁻16
(l) 10 + ⁻3
(m) 17 + ⁻6
(n) 9 + ⁻15
(o) 6 + ⁻20
(p) 4 + ⁻2 + ⁻1
(q) ⁻3 + ⁻5 + ⁻7
(r) ⁻3 + ⁻10 + 11

3 What does Rona score when she shoots:

(a) 4 fireballs **(b)** 7 missiles
(c) 6 robots **(d)** 3 dragons?

● **Remember**

A positive number multiplied by a negative number gives a negative number.

$$7 \times {}^-3 = {}^-21$$

A negative number multiplied by a positive number gives a negative number.

$${}^-6 \times 5 = {}^-30$$

4 Find:

(a) 6 × ⁻3 **(b)** ⁻4 × 5 **(c)** 4 × ⁻4
(d) 3 × ⁻7 **(e)** ⁻6 × 2 **(f)** 5 × ⁻1
(g) 0 × ⁻8 **(h)** ⁻9 × 3 **(i)** 7 × ⁻10

5 (a) Rona shoots 5 bombs giving a score of 20. What is the score for shooting a bomb?
(b) She shoots down 6 planes scoring ⁻30. What is the score for shooting a plane?

● **Remember**

A negative number divided by a positive number gives a negative number.

$${}^-20 \div 5 = {}^-4$$

6 Find:

(a) ⁻6 ÷ 3 **(b)** ⁻18 ÷ 6 **(c)** ⁻50 ÷ 2
(d) ⁻12 ÷ 4 **(e)** ⁻21 ÷ 7 **(f)** ⁻45 ÷ 9
(g) ⁻60 ÷ 5 **(h)** ⁻48 ÷ 8 **(i)** ⁻130 ÷ 10

7 Find:

(a) 4 − 9 **(b)** ⁻3 − 8 **(c)** 5 + ⁻2
(d) 7 + ⁻10 **(e)** 5 × ⁻4 **(f)** 6 × ⁻7
(g) 36 ÷ 4 **(h)** 70 ÷ 5 **(i)** 12 + ⁻4
(j) 6 + ⁻6 **(k)** ⁻16 ÷ 4 **(l)** ⁻80 ÷ 5

Rona's friends join in the game.

Rona has a score of 3 and it goes to 9. We can write this as
9 − 3 = ?
    ? = 6
Rona's score has gone **up 6** points.

(number line marked 9 down to 3, "up 6 points")

Trish has a score of ⁻5 and it goes to 3. We can write this as
3 − ⁻5 = ?
     ? = 8
Trish's score has gone **up 8** points.

(number line marked 3 down to ⁻5, "up 8 points")

Talat has a score of ⁻6 and it goes to ⁻10. We can write this as
⁻10 − ⁻6 = ?
      ? = ⁻4
Talat's score has gone **down 4** points.

(number line marked ⁻6 down to ⁻10, "down 4 points")

1 Copy and complete to find each person's change of score.

(a) Sally: ⁻2 to 7, 7 − ⁻2 = ☐
Sally's score goes ☐ ☐ points.

(b) Katy: ⁻4 to 9, 9 − ⁻4 = ☐
Katy's score goes ☐ ☐ points.

(c) Paul: ⁻9 to ⁻4, ⁻4 − ⁻9 = ☐
Paul's score goes ☐ ☐ points.

(d) Pierre: ⁻1 to ⁻7, ⁻7 − ⁻1 = ☐
Pierre's score goes ☐ ☐ points.

2 Write a subtraction to find Rona's change in score when it goes from:

(a) ⁻5 to 2   (b) ⁻6 to 1   (c) ⁻4 to ⁻9
(d) ⁻6 to ⁻3   (e) 4 to zero   (f) ⁻5 to 0

Subtracting a negative number is the same as adding the positive number.

6 − ⁻2	⁻3 − ⁻4
= 6 + 2	= ⁻3 + 4
= 8	= 1

3 Copy and complete.

(a) 6 − ⁻1
= 6 + 1
= ☐

(b) 4 − ⁻5
= 4 + 5
= ☐

(c) ⁻1 − ⁻4
= ⁻1 + 4
= ☐

(d) ⁻5 − ⁻3
= ⁻5 + 3
= ☐

(e) ⁻8 − ⁻7
= ⁻8 ☐
= ☐

(f) ⁻7 − ⁻3
= ⁻7 ☐
= ☐

(g) 5 − ⁻6
= ☐
= ☐

(h) ⁻7 − ⁻7
= ☐
= ☐

4 Find:

(a) 6 − ⁻2   (b) 2 − ⁻6
(c) ⁻5 − ⁻3   (d) ⁻3 − ⁻5
(e) ⁻4 − ⁻4   (f) 1 − ⁻7
(g) 7 − ⁻1   (h) ⁻6 − ⁻8
(i) ⁻8 − ⁻6   (j) ⁻3 − ⁻3

5 Find:

(a) 6 + 7 − 10   (b) 5 + 2 − 8
(c) 4 − 3 − 5   (d) 4 − 8 + 8
(e) 4 − 6 + ⁻3   (f) 7 + ⁻1 + ⁻4
(g) ⁻3 + ⁻5 + 7   (h) ⁻3 − ⁻2 + 5
(i) 8 − ⁻1 − 9   (j) 6 − ⁻2 − 4
(k) ⁻2 − ⁻5 + 6   (l) ⁻8 − ⁻4 + ⁻9

1 Copy and complete each of these number patterns.

(a)
2 × 3 =
2 × 2 =
2 × 1 =
2 × 0 =
2 × ⁻1 =
2 × ⁻2 =
2 × ⁻3 =

(b)
4 × ⁻3 =
3 × ⁻3 =
2 × ⁻3 =
1 × ⁻3 =
0 × ⁻3 =
⁻1 × ⁻3 =
⁻2 × ⁻3 =

(c)
⁻5 × 2 =
⁻5 × 1 =
⁻5 × 0 =
⁻5 × ⁻1 =
⁻5 × ⁻2 =
⁻5 × ⁻3 =
⁻5 × ⁻4 =

(d)
⁻3 × ⁻7 =
⁻2 × ⁻7 =
⁻1 × ⁻7 =
0 × ⁻7 =
1 × ⁻7 =
2 × ⁻7 =
3 × ⁻7 =

Look at your number patterns. Check that when you multiply two numbers

- the answer is **positive** when their **signs are the same**
- the answer is **negative** when their **signs are different**.

2 Find:

(a) 3 × ⁻4   (b) ⁻7 × 6   (c) ⁻6 × ⁻4
(d) 8 × ⁻2   (e) ⁻5 × ⁻9   (f) ⁻6 × ⁻6
(g) ⁻4 × 7   (h) 7 × ⁻5   (i) ⁻3 × ⁻3
(j) (⁻9)²   (k) (⁻5)²   (l) (⁻20)²

3 Copy and complete:

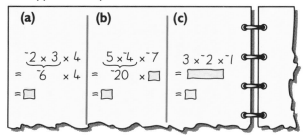

Since   5 × 3 = 15
then   15 ÷ 3 = 5
and   15 ÷ 5 = 3

Since   5 × ⁻3 = ⁻15
then   ⁻15 ÷ ⁻3 = 5
and   ⁻15 ÷ 5 = ⁻3

Since   ⁻5 × 3 = ⁻15
then   ⁻15 ÷ 3 = ⁻5
and   ⁻15 ÷ ⁻5 = 3

Since   ⁻5 × ⁻3 = 15
then   15 ÷ ⁻3 = ⁻5
and   15 ÷ ⁻5 = ⁻3

Look at these examples.
When you divide two numbers

- the answer is **positive** when their **signs are the same**
- the answer is **negative** when their **signs are different**.

5 Find:

(a) ⁻8 ÷ 2   (b) 20 ÷ ⁻5   (c) ⁻35 ÷ ⁻7
(d) ⁻24 ÷ 3   (e) ⁻36 ÷ ⁻6   (f) 5 ÷ ⁻1
(g) ⁻21 ÷ ⁻3   (h) ⁻63 ÷ ⁻3   (i) 56 ÷ ⁻8

6 Copy and complete:

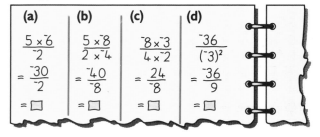

4 Find:

(a) 3 × ⁻4 × 2   (b) 5 × ⁻2 × ⁻1
(c) ⁻5 × ⁻1 × ⁻6   (d) (⁻4)³
(e) 0 × ⁻8 × ⁻9   (f) 2 × ⁻5 × ⁻1 × ⁻4
(g) 3 × ⁻2 × 4 × ⁻5   (h) (⁻5)³

7 Find:

(a) $\dfrac{4 \times {}^-6}{3}$ (b) $\dfrac{{}^-9 \times 5}{{}^-3 \times {}^-3}$ (c) $\dfrac{7 \times {}^-4}{({}^-2)^2}$

■ **Investigation**

8 (⁻1)² = ☐,   (⁻1)³ = ☐,
What do you notice? Test for other negative numbers.

● **Remember**

$$2(3a + 1)$$
$$= \quad 6a + 2$$

$$5(2b - 3)$$
$$= \quad 10b - 15$$

1 Multiply out the brackets.

(a) $5(a + 3)$ (b) $3(2b + 1)$
(c) $4(c - 7)$ (d) $2(5d - 3p)$

2 Copy and complete:

(a)

$^-2 (3+4)$ or $^-2 \times 3 + ^-2 \times 4$
$= ^-2 \times 7$ $= ^-6 + ^-8$
$= \square$ $= ^-6 - 8$
        $= \square$

(b)

$^-3 (5-1)$ or $^-3 \times 5 - ^-3 \times 1$
$= ^-3 \times \square$ $= ^-15 - ^-3$
$= \square$ $= ^-15 + 3$
        $= \square$

You can multiply brackets like this.

$$^-3(a + 4)$$
$$= \quad ^-3 \times a + ^-3 \times 4$$
$$= \quad ^-3a + ^-12$$
$$= \quad ^-3a - 12$$

$$^-3(a - 4)$$
$$= \quad ^-3 \times a - ^-3 \times 4$$
$$= \quad ^-3a - ^-12$$
$$= \quad ^-3a + 12$$

3 Copy and complete:

(a)   **(b)**   **(c)**   **(d)**

$^-3 (a+5)$ $^-2(5b+7)$ $^-5(c-2)$ $^-4 (3f-8)$
$= ^-3a + ^-15$ $= ^-10b + \square$ $= \square - ^-10$ $= \boxed{}$
$= \square - \square$ $= \boxed{}$ $= \boxed{}$. $= \boxed{}$

4 Multiply out the brackets.

(a) $^-4(p + 3)$ (b) $^-3(2q + 7)$
(c) $^-5(3r + 7s)$ (d) $^-7(x - 3)$
(e) $^-1(3w - 2z)$ (f) $^-7(4 - 5j)$
(g) $^-2(t + 2u + 3)$ (h) $^-4(3n - 7m + 5)$

You can simplify expressions like this.

$$6 - (a + 4)$$
$$= \quad 6 + ^-1(a + 4)$$
$$= \quad 6 - a - 4$$
$$= \quad 2 - a$$

$$2a - (a - 4)$$
$$= \quad 2a + ^-1(a - 4)$$
$$= \quad 2a - a + 4$$
$$= \quad a + 4$$

5 Copy and complete:

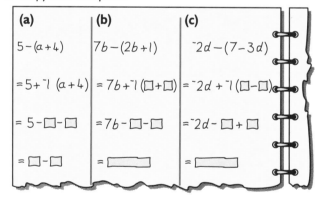

(a)   **(b)**   **(c)**

$5 - (a+4)$ $7b - (2b+1)$ $^-2d - (7-3d)$
$= 5 + ^-1 (a+4)$ $= 7b + ^-1 (\square + \square)$ $= ^-2d + ^-1 (\square - \square)$
$= 5 - \square - \square$ $= 7b - \square - \square$ $= ^-2d - \square + \square$
$= \square - \square$ $= \boxed{}$ $= \boxed{}$

6 Simplify:

(a) $4a - (a + 5)$ (b) $8f - (f - 8)$
(c) $4 - (3c + 7)$ (d) $^-5h - (7 - 3h)$

▶ **Challenge**

7 Multiply out the brackets and then simplify.

(a) $3(a + 1) - 2(a + 2)$
(b) $4(3b + 1) - 5(2b - 1)$
(c) $5(2 - 3c) - (c - 2)$
(d) $9(2d - 6) - (10 + 3d)$
(e) $7(1 - 2e) + (e - 1)$
(f) $6(2h - 3) + 2(15 - 4h)$

Up and down

Alan has x pounds in his bank account.
Dorothy has 3 times this amount.

You can make an equation and solve it.

	$3x + 6 = x - 10$
Subtract x from each side.	$2x + 6 = ^-10$
Subtract 6 from each side.	$2x\ \ \ \ = ^-16$
Divide each side by 2.	$x\ \ \ \ \ \ = ^-8$

Alan is **£8** overdrawn and Dorothy is **£24** overdrawn.

● **Remember**

Always do the opposite operation.

---

1 For each situation make an equation and solve it to find the answer.

(a) Duncan and Struan are divers. From the water surface Duncan is at $2t$ metres and Struan is at $4t$ metres. If Duncan dived 7 metres and Struan rose 13 metres they would meet. What position is each at?

(b) Carole and Ian are trying to find the freezing point of a liquid. The reading on Carole's thermometer is $6b°$C, the reading on Ian's is $3b°$C. The liquid froze when Carole decreased the temperature by 8°C and Ian decreased his by 20°C. What is the freezing point of the liquid?

2 Solve each equation.

(a) $3p + 4 = ^-2$ **(b)** $5 + 5p = ^-20$
(c) $6f + 18 = 6$ **(d)** $12 = 4v + 16$
(e) $3y - 5 = ^-29$ **(f)** $^-7 + 6r = ^-67$
(g) $2k + 15 = 3$ **(h)** $5 = 8c + 45$

3 Find the solution to each equation.

(a) $4c + 6 = 3c + 4$ **(b)** $8x + 5 = 3x - 30$
(c) $7p = 4p - 15$ **(d)** $2k - 7 = 5k + 2$
(e) $9 + 3y = ^-1 + y$ **(f)** $4a - 12 = 5a$

4 Solve:

(a) $^-4m = 16$ **(b)** $^-5t = 80$
(c) $^-6f = ^-36$ **(d)** $^-10b = ^-200$
(e) $^-5m + 3 = 8$ **(f)** $8 - 3r = 14$
(g) $^-29 = 4 - 3y$ **(h)** $^-47 = ^-4p - 3$
(i) $10 - 6d = ^-2$ **(j)** $26 = ^-7x + 5$

5 **(a)** $\frac{3t}{5} = ^-15$ **(b)** $\frac{6y}{7} = ^-36$

  (c) $\frac{^-2x}{3} = 12$ **(d)** $\frac{4y}{3} = 16$

  (e) $\frac{c}{^-4} = ^-6$ **(f)** $\frac{8v}{^-5} = ^-56$

  (g) $\frac{^-6h}{9} = ^-54$ **(h)** $\frac{3w}{^-2} = ^-99$

6 **(a)** $4(2n + 6) = ^-8$ **(b)** $5(4b - 7) = ^-55$
  (c) $^-6(4t + 7) = 30$ **(d)** $^-3(7m + 4) = 72$
  (e) $^-5(6y - 3) = 75$ **(f)** $^-2(8 - 5w) = ^-116$
  (g) $^-50 = ^-5(4s - 2)$ **(h)** $12 = 6(4a + 30)$
  (i) $^-80 = ^-8(4f - 10)$ **(j)** $18 = 9(8 - 3x)$

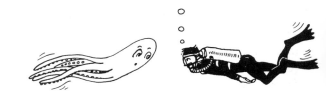

Barbara owns a shop which sells records, cassettes and CDs. She often takes newly released cassettes home so that she can listen to them.

1 One weekend she took 25 cassettes home and classified them in a table. Copy and complete her table.

	Rock	Easy listening	Classical	Total
Instrumental	2	6	2	
Vocal	9	3	3	
Total				25

● **Remember**

Probability is a measure of how likely something is to happen.

The probability that Barbara will pick, at random, a vocal, classical cassette to play is

P(vocal classical) = $\frac{3}{25}$ or **0·12** $3 \div 25 = 0·12$

Barbara selects a tape to listen to at random.

2 What is the probability that she will pick a tape which is:

(a) vocal rock   (b) classical instrumental
(c) instrumental easy listening?

3 Find these probabilities:

(a) P(rock)   (b) P(easy listening)
(c) P(classical)   (d) P(instrumental).

4 What is the probability that Barbara will pick a cassette which is:

(a) rock **or** classical
(b) easy listening **or** rock
(c) rock **or** easy listening **or** classical?

● **Remember**

The probability that Barbara will pick a cassette which is **not** rock is
P(not rock) = 1 − P(rock)

$$= 1 - \frac{11}{25} = \frac{14}{25} \text{ or } 0·56$$

5 Find:

(a) P(not classical)   (b) P(not instrumental)
(c) P(not vocal)   (d) P(not vocal classical).

After listening to a tape, Barbara puts it aside and picks another one at random from those she has not yet listened to.

6 What is the probability that the second tape is:

(a) classical vocal if the first was classical vocal
(b) rock if the first was easy listening
(c) easy listening if the first was also easy listening
(d) vocal if the first was vocal
(e) **not** rock if the first was rock
(f) **not** classical if the first was classical?

7 What is the probability that the third tape is:

(a) classical vocal if the first two were rock instrumental
(b) easy listening instrumental if the first was classical vocal and the second easy listening vocal
(c) instrumental if the first two were also instrumental
(d) rock if the first was easy listening and the second classical
(e) **not** instrumental if the first was instrumental and the second vocal
(f) **not** classical if the first two were not classical?

Face the music

Probably the Best sells albums in three formats – CD, cassette and record. When a customer comes into the shop Barbara sometimes tries to guess which format they will buy.

1 She thinks that the probability that a customer will buy a CD is $\frac{1}{3}$.
Do you agree with her? Explain.

Barbara notes the format of each album sold.
Of the next 100 albums sold, 48 were cassettes.

$\frac{48}{100}$ is the **relative frequency** of an album being sold in cassette format. It is an **estimate** of the probability that an album will be sold in cassette format.

2 ▶ Do Worksheets 12 and 13.

3 The table shows a summary of Barbara's album sales for one week.

	Easy listening	Classical	Rock	Jazz	Total
Records	10	12	12	4	38
Cassettes	35	24	58	17	134
CDs	23	20	29	6	78
Total	68	56	99	27	250

What is the relative frequency of selling:
(a) rock albums **(b)** classical albums
(c) albums in record format
(d) albums in cassette format
(e) jazz records **(f)** easy listening CDs?

There are three methods of allocating probabilities to events.
Method 1 Consider all possible events to be equally likely.
Method 2 Look at past records or existing data to determine relative frequencies which give estimates of probabilities.
Method 3 Carry out an experiment or survey to determine relative frequencies which give estimates of probabilities.

4 Barbara's assistant, Phil, enters information about albums on a computerised database.
For each sale he enters:
- title and artist
- manufacturer
- price paid
- date of sale
- type of music (rock etc)
- format (CD etc).

For each faulty album returned by a customer he enters:
- manufacturer
- format
- date of return.

Give the **method** of allocating probability which is most appropriate to each situation.
(a) At Christmas every customer's name is entered into a free prize draw. How could the probability of a particular customer winning be calculated?
(b) Barbara is considering changing the shop's opening hours. How would she find the probability of taking more than £100 between 8 am and 9 am on Mondays?
(c) How could the probability that a customer will buy more than one item be found?
(d) How could Barbara find the probability that a customer will buy an album in CD format?
(e) Listening booths are numbered 1 to 6. How could the probability that a customer will choose booth 6 at random, when none of the booths are in use, be found?
(f) How could the probability that a faulty item is a record be found?
(g) A customer does not know whether to buy a jazz or a classical cassette for a present. If one type is selected at random, how would the probability that it is jazz be found?
(h) How could the probability that a customer will purchase a classical album be found?

When ordering stock Barbara has to try to predict what will sell. To do this she has to calculate the expected sales.

I think I can sell 80 copies of this new album.

SOUNDS OF THE SEVENTIES

The probability of selling it in record format is 0·15.
The expected number of record sales is
E(record sales) = 0·15 × 80 = 12.
The probability of selling it in CD format is 0·28.
The expected number of CD sales is
E(CD sales) = 0·28 × 80 = 22·4

Expected value = probability × total number.

I From past sales of albums released by *The Mutande* Barbara knows that:
• P(record sale) = 0·2 • P(cassette sale) = 0·5
• P(CD sale) = 0·3.
She thinks that she can sell 200 copies of their latest release. How many copies should she order in:
(a) record **(b)** cassette **(c)** CD format?

2 These probabilities have been estimated for customers who buy CDs:
• P(buys rock) = 0·60 • P(buys jazz) = 0·06
• P(buys easy listening) = 0·26
• P(buys classical) = 0·08
Calculate the number of each type of CD which Barbara can expect to sell when the total CD sales are:
(a) 200 **(b)** 350 **(c)** 180 **(d)** 263.

3 Barbara has estimated these probabilities.

Amount spent	Under £10	£10 – £20	Over £20
Probability	0·60	0·25	0·15

Calculate to the nearest whole number the number of customers in each purchase range when the total number of customers is:
(a) 400 **(b)** 350 **(c)** 425 **(d)** 308.

Over the past year Phil has compiled this list of faulty CDs which were returned to the manufacturer.

Manufacturer	Number sold	Number returned
Peters	200	20
DMR	150	30
Epsilon	217	7

4 (a) For each manufacturer estimate the probability that a CD will be faulty.
(b) Barbara has received 45 CDs from Peters, 10 from DMR and 43 from Epsilon. For each manufacturer find to the nearest whole number the number of these CDs which Barbara can expect to return.

5 Before playing a cassette over the shop's loudspeakers Phil throws a die.

If it lands ⚀ I play jazz.
If it lands ⚁ or ⚂ I play easy listening, if ⚃ or ⚄ rock and if a ⚅ I play classical.

How many of each type will he expect to play when the number of tapes played is:
(a) 18 **(b)** 24 **(c)** 15 **(d)** 17?

6 Barbara was on holiday for a month. During this time Phil forgot to note the individual numbers of jazz, easy listening, classical and rock albums sold. He did, however, note the total numbers sold.

Week beginning	Total number sold
15 August	115
22 August	132
29 August	198
5 September	165

The week after Barbara returned the numbers sold were:
• jazz, 26 • easy listening, 37
• rock, 54 • classical, 19.
For each week of Barbara's holiday estimate to the nearest whole number the number of each type Phil sold.

Barbara wants to make sure that she is offering the service which her customers want. She also hopes to expand her business. Before making any changes in the shop she decides to ask her customers to complete a questionnaire.

> There are two types of question which can be used in a questionnaire:
>
> **closed response:** where you have to choose from a given selection of relevant answers, for example Q1 in Barbara's questionnaire
>
> **open response:** where it is possible to give any answer, for example Q3 in the questionnaire.

1 For each question in Barbara's questionnaire write whether it is *closed* or *open*.

2 List (a) the advantages
      (b) the disadvantages
of a closed response question.

3 List (a) the advantages
      (b) the disadvantages
of an open response question.

4 Re-write Q8 of Barbara's questionnaire as a closed response question.

5 Which two questions in the questionnaire could be asking for the same information? Explain.

I can't possibly ask all my customers to complete the questionnaire. I'll have to take a sample.

How shall we get a sample that isn't biased? If we only ask people who buy rock music to complete the questionnaire, it wouldn't represent the population in general.

Probably the ...

Q1 Which of these types of music do you usually listen to? Please tick one.

  A Pop ☐   B Easy listening ☐
  C Jazz ☐   D Classical ☐

Q2 Use the letters in Q1 to put the types of music into your preferred order. Start with the one you prefer most.

_____

Q3 Is there any type of music which we do not have which you might buy? Please specify.

_____

Q4 Which format do you usually buy? Please tick one.

  A CD ☐   B Cassette ☐   C Record ☐

Q5 Did you find the service in the shop satisfactory? Please circle one.

  Yes   No

  If 'No' please say why. _____

---

6 Barbara could have obtained a sample of people to complete her questionnaire in several ways. For each method explain any bias.
She could have:

(a) asked her friends
(b) asked members of her family
(c) asked regular customers
(d) asked only male customers
(e) asked customers who spent over £25
(f) carried out a telephone survey of people who live in her town
(g) interviewed people at random in the street
(h) sent a questionnaire to every hundredth person on the electoral register
(i) interviewed people as they left a rock concert.

7 Suggest some other methods of collecting a sample and identify any bias in them.

Questionnaire

Thank you for taking the time to complete this questionnaire.
When you have answered the questions, please place your completed questionnaire in the box provided.

6 Did you buy anything today? Please circle one.

Yes   No

If 'Yes', how much did you spend? £ _____

If 'No', please say why. _____

7 On average how much do you spend each month on recorded music? Please tick one.

A   Under £10 ☐   B   £10 – £20 ☐
C   Over £20 ☐

8 How many items did you buy today? _____

9 How old are you? Please tick one.

A   Under 17 ☐   B   17 – 24 ☐
C   25 – 32 ☐   D   33 – 40 ☐
E   Over 40 ☐

10 How far did you travel today to shop here? _____

_____

Barbara has to analyse the responses from her completed questionnaires.

1 ▶ Do Worksheet 14.

▶ You need the information on Worksheet 14 for questions 2–7.

2 Use the frequency tables.
  (a) What is the least popular type of music?
  (b) What fraction of customers usually listen to:
    • rock   • easy listening   • jazz   • classical?
  (c) What is the most popular format?
  (d) What percentage of customers usually buy:
    • CDs   • cassettes   • records?
  (e) What percentage of customers are 24 years old or under?
  (f) What fraction of customers are between 17 and 32 years old?

3 Draw a graph to show:
  (a) the numbers of people who usually listen to rock, easy listening, jazz and classical music
  (b) the percentages of people who buy records, cassettes and CDs
  (c) the ages of customers.

4 Use the responses to Q6 in the questionnaire to calculate the mean amount spent by those people who answered it.

5 (a) Analyse the responses to Q2.
  (b) Compare these results with those for Q1. Explain your findings.

6 What is the probability that a customer will:
  (a) spend £10 – £20 per month on music
  (b) not buy anything
  (c) be 32 years old or under
  (d) usually listen to classical music
  (e) find the service satisfactory
  (f) want to buy country music
  (g) buy more than 4 items?

7 In a week when there are 700 customers how many can be expected to:
  (a) spend £10 – £20 per month on music
  (b) not buy anything
  (c) be 32 years old or under
  (d) usually listen to classical music?

8 You are going to find out about the musical tastes of the students in your school.
  • Decide what information you want to gather.
  • Design a questionnaire which will allow you to collect the information. For each question decide whether it should be *open* or *closed*.
  • Decide on a suitable sample.
  • Carry out your survey.
  • Analyse your results and display them appropriately.
  • Write a report of your findings for your school magazine.

9 • Decide on an issue in which you are interested and design a questionnaire to help you carry out a survey.
  • Write a report of your survey.

Tied in Celtic Knots

Ancient Celtic monks used to decorate their manuscripts with decorative "knots", based on circles, such as those drawn here.

Follow these steps to make one of these "knots."

You need a ruler and compasses.

Step 1

- Draw a square, ABCD, of side 8 cm.
- Join the midpoints of the sides as shown.

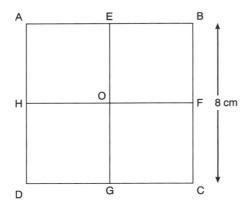

Step 2

- Draw a circle, centre O, with radius 4 cm.
- Keep your compasses at 4 cm. Draw semi-circles with centres E, F, G and H.

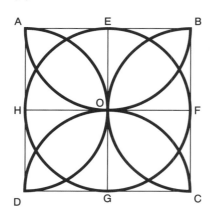

Step 3

- Keep your compasses set at 4 cm. Draw quarter-circles with centres A, B, C and D.

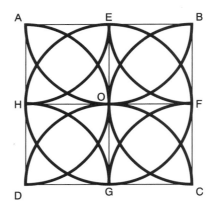

Step 4

- Repeat Steps **2** and **3** with your compasses set to 3·5 cm.
- Finish your "knot" by erasing any lines not required.
- Colour your "knot".

Ben is a trainee manager at Harrison's Hypermarket.
He is learning about the hypermarket's policies on
Hire Purchase (HP) from Jill, the senior salesperson.

We sell goods for cash or on Hire Purchase

H........ Harrison's.......H
Hire Purchase terms:
Deposit £150·00
Twelve instalments £80·40

To find the total HP price of this suite:

$$
\begin{array}{rl}
\text{Deposit} = & £150·00 \\
\text{12 instalments of } £80·40 = & £964·80 \\
\hline
\text{Total} = & £1114·80
\end{array}
$$

The HP price is **£1114·80.**

1 Find the total Hire Purchase price for each item.

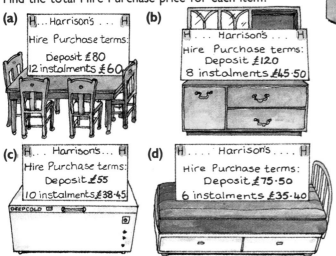

(a) H...Harrison's . . . H
Hire Purchase terms:
Deposit £80
12 instalments £60

(b) H . . . Harrison's . . . H
Hire Purchase terms:
Deposit £120
8 instalments £45·50

(c) H.. Harrison's... H
Hire Purchase terms:
Deposit £55
10 instalments £38·45

(d) H .... Harrison's .... H
Hire Purchase terms:
Deposit £75·50
6 instalments £35·40

H . . . Harrison's . . . H
Hire Purchase terms:
Deposit 15%
Ten instalments £48·35

Cash price £520

Jill finds the total HP price of this television like
this:

$$
\begin{array}{rll}
\text{Deposit 15\% of } £520 & = & £78·00 \\
\text{10 instalments of } £48·35 & = & £483·50 \\
\hline
\text{Total} & = & £561·50
\end{array}
$$

The total HP price is **£561·50.**

The **difference** between
the HP price and the cash price is
£561·50 − £520 = **£41·50**

2 For each item find:
  • the total HP price
  • the difference between the HP and the cash
    price.

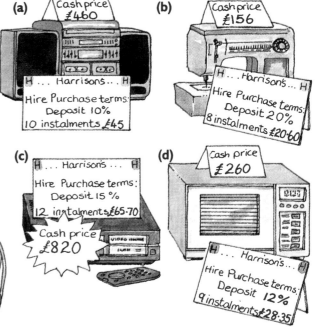

(a) Cash price £460

H . . . Harrison's . . . H
Hire Purchase terms:
Deposit 10%
10 instalments £45

(b) Cash price £156

H . . . Harrison's . . . H
Hire Purchase terms:
Deposit 20%
8 instalments £20·60

(c) H . . . Harrison's . . . H
Hire Purchase terms:
Deposit 15 %
12 instalments £65·70

Cash price £820

(d) Cash price £260

H . . . Harrison's . . . H
Hire Purchase terms:
Deposit 12%
9 instalments £28·35

Harrison's Hypermarket

Is the H P price always more than the cash price?

1 What do you think the answer to Ben's question will be?

2 Find the extra cost of buying each item on Hire Purchase.

(a)

H... Harrison's ... H
Cash price £2250
or
Deposit £800
20 instalments £95

(b)

H ... Harrison's ... H
Cash price £325
or
Deposit £60·50
9 instalments £40·25

(c)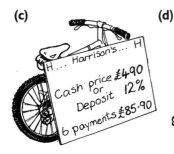

H ... Harrison's ... H
Cash price £490
or
Deposit 12%
6 payments £85·90

(d)

H ... Harrison's ... H
Cash price £980
or
deposit 25%
12 instalments £75

THE KENSINGTON   FREE FITTING

CASH PRICE £9 500

Harrison's policy is that the H P price for a kitchen should be 15% higher than the cash price.

For this kitchen,
15% of £9500 = £1425
Total HP price = £9500 + £1425 = **£10 925**

3 Calculate the total HP price for each kitchen.

(a)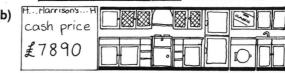

H... Harrison's... H
cash price
£4960

(b)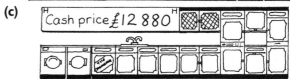

H... Harrison's... H
cash price
£7890

(c) Cash price £12 880

4 Find the HP price for each greenhouse.

(a)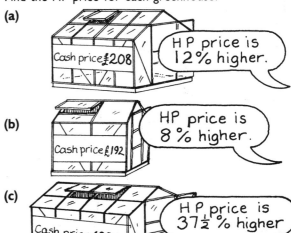

Cash price £208

H P price is 12% higher.

(b) Cash price £192

HP price is 8% higher.

(c) Cash price £324

H P price is $37\frac{1}{2}$% higher

5 The HP price of this fitted bedroom is 22% higher than the cash price.

H... Harrison's ... H
Cash price £6890
Hire Purchase terms
Deposit 20%
20 equal instalments

(a) How much is the total HP price?
(b) Calculate the deposit.
(c) How much is each instalment?

▶ Challenge

6 The HP price of a computer is £1176, which is 20% higher than the cash price. What is the cash price of the computer?

The difference between the HP price and the cash price of this garden furniture is £350.

To compare the difference with the cash price Jill writes:

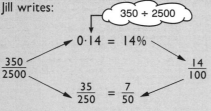

$$\frac{350}{2500}$$

$$350 \div 2500$$

$$0{\cdot}14 = 14\%$$

$$\frac{14}{100}$$

$$\frac{35}{250} = \frac{7}{50}$$

The HP price is 14% or $\frac{7}{50}$ more than the cash price.

H Harrison's
Cash price £2500
HP price £2850

1 For each television calculate:

• the actual increase in price

• the percentage increase in price

• the fractional increase in price

if it is bought on Hire Purchase.

(a)

H Harrison's
Cash price
£360
HP price
£450

(b)

Cash price
£240
HP price
£276

(c)

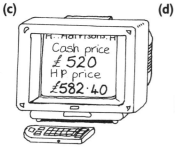

H Harrison's
Cash price
£520
HP price
£582·40

(d)

Cash price
£480

HP terms:
No deposit!
18 payments
£32

(e)

Cash price
£440

H Harrison's
HP terms:
Deposit £135
8 instalments
£45

(f)

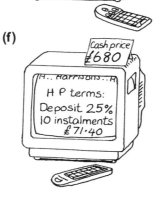

Cash price
£680

H Harrison's
HP terms:
Deposit 25%
10 instalments
£71·40

2 For each item in the sale find:

• the actual decrease in price

• the percentage decrease in price

• the fractional decrease in price.

(a)

H Harrison's
Normal price
£86
Sale price
£77·40

(b)

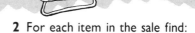

H Harrison's
Normal price
£280
Sale price
£238

(c)

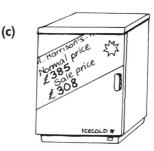

H Harrison's
Normal price
£385
Sale price
£308

ICECOLD

(d)

H Harrison's
Normal price
£198
Sale Price
£148·50!

(e)

H Harrison's
Normal price
£86·50
Sale price
£69·20

(f)

H Harrison's
Normal price
£480
Sale price
£420!

Ellerman Electrical

William works at Ellerman Electrical.
One of his tasks is to price out invoices.

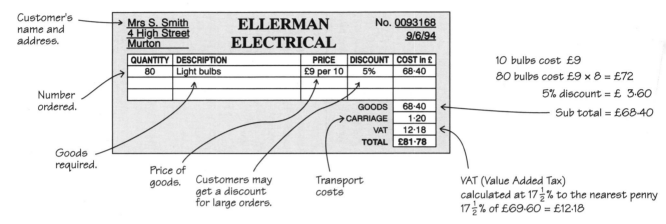

Customer's name and address.

Number ordered.

Goods required.

Price of goods.

Customers may get a discount for large orders.

Transport costs

10 bulbs cost £9
80 bulbs cost £9 × 8 = £72
5% discount = £ 3·60
Sub total = £68·40

VAT (Value Added Tax)
calculated at $17\frac{1}{2}$% to the nearest penny
$17\frac{1}{2}$% of £69·60 = £12·18

QUANTITY	DESCRIPTION	PRICE	DISCOUNT	COST in £
80	Light bulbs	£9 per 10	5%	68·40
			GOODS	68·40
			CARRIAGE	1·20
			VAT	12·18
			TOTAL	£81·78

ELLERMAN ELECTRICAL
Mrs S. Smith
4 High Street
Murton
No. 0093168
9/6/94

1 ▶ Do Worksheet 15.

2 William also has to check and pay bills and expenses.
Find the total cost of each.

(a)

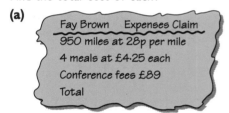

Fay Brown   Expenses Claim
950 miles at 28p per mile
4 meals at £4·25 each
Conference fees £89
Total

(b)

D. Rain Plumbers		
PARTS	£83·00	
LABOUR	5 hours at £17 per hour	
VAT		
TOTAL		

(c)

Parkers Garage

Parts	£176
Labour 8 hours at £19·50 per hour	
MOT test	£35
VAT	
TOTAL	

(d)

MPI FURNITURE

4 desks at £172 each	
2 filing cabinets at £110 each	
Discount 2%	
VAT	
Total	

(e)

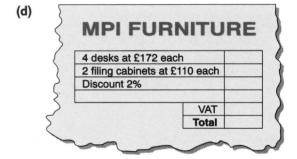

SANDERSON STATIONERY

250 folders at £7·50 per 50	
40 reams of paper at £4·80 per ream	
8 boxes of pens at £9 per box	
Discount 8%	
VAT	
TOTAL	

3 William is given a discount for paying bills within 28 days. Using your answers to question **2** calculate what he pays:

(a) D. Rain if the discount is 5%
(b) Sanderson Stationery if the discount is $2\frac{1}{2}$%
(c) Parkers Garage if the discount is $4\frac{1}{2}$%.

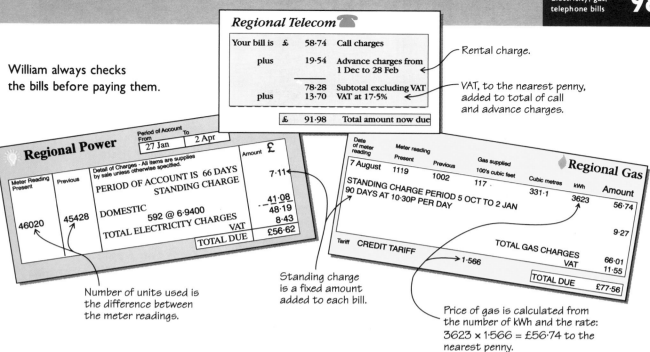

William always checks
the bills before paying them.

Regional Telecom ☎

Your bill is	£	58·74	Call charges
plus		19·54	Advance charges from 1 Dec to 28 Feb
		78·28	Subtotal excluding VAT
plus		13·70	VAT at 17·5%
	£	91·98	Total amount now due

Rental charge.

VAT, to the nearest penny,
added to total of call
and advance charges.

Regional Power

Period of Account
From 27 Jan To 2 Apr

Meter Reading Present	Previous	Detail of Charges - All items are supplies by sale unless otherwise specified.	Amount £
		PERIOD OF ACCOUNT IS 66 DAYS STANDING CHARGE	7·11
46020	45428	DOMESTIC 592 @ 6·9400	41·08
		TOTAL ELECTRICITY CHARGES	48·19
		VAT	8·43
		TOTAL DUE	£56·62

Regional Gas

Date of meter reading	Meter reading Present	Previous	Gas supplied 100's cubic feet	Cubic metres	kWh	Amount
7 August	1119	1002	117	331·1	3623	56·74
STANDING CHARGE PERIOD 5 OCT TO 2 JAN 90 DAYS AT 10·30P PER DAY						9·27
Tariff CREDIT TARIFF			1·566	TOTAL GAS CHARGES		66·01
				VAT		11·55
				TOTAL DUE		£77·56

Number of units used is
the difference between
the meter readings.

Standing charge
is a fixed amount
added to each bill.

Price of gas is calculated from
the number of kWh and the rate:
3623 × 1·566 = £56·74 to the
nearest penny.

1 Find the total amount due for each bill.

(a)

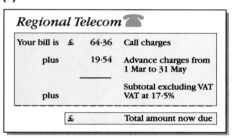

Regional Telecom ☎

Your bill is	£	64·36	Call charges
plus		19·54	Advance charges from 1 Mar to 31 May
plus			Subtotal excluding VAT VAT at 17·5%
	£		Total amount now due

(b)

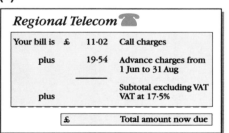

Regional Telecom ☎

Your bill is	£	11·02	Call charges
plus		19·54	Advance charges from 1 Jun to 31 Aug
plus			Subtotal excluding VAT VAT at 17·5%
	£		Total amount now due

(c)

Regional Power

Period of Account
From 3 Apr To 7 Jun

Meter Reading Present	Previous	Detail of Charges - All items are supplies by sale unless otherwise specified.	Amount £
		PERIOD OF ACCOUNT IS 66 DAYS STANDING CHARGE	7·11
53251	52836	DOMESTIC 415 @ 6·9400	- - - -
		TOTAL ELECTRICITY CHARGES	
		VAT	
		TOTAL DUE	

(d)

Regional Power

Period of Account
From 8 Jun To 12 Aug

Meter Reading Present	Previous	Detail of Charges - All items are supplies by sale unless otherwise specified.	Amount £
		PERIOD OF ACCOUNT IS 66 DAYS STANDING CHARGE	7·11
62538	61825	DOMESTIC @ 6·9400	- - - -
		TOTAL ELECTRICITY CHARGES	
		VAT	
		TOTAL DUE	

(e)

Regional Gas

Date of meter reading	Meter reading Present	Previous	Gas supplied 100's cubic feet	Cubic metres	kWh	Amount
2 April	1235	1084	151	412	4525	
STANDING CHARGE PERIOD 3 JAN TO 2 APR 90 DAYS AT 10·30P PER DAY						9·27
Tariff CREDIT TARIFF			1·566	TOTAL GAS CHARGES		
				VAT		
				TOTAL DUE		

(f)

Regional Gas

Date of meter reading	Meter reading Present	Previous	Gas supplied 100's cubic feet	Cubic metres	kWh	Amount
25 June	2106	1856	250	682	7602	
STANDING CHARGE PERIOD 28 MAR TO 25 JUN 90 DAYS AT 10·30P PER DAY						
Tariff CREDIT TARIFF			1·566	TOTAL GAS CHARGES		
				VAT		
				TOTAL DUE		

2 ▶ **Do Worksheet 16.**

High Finance

The charge for borrowing money is called **interest**.

Lisa works for High Finance calculating the simple interest on loans. The interest is calculated as a percentage of the amount borrowed.

High Finance
Loan Terms

6% per annum

10% per annum

15.5% per annum

I'd like to borrow £650 over 3 years.

The interest rate will be 7½ % pa.

pa is short for per annum which means for each year.

John wants to borrow £650.

Lisa calculates the simple interest like this.

Interest for 1 year	= 7½% of £650	= £48·75
Interest for 3 years	= £48·75 × 3	= £146·25
Total amount due	= £650 + £146·25	= £796·25

John will pay back **£796·25** over 3 years.

1 List reasons why people might borrow money.

2 Copy and complete Lisa's calculations for each borrower.

(a) *Peter*
Loan: £2500 at 8% pa over 4 years.
Interest for 1 year = 8% of £2500 = ☐
Interest for 4 years = ☐ × 4 = ☐
Total amount due = £2500 + ☐ = ☐

(b) *Kelly*
Loan: £3200 at 9½% pa over 6 years.
Interest for 1 year = 9½% of £3200 = ☐
Interest for 6 years = ☐
Total amount due = £3200 + ☐

(c) *Sam*
Loan: £980 over 3 years at 6% pa.
Interest for 1 year = ☐
Interest for ☐
Total amount due ☐

(d) *Shona*
Loan: £8400 over 9 years at 13·25% pa
Interest for 1 year = ☐
Interest for ☐
☐

3 Sheila borrows £800 at 5% pa to buy a Hi-Fi system. Find the interest and the total amount which she will pay if she borrows the money for a term of:

(a) 1 year **(b)** 2 years **(c)** 3 years **(d)** 7 years.

4 In February the interest rate was 11%. Find the interest Lisa calculated for:

(a) Trevor who borrowed £4300 over 5 years, to buy a motor bike
(b) Glenda who borrowed £970 over 2 years, to go on holiday
(c) Alan who borrowed £6350 over 8 years, to invest in a time-share flat.

5 Find the interest on:

(a) £2200 borrowed for 4 years at 9% pa
(b) £12 000 borrowed at 14·75% pa for 10 years
(c) £475 borrowed for 2 years at 4% pa
(d) £9500 borrowed at 8½% pa for 7 years.

6 Delia borrows money to buy a car.

(a) How much interest will she be charged?

(b) What is the total amount Delia has to pay High Finance?

(c) She agrees to pay the total amount in equal monthly instalments.
What is the amount of each instalment?

7 Calculate the amount of each equal monthly instalment to repay:

(a) £900 borrowed at 7% pa for 1 year

(b) £4800 borrowed over 2 years at 6·75% pa

(c) £18 000 borrowed at 9% pa for 5 years

(d) £3720 borrowed at $12\frac{1}{2}$% pa for 4 years.

8 Gordon wants to borrow money to buy a windsurfer. Copy and complete Lisa's calculations.
Gordon
Loan: £470 at 15% pa over 6 months.
Interest for 1 year   =   15% of £470   = ☐
Interest for $\frac{1}{2}$ year   = ☐   × $\frac{1}{2}$ = ☐
Total amount due   = ☐

9 What fraction of a year is:

(a) 4 months   (b) 3 months   (c) 9 months

(d) 5 months   (e) 2 months   (f) 1 month?

10 Copy and complete Lisa's calculations for each borrower.

(a) *Theresa*
Loan: £3500 at 3% pa over 7 months.
Interest for 1 year   =   3% of £3500   = ☐
Interest for 7 months   = ☐   × $\frac{7}{12}$ = ☐
Total amount due   = ☐

(b) *Kim*
Loan: £1600 at $4\frac{1}{4}$% pa over 2 years and 9 months.
Interest for 1 year   = $4\frac{1}{4}$% of £1600   = ☐
Interest for $2\frac{3}{4}$ years   = ☐
Total ☐

11 Kaye borrows £2400 at 9% pa to install new windows. Find the interest and the total amount due if she borrows the money for a term of:

(a) 2 months   (b) 5 months   (c) $3\frac{1}{2}$ years

(d) 4 years and 3 months.

12 Calculate the amount of each equal monthly instalment on:

(a) £720 borrowed for 9 months at 18% pa

(b) £3000 borrowed at 5% pa for $2\frac{1}{2}$ years

(c) £3400 borrowed at 7·5% pa for 16 months

(d) £8700 borrowed at 11% pa for 7 years and 3 months.

Insure with Smartsure

Valuable property is insured against theft, loss, fire or other damage. The cost of insurance is worked out annually and is called the **premium**.

There are two types of House Insurance:
buildings insurance covers the actual building and fixtures
contents insurance covers property inside your home.

The table shows the premiums per £100 to insure buildings in different areas with Smartsure.

Smartsure Buildings Insurance	
Rating area	Premiums for each £100 of Sum Insured
A	18p
B	21p
C	24p
D	28p
E	32p
F	38p

John lives in area C. He wants to insure his flat for £36 000. He calculates the premium like this:

Premium per £100 = 24p
Premium for £36 000 = 24p × 360
= 8640p or £86·40

John will pay **£86·40** to insure his flat.

1 Buildings insurance is cheaper than contents insurance. Why should this be?

2 Theresa lives in area F and has insured her house for £72 000. Find:
   (a) the premium per £100 for area F
   (b) the premium to insure Theresa's house.

3 Find the amount of each building insurance premium with Smartsure.
   (a) Thelma lives in area D. Her house is insured for £91 800.
   (b) Philip has a bungalow in area B insured for £124 000.
   (c) Kay lives in area E, in a house which is insured for £154 200.
   (d) Ian has insured his flat in area A for £76 600.
   (e) Peter is insuring his house in area C for £56 700.
   (f) Jan has a flat in area D insured for £67 800.

4 If each person in question 3 paid their premium in equal monthly instalments, find the amount of each instalment.

5 Wilma lives in area C.
   (a) How much is the premium for her house, insured for £46 500?
   (b) To cover costs, Smartsure now offer equal monthly payment terms at 10% extra on the annual premium.
   How much will Wilma's premium cost per month?

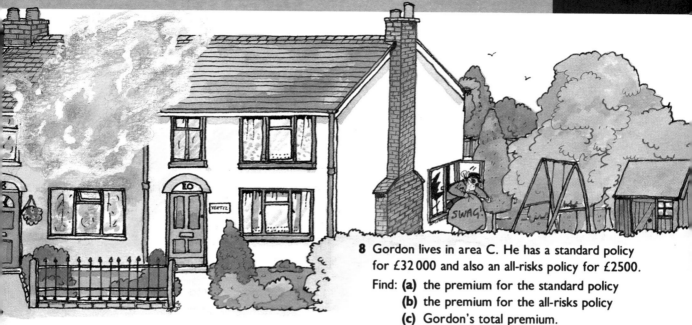

8 Gordon lives in area C. He has a standard policy for £32 000 and also an all-risks policy for £2500.

Find: **(a)** the premium for the standard policy

(b) the premium for the all-risks policy

(c) Gordon's total premium.

The table shows the premiums per £100 to insure the contents of a home with Smartsure. An all-risks policy covers property both inside and outside the home.

Smartsure Contents Insurance		
Rating area	Premiums for each £100 of Sum Insured	
	Standard	All-risks
A	32p	57p
B	35p	60p
C	40p	65p
D	45p	70p
E	50p	75p
F	60p	85p

6 (a) List some items which might be insured with an all-risks policy.

(b) Why is the premium for an all-risks policy higher than that for a standard policy?

7 Find the premium for each contents policy with Smartsure.

(a) Carole lives in area B and has a standard policy for £24 000.

(b) Trevor lives in area F and has an all-risks policy for £5000.

(c) Joanne lives in area A and has a standard policy for £16 500.

(d) Pierre lives in area D and has an all-risks policy for £3450.

9 Find the **total** premium for each person.

(a) Andrew. Area E:
standard policy £16 400, all-risks policy £2000.

(b) Gerald. Area A:
standard policy £45 000, all-risks policy £16 000.

(c) Dianne. Area B:
standard policy £38 000, all-risks policy £7450.

10 Margaret lives in area E. She has a **buildings policy** for £64 000 and a standard contents policy for £35 000. Find her total premium.

11 For each person, find the total premium with Smartsure.

(a) Fred. Area F:
buildings policy   £52 000,
standard contents £25 000, all-risks £4500.

(b) Ann. Area C:
buildings policy   £68 500,
standard contents £18 750, all-risks £3800.

12 Smartsure are offering 20% discount on **contents insurance** to customers who install a burglar alarm. Use your answers to question 11 to calculate the new premiums for Fred and Ann if they each install an alarm.

■ Investigation

13 Many insurance policies have an **excess**. Find out what this means.

Quinn's Mini-market

Jan sells bags of rolls at the bakery counter.

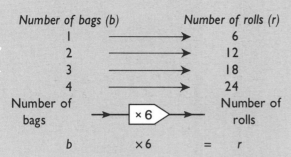

Number of bags (b)		Number of rolls (r)
1	$\longrightarrow$	6
2	$\longrightarrow$	12
3	$\longrightarrow$	18
4	$\longrightarrow$	24

Number of bags $\longrightarrow$ ×6 $\longrightarrow$ Number of rolls

$b \qquad ×6 \qquad = \qquad r$

The number machine shows how the number of rolls can be found from the number of bags.
This can be written as a formula: $b × 6 = r$
or $r = 6b$

The formula can be used to find the number of rolls in 7 bags.
When $b = 7$, $\qquad r = 6 × 7$
$r = 42$
So 7 bags hold **42** rolls.

1 Quinn's sells 3 kg bags of potatoes.
  (a) Copy and complete:
  • the table   • the number machine.

Number of bags (n)		Weight of potatoes (w)
1	$\longrightarrow$	3
2	$\longrightarrow$	6
3	$\longrightarrow$	
4	$\longrightarrow$	

$n \longrightarrow$ ⬡ $\longrightarrow w$

  (b) Find a formula for the weight of potatoes.
  (c) Use your formula to find the weight of potatoes in:
  • 5 bags   • 25 bags   • 32 bags

2 The shop stocks packets of 16 fish fingers.
  (a) Make a table to show the number of fish fingers in 1, 2, 3 and 4 packets.
  (b) Draw a number machine showing how the number of fish fingers (f) can be found from the number of packets (p).
  (c) Write a formula for the number of fish fingers.
  (d) Use your formula to find the number of fish fingers in: • 10 packets   • 22 packets.

3 Quinn's sells packs of 10 tangerines.
  (a) Copy the table and use the information from the graph to complete it.

Number of packs (p)		Number of tangerines (t)
1	$\longrightarrow$	10
2	$\longrightarrow$	
3	$\longrightarrow$	
4	$\longrightarrow$	

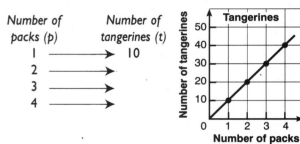

  (b) Copy and complete:
  • the number machine   • the formula.

Number of packs $\longrightarrow$ ⬡ $\longrightarrow$ Number of tangerines

$p \qquad × \qquad =$
or $\qquad t =$

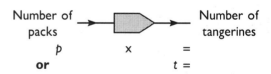

  (c) Use your formula to find the number of tangerines in: • 9 packs   • 14 packs.

4 Jan made bags of 25 fun-size mini-chocs.
  (a) Use the graph. Make a table showing the number of mini-chocs in 1, 2, 3 and 4 bags.

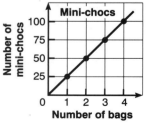

  (b) Draw a number machine to show how the number of mini-chocs can be found from the number of bags.
  (c) Using suitable letters, write a formula for the number of mini-chocs.
  (d) Use your formula to find the number of mini-chocs in:
  • 6 bags   • 10 bags   • 25 bags.

Mrs Bain called Fast Fix to repair her washing machine. They have a "call-out" charge of £35 plus a charge of £9 per hour of work.

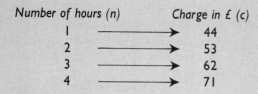

Number of hours (n)		Charge in £ (c)
1	⟶	44
2	⟶	53
3	⟶	62
4	⟶	71

Number of hours ⟶ ×9 ⟶ +35 ⟶ Charge in £

Formula: $n \times 9 + 35 = c$

The number machine shows how the charge can be found from the number of hours.
This can be written as a formula $9n + 35 = c$

or $c = 9n + 35$

The formula can be used to find the cost of an 8-hour repair.

When $n = 8$, $c = 9 \times 8 + 35$
$c = 72 + 35$
$c = 107$

The cost of an 8-hour repair is **£107**.

1 Mr Bain is building a garden wall. He hired a cement mixer at a fixed charge of £25 plus a charge of £10 per day.

(a) Copy and complete:
  • the table
  • the number machine.

Number of days (x)		Charge in £ (c)
1	⟶	35
2	⟶	
3	⟶	
4	⟶	

Number of days ⟶ ▢ ⟶ ▢ ⟶ Charge in £

(b) Find a formula for the charge.

(c) Use your formula to find the charge for:
  • 7 days • 10 days • 25 days.

2 For their holiday last year the Bains hired a four-berth caravan at Clifton Park holiday village. They paid a fixed charge of £80 plus £40 per day.

(a) Make a table to show the cost for different numbers of days.

(b) Draw a number machine to show how the cost can be found from the number of days.

(c) Write a formula for the cost of a four-berth caravan holiday at Clifton Park.

(d) Use your formula to find the cost of a holiday lasting: • 7 days • 24 days.

3 Graham Bain works in a toy shop. Staff are paid an hourly rate plus a bonus.

(a) Use the graph. Make a table showing the wages earned for 10, 20, 30 and 40 hours.

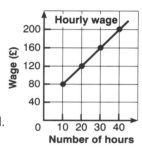

(b) Draw a number machine to show how the wage can be found from the number of hours worked.

(c) Write a formula for the wage.

(d) Use your formula to find Graham's wage when he works: • 12 hours • 45 hours.

4 Hilary Bain is a salesperson for Cherry Computers. She earns a basic weekly wage plus an amount for each computer she sells.

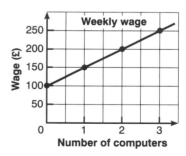

(a) Use the graph. Make a table showing her wage when she sells 0, 1, 2 and 3 computers.

(b) Draw a number machine and write a formula to show how Hilary Bain calculates her weekly wage.

(c) Use your formula to find Hilary's weekly wage when she sells: • 5 computers • 7 computers.

Bargain basement

Mrs Wills is going to make new curtains. She chooses fabric which costs £8 per metre and finds that if she pays in cash immediately she will be given a discount of £5 on her total bill.

Number of metres (n)		Cost in £ (c)
1	$\longrightarrow$	3
2	$\longrightarrow$	11
3	$\longrightarrow$	19
4	$\longrightarrow$	27

Number of metres $\longrightarrow \boxed{\times 8} \longrightarrow \boxed{-5} \longrightarrow$ Cost in £

Formula: $\quad n \quad \times 8 \quad - 5 \quad = \quad c$

The number machine shows how the cost of fabric can be found from the number of metres needed.

The formula can be written as $c = 8n - 5$
It can be used to find the cost of 5 m of fabric.
When $n = 5$, $\quad c = 8 \times 5 - 5$
$\qquad\qquad c = \quad 40 - 5$
$\qquad\qquad c = \qquad 35$
The cost of 5 m of fabric is **£35**.

£9 off your total bill on all discontinued wallpaper.

WALLPAPER £12 a roll

One purchase per household only

1 (a) Mrs Wills buys discontinued wallpaper. Copy and complete:
• the table • the number machine.

Number of rolls (x)		Cost in £ (c)
1	$\longrightarrow$	3
2	$\longrightarrow$	15
3	$\longrightarrow$	
4	$\longrightarrow$	

Number of rolls $\longrightarrow \boxed{} \longrightarrow \boxed{} \longrightarrow$ Cost in £

(b) Find a formula for the cost.
(c) Use your formula to find the cost of:
• 7 rolls • 10 rolls • 18 rolls.

2 The Wills family take their summer holiday at Lupin's Holiday Camp out of season. They are given a £50 discount. The cost for the family is £70 per day before discount.
(a) Make a table to show how the cost varies for different numbers of days.
(b) Draw a number machine and write a formula to show how the cost can be found from the number of days.
(c) Use your formula to find the cost of a holiday lasting: • 7 days • 14 days.

3 The Wills family are going to the panto at the Kings Theatre with a group of friends. For parties of 10 or more a discount is given.

(a) Use the graph. Make a table showing the cost of tickets for 10, 11, 12 and 13 people.
(b) Draw a number machine and write a formula to show how the cost of tickets can be found from the number of people.
(c) Use your formula to find the cost of tickets for:
• 15 people • 18 people • 23 people.

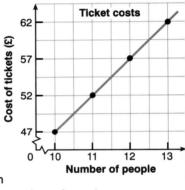

Ticket costs

Cost of tickets (£) / Number of people

4 At the Kirkie Mahal restaurant the gourmet night has a fixed-price meal. In January, they also distributed Family Discount vouchers which the Wills family used.

(a) Use the graph. Make a table showing the cost of a meal for a family of 3, 4, 5 and 6.
(b) Draw a number machine and write a formula to show how the cost of a meal can be found from the number of people in the family.
(c) Use your formula to find the cost for a family of: • 7 people • 12 people.

Restaurant bill

Cost of meal (£) / Number of people

1 For this square: Area = 3 × 3
= 9 cm²

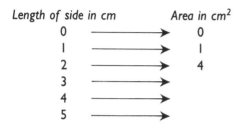

3 cm

(a) Copy and complete this table for areas of squares.

Length of side in cm		Area in cm²
0	⟶	0
1	⟶	1
2	⟶	4
3	⟶	
4	⟶	
5	⟶	

(b) Copy and complete the graph.

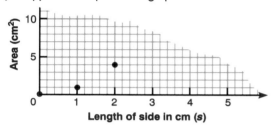

(c) Using A for area and s for length of side write a formula for the area of a square.

(d) Use your formula to find the area of a square of side: • 9 cm • 12 cm • 3·2 cm.

2 A charity football match is started by dropping the ball from a hot-air balloon to the field below. The table shows the distance fallen by the ball after 1, 2, 3, and 4 seconds.

Time in seconds		Distance fallen in m
0	⟶	0
1	⟶	5
2	⟶	20
3	⟶	45
4	⟶	80

(a) Copy and complete the graph.

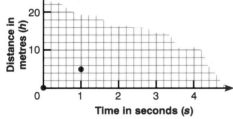

(b) Copy and complete this formula for the distance fallen, h, after t seconds: $h = \boxed{} \, t^2$

3 The table shows the approximate areas of circles with radii up to 4 cm.

Radius in cm		Area of circle in cm²
0	⟶	0
1	⟶	3
2	⟶	12
3	⟶	27
4	⟶	48

(a) Copy and complete the graph.

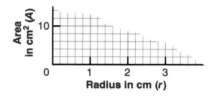

(b) Copy and complete this formula for finding the approximate area of a circle: $A = 3 \boxed{}$

4

The road across a bridge is supported by vertical steel cables. The cables increase in length as you move away from the centre.

Distance from centre in metres		Length of cable in metres
0	⟶	5
2	⟶	9
4	⟶	21
6	⟶	41
8	⟶	69

(a) Copy and complete the graph.

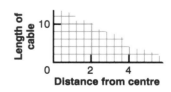

(b) Copy and complete this formula for the length, l, of the cable at a distance, d, from the centre of the bridge: $l = d^2 + \boxed{}$

Every picture tells a story

1 Which of these descriptions best fits the graph?
  A Hamish leaves his croft, climbs up the steep hill, walks across the plateau and strolls down the other side.
  B Hamish leaves his croft, runs down to the village, has a bowl of porridge for breakfast in the cafe and walks back home.

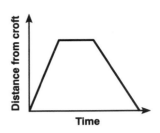

2 Match each explanation to a graph.
  A Hamish walks to the jetty then turns and walks home again. He walks at the same speed all the way.
  B Hamish ran to the post box. On his walk back home he stopped to speak to Morag.
  C Hamish had walked part of the way to the bus stop when he realised he was late and ran the rest of the way. He waited quarter of an hour but he had missed the bus and so he walked back home.
  D Hamish left his croft and climbed to the top of Ben More where he stopped to eat his haggis. Half-way down again he stopped for a rest.
  E Hamish walked to the shop where he bought some bread. He went on to the hotel where he stopped for a glass of lemonade. He ran home for his tea.
  F Hamish carried a sack of peat up the hill to Granny MacSporran's cottage. He started by walking quickly but gradually slowed down. On the way home he ran all the way.
  G Hamish leaves home and starts walking slowly down hill but he gets faster and faster until he reaches the harbour. He turns round immediately and runs home at a steady speed.
  H Hamish walks to the next village to visit his friend Demon Donald. They watch a video together. Donald gives Hamish a lift home on his motor bike.

Graph 1
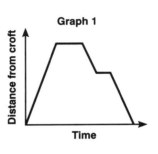

Graph 2
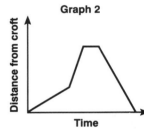

Graph 3
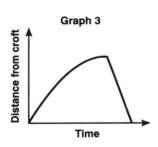

Graph 4
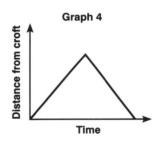

Graph 5
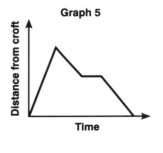

Graph 6
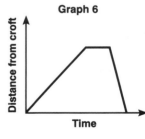

Graph 7
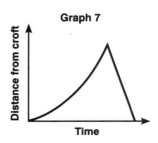

Graph 8
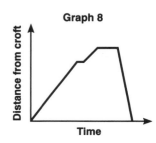

A graphic description

Mappings,
functions and
formulae:
Sketching graphs

108

1 This tank is being filled at a constant rate with fuel oil from a hose. Copy and complete the graph.

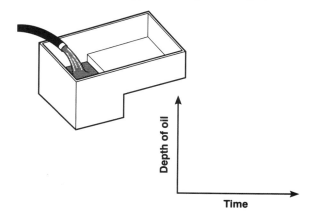

2 Water is leaking from this tank at a constant rate. Copy and complete the graph.

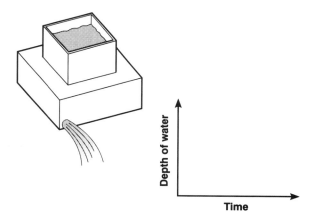

3 A cross-country runner is just about to start running down a hill. At the bottom of the hill she has to cross some flat ground then climb a steep hill. Copy and complete the graph.

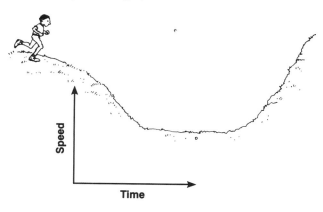

4 Copy and complete this graph to show the speed of a train as it travels between two stations.

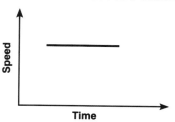

5 A car is travelling along a straight, flat road towards a jack-knifed lorry which is blocking the road.

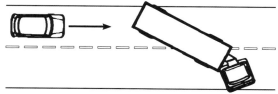

(a) The driver of the car is not looking where he is going. Draw a possible graph of speed against time for the car.

(b) A second car comes along soon afterwards but this driver is alert. Draw a possible graph of speed against time for the second car.

6 This is a sketch of a motor-racing circuit.

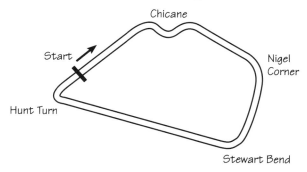

(a) Copy and complete the graph to show Ann's first lap in a race.

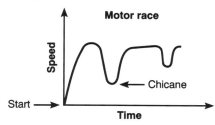

(b) On her third lap Ann spins off the track at Stewart Bend. Draw another graph of speed against time for Ann's third lap.

Going places

1 Bob drove his van from Glasgow to Kendal.
   Which sections of the graph represent:
   (a) the fastest part of his journey
   (b) his lunch stop
   (c) the three stretches of clear motorway
   (d) ten miles through a built-up area
   (e) being slowed by motorway repairs for half an hour?

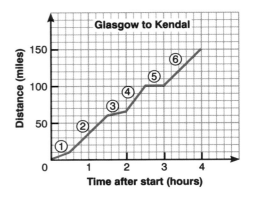

2 Use the Glasgow to Kendal graph.
   (a) Find the total distance Bob travelled.
   (b) Find how long the journey took.
   (c) Calculate Bob's average speed over the whole journey.

3 Bob left Kendal in his van at 10 am heading for Birmingham. At the same time Sally left Birmingham in her truck, heading for Kendal.
   (a) What happened at 11.48 am?
   (b) Who was first to complete their journey?
   (c) Why do you think this was?

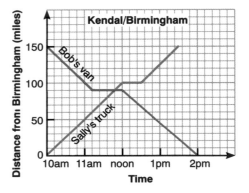

4 At 9 am Bill on his motorbike and Sam in his car are both travelling south on the M6 on their way to London.
   (a) Bill leaves the Southwaite services at 9 am. How far away is Sam at this time?
   (b) Describe:
      • Sam's journey   • Bill's journey.
   (c) What happens at 11 am?
   (d) Describe events between 11.30 am and 12.30 pm.
   (e) What reason did the police have for stopping Bill at 1 pm?

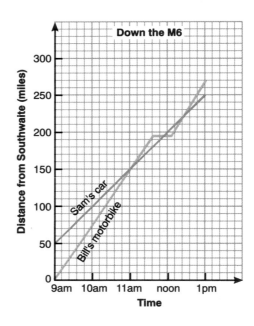

Jenny has been asked to investigate photocopying costs by her boss Fiona.

1 (a) Use Fastprint's photocopying charges. Copy and complete the table.

Number of copies	Cost in pence
10	
20	260
30	

100	

(b) Use an A4 page of 2 mm squared paper to draw a graph of cost against number of copies.

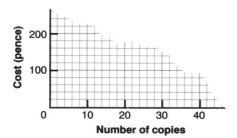

(c) How much would it cost for:
- 75 copies
- 250 copies?

2 (a) Use Speedprint's photocopying charges. Copy and complete the table:

Number of copies	Cost in pence
10	
20	
30	
40	
50	600
60	650

100	

(b) On the **same diagram** that you used for Fastprint, draw a graph of Speedprint's costs.

(c) How much would it cost at Speedprint for:
- 35 copies
- 75 copies
- 250 copies?

3 (a) For the following numbers of copies, which firm is the cheaper and what is the cost?
- 16
- 45
- 63
- 98

(b) Write Jenny's memo to Fiona giving her advice about which firm to use for the most economical photocopying.

Catch the Hare

This game *"De Cercar La Liebre"* or Catch the Hare was first recorded over 700 years ago in the 1283 Alfonso manuscript.

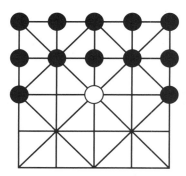

Play this board game with a partner.

You need a white counter and 12 black counters, arranged as shown.

One player is the hare (white counter) and the other player is the hunters (black counters).

- Both hare and hunters can move along a line in any direction to an empty point.
- Only the hare can capture and this is done by jumping as in draughts.
- The hunters try to trap the hare so that it is impossible for it to jump or move.
- The hare tries to capture the hunters until it cannot be trapped.

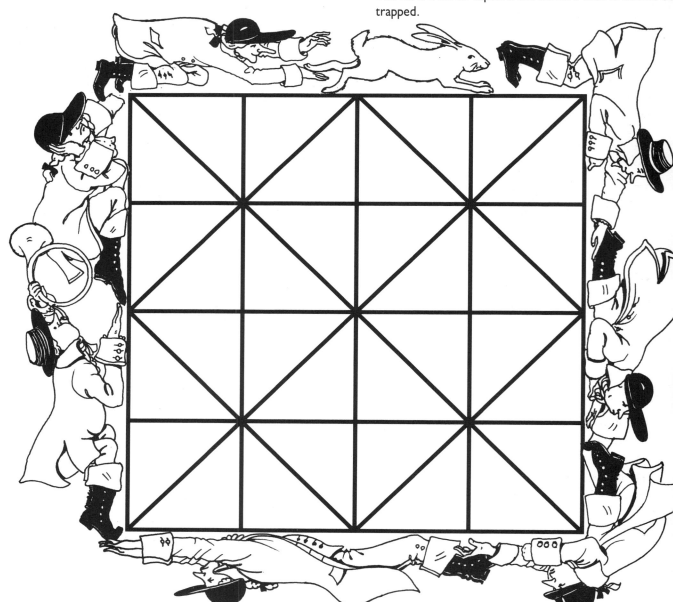

● Remember

To find the circumference of a circle use the formula, $C = \pi d$ where $\pi = 3.14$ and d is the diameter of the circle.

The diameter of this coin is 2·4 cm.
Calculate its circumference.
$C = \pi d$
$C = 3.14 \times 2.4$
$C = 7.536$

←——2·4 cm——→

The circumference is **7·54 cm**, to two dp.

1 Use the formula $C = \pi d$ to calculate the circumference of each of these coins, to two decimal places.

(a)

diameter
= 2·3 cm

(b)

diameter
= 3·2 cm

(c)

diameter
= 2·0 cm

(d)

diameter
= 1·8 cm

(e)

diameter
= 2·4 cm

2 Calculate the circumference, to two decimal places, of a circle with:

(a) diameter = 11 cm   **(b)** diameter = 4·7 cm
(c) diameter = 67 cm   **(d)** diameter = 16 cm
(e) diameter = 315 mm   **(f)** diameter = 4·3 m

The radius of this coin is 10·4 mm.
Calculate its circumference.
$d = 2 \times$ radius
$d = 2 \times 10.4$
$d = 20.8$ mm

$C = \pi d$
$C = 3.14 \times 20.8$
$C = 65.312$

radius
= 10·4 mm

The circumference is **65·3 mm**, to one dp.

3 Calculate the circumference of each of these coins, to one decimal place.

(a)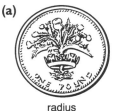

radius
= 11 mm

(b)

radius
= 10 mm

(c)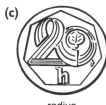

radius
= 11·8 mm

(d)

radius
= 9·5 mm

(e)

radius
= 13·1 mm

4 Calculate the circumference, to one decimal place, of a circle with:

(a) radius = 11·6 cm   **(b)** radius = 2·3 m
(c) radius = 34 mm   **(d)** radius = 12 cm
(e) radius = 23·4 cm   **(f)** radius = 4·3 m

Revolution!

This wagon wheel has a diameter of 1·7 metres. How many revolutions, or turns of the wheel, would be made if the wagon travelled 200 metres?

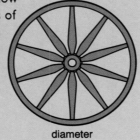

diameter =1·7 m

$C = \pi d$
$= 3·14 \times 1·7$
$= 5·338$ m

To travel 200 metres, the number of revolutions
$= \dfrac{200}{5·338} = 37·467$

37 complete revolutions of the wheel will be made.

1 A bicycle has wheels of diameter 90 cm.

90 cm

(a) How far, in metres, would the bicycle travel in one revolution of the wheel?
(b) How far would the bicycle travel in 20 revolutions?
(c) How many complete revolutions of the wheel would be made if the bicycle travelled 300 m?

2 A car has wheels of diameter 72 cm.
(a) How far would the car travel in one revolution of the wheel?
(b) How many complete revolutions of the wheel will be made when the car has travelled:
  • 500 m • 1 km • 50 km?

3 How many complete revolutions would be made if each of these wheels travelled 1 km?

(a)
diameter = 52 cm

(b)
diameter = 1·5 m

(c)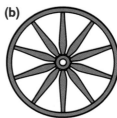
radius = 0·7 m

4 The front wheel of a Penny-farthing bicycle has a diameter of 155 cm and a rear wheel of radius 19 cm.
(a) How far would the bicycle travel in 50 revolutions of the front wheel?
(b) How many complete revolutions of the rear wheel would be made over the same distance?

5 The winch for this mine shaft has a diameter of 4·8 metres.

(a) How far would the lift go down in one revolution of the wheel?
(b) How many complete revolutions of the wheel would be needed for the lift to travel from the surface to the bottom of the shaft, a distance of 130 m?

This birthday cake has a ribbon round it.
The length of the ribbon is 92 cm.
Find the diameter of the cake.

$C = \pi d$
$92 = 3 \cdot 14 \times d$
$\dfrac{92}{3 \cdot 14} = d$
$d = 29 \cdot 299 \ldots$

The diameter is **29·3 cm**, to one dp.

This bicycle wheel has a circumference of
1·56 metres. Find the radius of the wheel.

$C = \pi d$
$1 \cdot 56 = 3 \cdot 14 \times d$
$\dfrac{1 \cdot 56}{3 \cdot 14} = d$
$d = 0 \cdot 496 \ldots$
$r = 0 \cdot 248 \ldots$

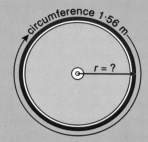

The radius of the wheel is **0·25 m**, to two dp.

1 Find the diameter, to one decimal place, of each of
these cakes.

(a)

circumference
= 69 cm

(b)

circumference
= 115 cm

(c)

circumference
= 178 cm

2 Find the diameter, to one decimal place, of a circle
with circumference:

(a) 45 cm **(b)** 23 mm **(c)** 65 m
(d) 5·7 cm **(e)** 100 km **(f)** 9·8 mm
(g) 4·62 cm **(h)** 2460 mm **(i)** 23·1 cm.

3 A strip of plastic is put round the edge of a circular
table. Find the diameter, to one decimal place, of
the table if the length of the plastic strip is:

(a) 324 cm **(b)** 676 cm **(c)** 419 cm.

4 Find the radius, to two decimal places, of each of
these wheels.

(a) *Water wheel*
Circumference = 25 m
(b) *Trundle wheel*
Circumference = 1 m
(c) *Big wheel*
Circumference = 98 m

5 Find the radius, to two decimal places, of a circle
with circumference:

(a) 12 cm **(b)** 23·5 m **(c)** 1·06 km.

Squaring the circle

Ian investigated the connection between the area and the radius of a circle. On 1 cm squared paper he drew a circle with radius 2 cm.
He estimated its area by counting squares.

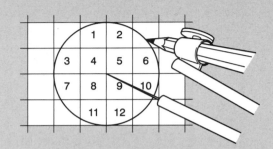

1 (a) On 1 cm squared paper draw circles of radius 3 cm, 4 cm, 5 cm and 6 cm.
  (b) Estimate their areas by counting squares.
  (c) Copy and complete the table.

Radius, r	r²	Area, A
2 cm	4 cm²	12 cm²
3 cm		

  (d) Copy and complete:
      The area of a circle is about ☐ × r².

It is more accurate to say that the Area, A = πr², where π = 3·14.

The radius of this circle is 1·2 m.
Find its area.

A = πr²
A = 3·14 × 1·2²
A = 3·14 × 1·44
A = 4·5216

The area is **4·5 m²**, to one dp.

2 Find the area of each of these circles, to one decimal place.
  (a)

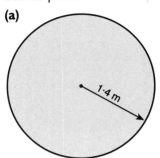

  (b)

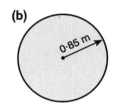

  (c)

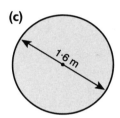

3 Find the area, to one decimal place, of a circle with:
  (a) radius = 11 cm   (b) radius = 25 km
  (c) diameter = 20 m   (d) diameter = 4·5 mm
  (e) radius = 6·8 mm   (f) radius = 0·61 cm
  (g) diameter = 210 m   (h) diameter = 7·13 m
  (i) radius = 0·314 cm.

4 Find the area of each of these semi-circles, to one decimal place.
  (a)

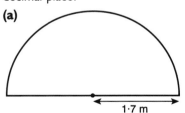

  (b)

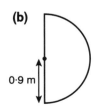

  (c)

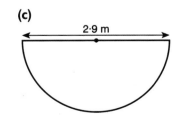

This shape is used in the construction of a model train. Find the area of the shape.

Semi-circle

$A = \frac{1}{2} \times \pi r^2$

$A = \frac{1}{2} \times 3\cdot14 \times 2\cdot4^2$

$A = 18\cdot0864$

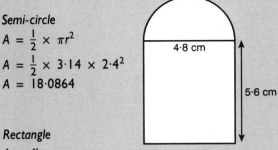

4·8 cm

5·6 cm

Rectangle

$A = lb$

$A = 5\cdot6 \times 4\cdot8$

$A = 26\cdot88$

Total area = 9·0432 + 26·88
         = 35·9232
The area of the shape is **35·9 cm²**, to one dp.

1 Each of these model train parts is made from rectangles and parts of circles. Find the area, to one decimal place, of each part.

(a) Front section

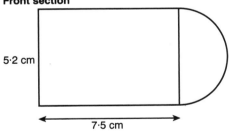

5·2 cm

7·5 cm

(b) Baseplate

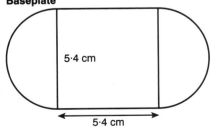

5·4 cm

5·4 cm

(c) Nameplate

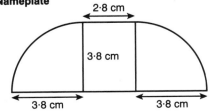

2·8 cm

3·8 cm

3·8 cm   3·8 cm

This metal washer is used in the construction of a bicycle. Find the area of the shaded part.

Large circle

$A = \pi r^2$

$= 3\cdot14 \times 2\cdot5^2$

$= 19\cdot625$ cm²

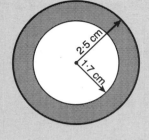

2·5 cm

1·7 cm

Small circle

$A = \pi r^2$

$= 3\cdot14 \times 1\cdot7^2$

$= 9\cdot0746$ cm²

Area of shaded part = 19·625 − 9·0746
            = 10·5504
Area of shaded part is **10·6 cm²**, to one dp.

2 Find the area, to one decimal place, of the shaded part in each of these wheels

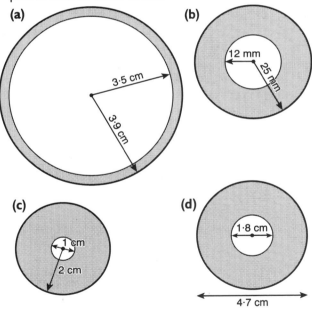

(a)

3·5 cm

3·9 cm

(b)

12 mm

25 mm

(c)

1 cm

2 cm

(d)

1·8 cm

4·7 cm

3 The shapes below are made from rectangles, circles and semi-circles. Find the area, to one decimal place, of each shaded part.

(a)

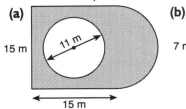

15 m

11 m

15 m

(b)

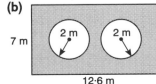

7 m

2 m   2 m

12·6 m

Problems, problems . . .

1 A circular garden table has a radius of 75 cm. Jane puts a strip of edging around its circumference. How long is the edging?

2 Martha makes a cloth of diameter 1·8 m for the table.

(a) What is the area of the cloth to one decimal place?

(b) She sews a fringed edge round the circumference of the cloth. What is the length of the fringe, to two decimal places?

(c) The fringe costs £1·30 per metre. How much will it cost Martha to put a fringe on the cloth?

3 Ken is working on his garden. He is making a lawn with an ornamental border fence.

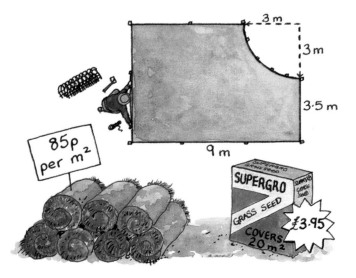

85p per m²

SUPERGRO GRASS SEED £3.95 COVERS 20 m²

(a) What is the length of the fence, to one decimal place?

(b) What is the area of the lawn, to one decimal place?

(c) How much would it cost to make the lawn using: • turf   • seed?

4 The manufacturer claims that a rotary water sprinkler can cover 25 square metres. Ken finds that it sprays water to a radius of 2·9 m. Is the manufacturer's claim correct? Explain.

5 This circular model race track has two lanes. The inside lane has a diameter of 86 cm.

86 cm

(a) How far, to the nearest centimetre, would a car travel in one lap of the inside lane?

(b) One lap of the outside lane is 3·3 metres. What is the diameter, in centimetres, of the outside lane?

6 Bill, the groundsman, is lining the pitch for a five-a-side football tournament.

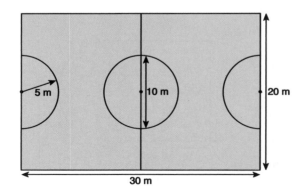

5 m   10 m   20 m

30 m

(a) What is the total distance he needs to line?

(b) It takes 2 litres of white paint to make a line 20 metres long. The paint is sold in 5-litre tins. How many tins of paint does he need to line the whole pitch?

A **tangent** is a straight line which touches the circumference of a circle at one point only. This is called a **point of contact**.

Line AT is a tangent A

Lines AR and AS are **not** tangents.

1 ▶ **You need Worksheet 17, Tangents.**

(a) For each circle:

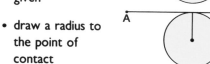

- draw a tangent from the point given

- draw a radius to the point of contact

- measure the angle between the radius and the tangent. Record your answers in the table.

Circle	Size of Angle
1	
2	

(b) Copy and complete this statement.
The angle between a tangent and the radius drawn to its point of contact is [____] degrees.

(c) Draw three diagrams of your own to test your statement.

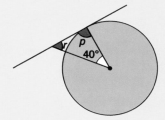

In this diagram
$p = 90°$ since it is the angle between the radius and the tangent

$r = 180 - (90 + 40)$ since the angles of a
$\ = 50°$ triangle add up to 180°.

2 Find the size of each of the angles *a* to *j*.

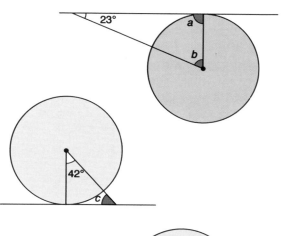

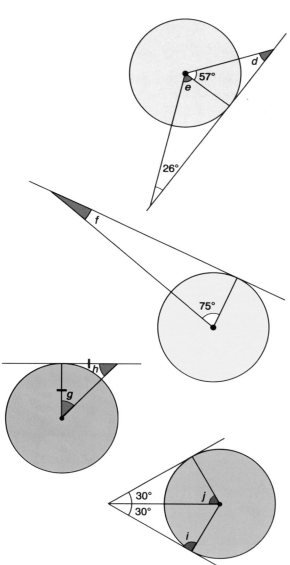

Angles, all right!

▶ **You need Worksheet 17,**
Angles in a semi-circle.

1 (a) • For each circle draw lines from points A and
B to each of the points marked on the
circumference.
• Each of the angles at K, L, M, X, Y and Z is
called **an angle in a semi-circle**.
• Measure each of these angles. Record your
answers in the table.

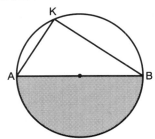

Angle	Size
AK̂B	
AL̂B	
AM̂B	

(b) Copy and complete this statement.
The angle in a semi-circle is ☐ degrees.
(c) Draw three diagrams of your own to test your
statement.

2 Calculate the size of each marked angle *a* to *f*.

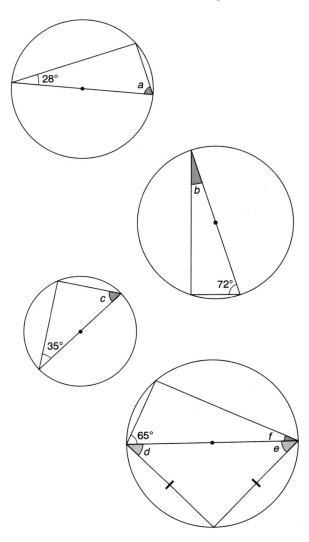

3 Find the size of each marked angle *a* to *r*.

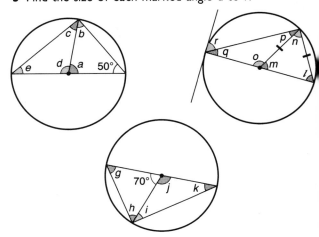

1 The bottom of the wheel just touches the base of the wheelclamp. Find the size of angle AB̂C.

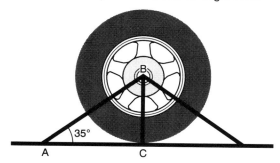

2 The rear mudguard of Leona's bicycle forms part of a circle. It has a rack attached which touches the mudguard at point P. The struts supporting the rack and mudguard are connected to the centre of the wheel.

Find the sizes of angles a and b.

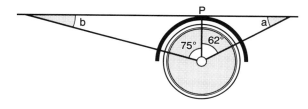

3 Simon makes a clown's face by taking a circle and a kite of coloured paper and sticking them together. QR and QT are tangents to the circle and angle RŜT is 120°.

Find the size of:

(a) angle QR̂S
(b) angle QT̂S
(c) angle RQ̂T.

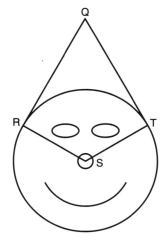

4 Eric designs earrings based on circles and triangles. Calculate the size of each marked angle a to f.

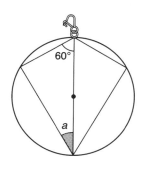

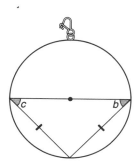

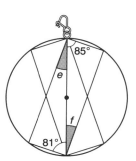

5 The arch above a door is in the shape of a semi-circle. The arch is in need of repair and is being supported by two beams until repair work can be carried out. What is the size of angle XẐY?

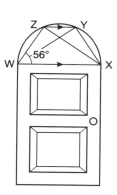

6 PQ is a tangent to the circle.

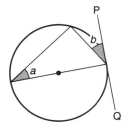

(a) Find the value of b when a is:
• 10° • 20° • 30° • 40° • 50° • 60°
(b) What do you notice about a and b?
(c) Test this for other values of a.

Solve it!

1 In April 1979 at Tummel Bridge in Perthshire the minimum temperature was ⁻9°C and the maximum was 24°C. What was the temperature range during April?

2 Susan paid a total HP price of £8120 for her car. She paid a deposit of 20% of the cash price and then 24 instalments of £280. What was the cash price?

3 For machines A and B, the formulae give the number of cards sorted, c, in time, t, minutes.

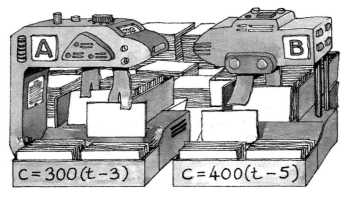

$$c = 300(t-3) \qquad c = 400(t-5)$$

(a) How many cards does machine A sort in 5 minutes?
(b) Which machine sorts more cards in 7 minutes?
(c) For how many cards do the two machines take the same length of time?

4 Colin invested £600 in a bank account with a fixed interest rate of 7% pa. He earned £14 in interest. How long did he leave his money in the bank?

5 Liz has triplets.

(a) Draw a tree diagram to show all the possible combinations of boys (b) and girls (g).
(b) If the sex of each child is taken to be random what is the probability of Liz having two boys and a girl?

6 What percentage of £500 is the same as 40% of £1000?

7 Find the area of the coloured region which is formed from a square and a quarter circle.

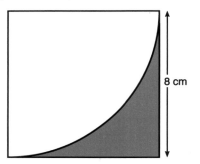

8 cm

8 Altogether Sandy, Heather and Gavin earn £610 per week. How much does each person earn per week?

I earn £25 more than Sandy and £40 more than Gavin

9 The Triangle Rule states that the sum of any two sides of a triangle must be greater than the third side. So for any triangle with sides a, b and c

$$a + b > c$$
$$b + c > a$$
$$a + c > b.$$

(a) Is it possible to make a triangle with sides 12 cm, 15 cm and 8 cm?

(b) Which of these triangles would be impossible to make? Explain.

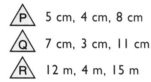

P   5 cm, 4 cm, 8 cm

Q   7 cm, 3 cm, 11 cm

R   12 m, 4 m, 15 m

(c) Two sides of a triangle are of lengths 10 cm and 15 cm. Between which two lengths must the third side lie?

10 The area of a shape drawn on square dot paper can be found using Pick's Formula $A = \frac{1}{2}b + i - 1$ where b is the number of dots on the boundary and i is the number of dots inside the shape. For this shape $b = 8$ and $i = 3$

So $A = \frac{1}{2}b \quad + i - 1$

$\quad = \frac{1}{2} \times 8 + 3 - 1$

$\quad = \quad 4 \quad + 3 - 1$

$\quad = 6$

Use Pick's Formula to find the area of these shapes.

(a)   **(b)**

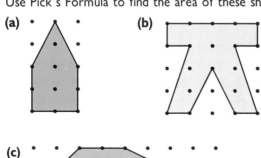

(c)

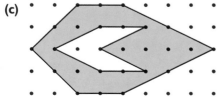

11 A band fits tightly around two wheels of identical radius. What is the length of the band?

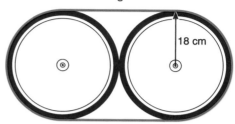

18 cm

12 Before decimalisation of money there were 12 (old) pennies in a shilling and 20 shillings in a pound. Change 288 pennies to pounds and shillings.

13 (a) Copy and complete this ready reckoner for Quickcopy.

QUICK COPY

| Up to 12 copies | 10p per copy |
| Additional copies | 3p per copy |

Number of copies	Cost (p)
6	60
12	
18	
24	156
30	
36	
42	
48	

(b) Draw a graph to show the cost against number of copies.

(c) For 60 copies what is the average cost per copy?

14 Use the diagram.

(a) What is the area of square ABCD?

(b) What fraction of square ABCD is the coloured region?

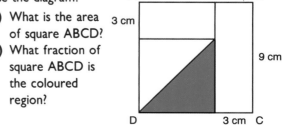

A   B

3 cm

9 cm

D   3 cm C

The Gullivers' travels

Bob and Janine Gulliver and their two children, Scott, aged 15, and Ruth, aged 12, have decided to go abroad for their summer holiday.
Bob has collected some holiday brochures. These tables, from two of the brochures, give the basic costs for different types of accommodation.

Hotels of the Neapolitan Riviera

Accommodation	Therma		La Solara		Minerva		Child reduction as a %
Board Basis	Self-catering		Bed & B/fast		Bed & B/fast		
No of weeks	1	2	1	2	1	2	
Departure dates							
27 Apr – 13 May	174	199	184	214	209	249	30
14 May – 1 Jun	214	231	224	247	252	284	20
2 Jun – 17 Jun	228	254	255	284	267	306	18
18 Jun – 1 Jul	273	294	294	319	297	331	16
2 Jul – 15 Jul	324	359	349	389	362	409	15
16 Jul – 1 Aug	333	379	359	409	372	429	5
2 Aug – 19 Aug	315	352	342	379	355	399	5
20 Aug – 9 Sep	308	333	338	369	352	391	10
10 Sep – 16 Sep	293	317	309	334	322	356	16
17 Sep – 23 Sep	284	299	297	319	312	341	18
24 Sep – 14 Oct	244	259	269	274	282	304	25
15 Oct – 31 Oct	229	–	245	–	265	–	25

Prices are per person in £'s. Remember to add holiday insurance and add any applicable supplements. Child reductions apply only to children aged 12 and under.

CAMPING AT CAMPESI, NAPLES

Nights	7		10		14		Child discount: deduct from adult price
Accomodation	Tent	C/van	Tent	C/van	Tent	C/van	
Departure dates on or between							
1 – 4 May	99	104	99	109	99	119	30
5 – 11 May	99	114	101	119	104	129	30
12 – 25 May	99	124	104	129	109	139	30
26 – 31 May	114	129	119	139	124	159	30
1 – 8 Jun	104	114	109	119	114	129	30
9 – 29 Jun	114	124	119	129	124	139	30
30 Jun – 16 Jul	154	159	159	169	174	189	50
17 Jul – 1 Aug	184	209	189	219	199	239	50
2 Aug – 10 Aug	184	219	189	229	199	249	40
11 – 18 Aug	164	199	169	209	184	299	40
19 – 24 Aug	134	189	139	199	154	219	40
25 Aug – 14 Sep	114	169	119	179	134	199	40
15 – 28 Sep	114	139	119	149	124	169	40

Prices are per person in £'s. Remember to arrange your own holiday insurance.
A cleaning/breakage refundable deposit of £40 is payable on arrival. Child reductions apply to children aged 12 and under.

1 Find the basic cost for one person of each of the holidays listed below.

Departure date	Accommodation	No of weeks
1st May	La Solara	2
2nd June	Therma	1
15th July	Minerva	2
8th August	La Solara	1
24th Sept	Minerva	2
3rd May	tent at Campesi	2
2nd June	tent at Campesi	2
28th July	caravan at Campesi	1
18th August	caravan at Campesi	2
5th Sept	tent at Campesi	1

2 Which hotel is cheapest for bed and breakfast? Explain.

3 If the Gullivers were to stay at any of the hotels, between which two departure dates are the basic costs highest? Why do you think this is?

4 Is the cost of a tent at Campesi for 2 weeks double the cost for 1 week? Why do you think this is?

Holiday insurance

Holiday insurance from Euro–Insurance must be added to the cost of all holidays.

Length of stay	Insurance (per person)
up to 9 days	£22·50
10 - 17 days	£23·95
18 - 24 days	£27·50
25 - 31 days	£30·95

To find the cost, inclusive of insurance, of a 2 week holiday departing on 4th July for the Gulliver family at the Minerva

Bob, Janine and Scott   *Ruth*

Cost for 1 adult	= £409	
Cost for 3 adults	= 3 × £409	= £1227
Cost for 1 child	= 85% of £409	= £ 347·65
Insurance	= 4 × £23·95	= £ 95·80
Cost inclusive of insurance		= **£1670·45**

5 If the Gullivers take a 2 week holiday from 20th July to 3rd August, find the cost of their holiday inclusive of insurance of staying at:

  (a) a tent at Campesi   **(b)** the Minerva.

6 Find the cost inclusive of insurance for each of these holidays.

Departure Date	Accommo- dation	No of people		No of weeks
		Adults	Children under 12	
3rd May	tent	2		1
5th Aug	Minerva	2	1	2
15th July	La Solara	1	2	1
30th June	caravan	3	4	2
21st May	Therma	2	3	1
13th Sep	La Solara	1	1	2
4th Aug	tent	1	3	1

7 The Gullivers have £1000 to spend on a holiday. They would like to go to either La Solara or a tent at Campesi, for 2 weeks, leaving on 8th August. Which of these holidays, if either, can they afford? Explain.

Conditions of payment

- 20% deposit required when booking.
- the remainder to be paid at least 8 weeks before departure.

8 The Gullivers are considering a holiday in a tent at Campesi for a fortnight departing on 23rd August.

  (a) What would be the total cost of this holiday?
  (b) How much is the deposit?
  (c) Calculate the remainder.
  (d) When is the remainder due to be paid by?

9 Janine notices the list of supplements in small print at the bottom of the page.

Hotel supplements per person per night	En-suite bath £1·20 Sea view £0·70 Balcony £2·40

Campesi supplements per night	£0·50 per car space £2·00 Grade 1 site £1·50 for electricity £1·20 caravan with WC

What would be the total cost, including insurance and any supplements, of each of these holidays for the Gullivers?

  (a) 14 days at the Minerva with a sea view and en-suite bath, departing 23rd May.
  (b) One week at the Therma with sea view and balcony, departing 28th August.
  (c) 2 weeks in a caravan at Campesi with electricity, departing 16th July.

10 The Gullivers have decided on a 2 week holiday in Naples, starting on 14th July. What is the total cost for the family of a tent at Campesi on a grade 1 site with electricity?

The sunshine factor

In choosing their holiday the Gullivers took account of these graphs which give average temperature and hours of sunshine for different resorts.

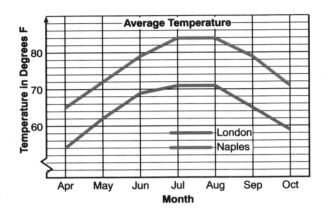

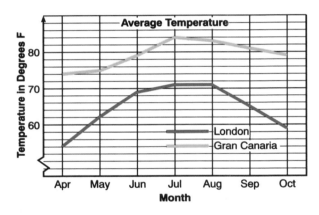

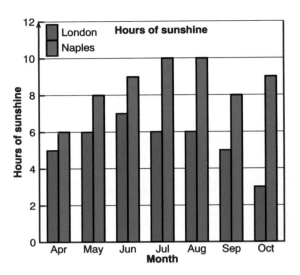

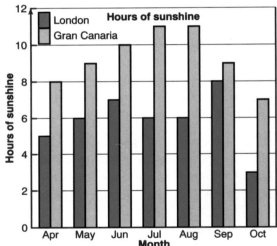

1 What is the average temperature in June in:

   (a) Naples   **(b)** Gran Canaria?

2 What is the average number of hours of sunshine during September for:

   (a) Naples   **(b)** Gran Canaria?

3 For the month of July, what is the difference between the average number of hours of sunshine in:

   (a) London and Naples
   (b) London and Gran Canaria?

4 During the month of August, what is the difference in average temperature between:

   (a) London and Naples
   (b) London and Gran Canaria?

5 If you were to go on holiday in July which of these two resorts would you choose? Explain.

6 Draw a bar chart to show the average number of hours of sunshine in Majorca and in London.

	April	May	June	July	Aug	Sep	Oct
Majorca	7	10	10	11	11	8	6
London	5	6	7	6	6	5	3

7 Draw a line graph to show the average daily temperatures in Kenya and London.

	April	May	June	July	Aug	Sep	Oct
Kenya	85	83	82	81	81	82	84
London	56	62	69	71	71	65	59

FOREIGN · NEXT

Exchange rate per £ sterling

Austria (sch)	16·95
Denmark (kr)	9·38
France (fr)	8·18
Germany (Dm)	2·42
Greece (dr)	307
Ireland (punts)	0·923
Italy (lire)	2165·00
Spain (pes)	171·00
Switzerland (Sfr)	2·145
United States ($)	1·643

For their trip, Bob and Janine need to change money from sterling into foreign currencies. The table gives exchange rates.

How many Italian lire would Janine exchange for £50?

£	Lire
1	2165
50	$2165 \times 50 = 108\,250$

She would receive **108 250 lire**

1 How many Italian lire would be exchanged for:
(a) £100   **(b)** £150   **(c)** £250   **(d)** £125?

2 The family decides to travel to Italy by car, stopping off for a day at Euro-Disney in France and a night in Montreux in Switzerland. They will need some French francs and some Swiss francs.
(a) How many French francs will they get for:
 • £50   • £75   • £90   • £100?
(b) How many Swiss francs will they get for:
 • £40   • £80   • £100   • £135?

3 Change each amount into the currency given:
(a) £60 into Austrian schillings
(b) £150 into German marks
(c) £225 into American dollars
(d) £175 into Spanish pesetas
(e) £163 into Irish punts.

The travel agent has advised Bob to take travellers cheques abroad instead of large amounts of cash. These can be exchanged for foreign currency in most countries.

There is a charge of 1% commission on travellers cheques.

How much would it cost the Gullivers to buy £200 of travellers cheques?

Commission = 1% of £200
      = £2
Total cost = £200 + £2
      = £202
or Total cost = 101% of £200
      = **£202.**

4 How much would it cost to buy travellers cheques worth:
(a) £300   **(b)** £250   **(c)** £125   **(d)** £375?

5 Bob and Janine decide to take £350 in travellers cheques, £100 in French francs, £150 in Swiss francs and £200 in lire. How much in sterling will this cost them?

■ Investigation

6 Investigate the advantages and the disadvantages of taking travellers cheques abroad instead of foreign currency.

Planning the trip

The Gullivers come from Manchester. They will be travelling to Dover to catch the ferry to France.

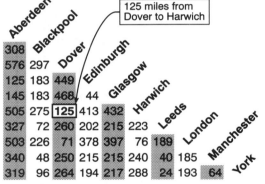

> 125 miles from Dover to Harwich

	Aberdeen	Blackpool	Dover	Edinburgh	Glasgow	Harwich	Leeds	London	Manchester	York
Aberdeen	308									
Blackpool	576	297								
Dover	125	183	449							
Edinburgh	145	183	468	44						
Glasgow	505	275	125	413	432					
Harwich	327	72	260	202	215	223				
Leeds	503	226	71	378	397	76	189			
London	340	48	250	215	215	240	40	185		
York	319	96	264	194	217	288	24	193	64	

The chart shows the distances, in miles, between major towns in Britain.

1 Find the distance between:
- **(a)** Manchester and Dover
- **(b)** Aberdeen and York
- **(c)** Edinburgh and London
- **(d)** Leeds and Aberdeen
- **(e)** Manchester and Edinburgh
- **(f)** Glasgow and Harwich
- **(g)** York and London.

2 How much further is it from Manchester to Aberdeen than from Manchester to London?

3 How long should it take to travel from Manchester to:
- **(a)** Leeds at 40 mph
- **(b)** Dover at 50 mph
- **(c)** Harwich at 30 mph
- **(d)** Aberdeen at 40 mph?

Channel Ferry Departures

The crossing times are given in brackets.

Dover-Calais (1hr15min)	Calais-Dover (1hr15min)
0200 0400 0600 0730 0900	0015 0200 0400 0550 0730
1030 1200 1330 1500 1630	0900 1045 1215 1345 1515
1800 1930 2100 2230 2359	1645 1815 1945 2115 2245

Dover-Boulogne (1hr40min)	Boulogne-Dover (1hr40min)
0445 0830 1015 1400 1545	0645 0830 1215 1400 1815
2000	2015

Felixstowe-Zeebrugge (5hr45min)	Zeebrugge-Felixstowe (5hr45min)
1100 2300	0830 1645 2300

Harwich-Hook of Holland (7hr30min)	Hook of Holland-Harwich (7hr30min)
1100 2100	1200 2130

4 Find the arrival time of these sailings:
- **(a)** 1630 sailing from Dover – Calais
- **(b)** 2359 sailing from Dover – Calais
- **(c)** 1545 sailing from Dover – Boulogne
- **(d)** 2300 sailing from Felixstowe – Zeebrugge
- **(e)** 2100 sailing from Harwich – Hook of Holland.

5 Janine estimates that she can drive from Manchester to Dover at an average speed of 50 mph. She also allows for one stop of 20 minutes and one stop of 35 minutes for refreshments.
- **(a)** How long should the journey take?
- **(b)** The ferry she wants to catch leaves at 1330. What is the latest time they should leave Manchester for checking in at least 30 minutes before departure time?

6 (a) At what time will the Gullivers' ferry arrive in Calais?
- **(b)** The ferry takes 15 minutes to unload, and the journey to their first campsite takes three and a half hours. At what time do they expect to arrive at the campsite?

	Exchange rate per £ sterling
Denmark(kr)	9·38
France(fr)	8·18
Germany(Dm)	2·42
Italy(lire)	2165
Spain(pes)	171
Switzerland(Sfr)	2·145
United States($)	1·643

The Gullivers spend their first two nights at 'Camp des Anglais', near Euro-Disney. Scott spends 32·15 francs on amusements.
How much is this in sterling?

francs	£
8·18	1
1	1 ÷ 8·18
32·15	32·15 × 1 ÷ 8·18 = 3·93

Scott spent **£3·93** to the nearest penny.

1 How much is each amount in sterling?
   (a) 50 francs   **(b)** 72·16 francs   **(c)** 85·21 francs

2 Calculate how much each of the following is worth in sterling.
   (a) 25 Dm   **(b)** 300 pes   **(c)** 56·85 kr   **(d)** $ 200

3 The Gullivers spend the day at Euro-Disney. Entry to the theme-park is 250 francs per adult and 204 francs per child. What is the total cost of entry for the Gullivers in sterling?

4 Scott and Ruth buy presents from one of the Euro-Disney shops.
   Find the cost, in sterling, of each of the following.
   (a) T-shirt   **(b)** cap   **(c)** 2 pennants.

5 Next morning they pack up early and head for Montreux. They follow this route, to take in some of rural France:

   Paris (Camp des Anglais) → Châlons-sur-Marne → Dijon → Besançon → Montreux

   (a) Use the map to calculate the distance they travel from Paris to Montreux.

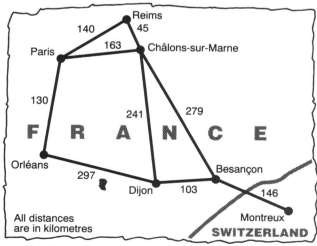

   (b) Bob estimates that the car will travel 12·5 kilometres on one litre of petrol. How much petrol will they need for this journey?

   (c) Petrol costs 6·75 francs per litre. How much will petrol cost for this journey in:
   • francs   • sterling?

Francly speaking

5 miles is about 8 kilometres.

Bob drives through France at 55 mph.
What is his speed in km/h?

miles	kilometres
5	8
55	8 ÷ 5 × 55 = 88

His speed is **88 km/h.**

1 Change each speed into km/h.
   (a) 25 mph   (b) 40 mph   (c) 86 mph

2 Change each speed into mph.
   (a) 32 km/h   (b) 40 km/h   (c) 124 km/h

3 The table gives the speed limits for different types of road in France and Britain.

Road	Maximum Speed Limit	
	France (km/h)	Britain (mph)
motorways	130	70
dual carriageways	110	70
other roads	90	60
built-up areas	50	30

On what types of road are you allowed to travel faster in France than in Britain?

4 On what types of road in France would Bob be breaking the speed limit if he was travelling at 65 mph?

5 When they reach Montreux, in Switzerland, they have a meal in a traditional Swiss restaurant.

Menu

	Swiss Francs
Baslermehl soppe	5·25
Fondue	19·10
Raclette	23·40
Berner Rosti	25·30
Apfel Kuchen	25·95
Geschnatzeles	6·50
Glace	8·50

Service charge 8% extra.

(a) What is the **total** bill for the family, in Swiss francs, if each has the following meal?

Bob   Baslermehl soppe, Raclette, Glace
Janine Fondue, Glace
Scott   Fondue, Apfel Kuchen
Ruth   Berner Rosti, Glace

(b) What is this cost in sterling?

6 The night before they complete the last leg of their journey to Italy, Janine takes Scott and Ruth to see The BOFs at the Montreux Rock and Pop Festival. The price of a ticket is 30 francs. Ruth buys a T-shirt at 21·50 francs and Scott buys a poster costing 9·80 francs.

(a) How much, in Swiss francs, did they spend altogether?
(b) How much is this in sterling?

On arrival at Campesi, the family see these advertisements in the camp shop window.

1 Find the cost for each of the following in:
  • lire   • sterling.
  (a) The Gullivers to visit Pompei.
  (b) The family to hire a boat for 5 hours.
  (c) Scott and Ruth to hire water-ski equipment and have tuition for 2 hours.

2 The family plan a day trip to Rome.
  (a) What would be the total cost for the family?
  (b) The coach trip takes 2 hours 15 minutes each way. If they take the coach leaving at 0845, when should they arrive back at the campsite?

3 (a) Before visiting Pompei, Janine exchanged £150 in travellers cheques for lire and the local bank charged 1·5% commission. The exchange rate was 2155 lire to the £. How many lire did Janine receive?
  (b) How many lire would she receive in exchange for travellers cheques of value:
  • £75   • £100   • £225?

4 (a) Find the sale price of each of these gifts in lire.

(b) Ruth has £25 left in travellers cheques. Does she have enough to buy these presents for her friends? Explain.

■ Investigation

5 Investigate the cost of a holiday abroad for your family.

Marking time

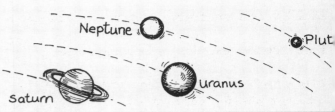

Before 1752 the Julian calendar was used to record dates. This calendar assumed that the earth took exactly $365\frac{1}{4}$ days to travel round the sun. In fact it takes 11 minutes and 14 seconds less than this.

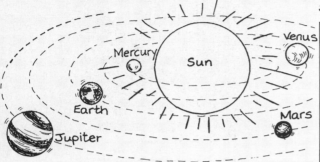

As the centuries passed, the error built up and by the middle of the eighteenth century it amounted to 11 days.

In 1752 it was decided to introduce a more accurate calendar, the Gregorian calendar, and correct the 11 days' error at the same time. It was therefore declared that 2nd September would be followed by 14th September. Many people thought they were being robbed of eleven days of their life and rioted in the streets.

The Gregorian calendar is still in use today. A leap year occurs every 4 years to account for the extra $\frac{1}{4}$ day the earth takes to travel round the sun. The 11 minutes and 14 seconds is allowed for by not having a leap year at the beginning of some centuries. The years 1800 and 1900 were not leap years. The year 2000 will be a leap year. The year 2100 will not.

1 Printers need to know how many possible calendars there are. A year could start on a Monday, Tuesday, Wednesday, . . .
  (a) On how many different days could a year begin?
  (b) On how many different days could a leap year begin?
  (c) How many possible calendars are there?

> 30 days has September,
> April, June and November.
> All the rest have 31 except February alone.
> Which has but 28 days clear,
> And 29 in each leap year.

2 List the months in order. Beside each month write the number of days it has in a year which is not a leap year.

3 The Gregorian calendar is now used throughout the world. Some people think it could be improved. What do you think is wrong with the Gregorian calendar?

4 Many businesses produce statistics each quarter:
  • January – March   • April – June
  • July – September   • October – December.
  (a) Does each quarter contain the same number of days?
  (b) Does each half of the year contain the same number of days?

5 A balanced calendar would have the same number of days in each quarter. Keeping the 12 months we have, but changing the number of days in some of the months, design a new calendar which is more balanced.

■ Investigation

6 Investigate how a calendar with 13 months could be designed. Call the new month Sol.

Ali designs logos for advertising stationery and posters.

1 Copy this logo **exactly**, on $\frac{1}{2}$ cm squared paper.

2 Ali wants to enlarge the logo for box labels. Draw the logo when the scale factor is 2.

3 The business stationery will contain the same logo. Draw the logo for:

   (a) the letter heading, scale factor $\frac{1}{2}$.
   (b) the business cards, scale factor $\frac{1}{4}$.
   (c) the compliments slips, scale factor $\frac{3}{4}$.

4 The carpeting in reception will have the same design. Draw the logo when the scale factor is $3\frac{1}{2}$.

5 Copy and complete:

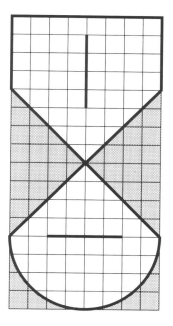

	Scale factor	Logo size
Leaflet	1	original
Box label		
Letter heading		
Business card	$\frac{1}{4}$	
Compliments slip		smaller
Carpeting		larger

- When the scale factor is greater than 1 the logo becomes [   ].
- When the scale factor is less than 1 the logo becomes [   ].

6 This is the top of the logo for the poster. What scale factor has Ali used?

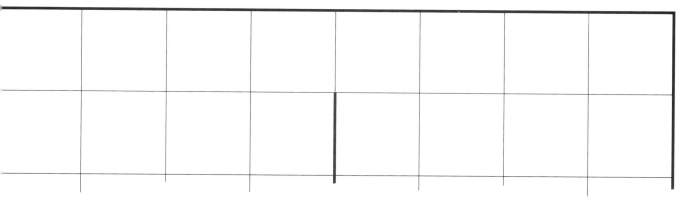

Ali is also using these shapes for logos.

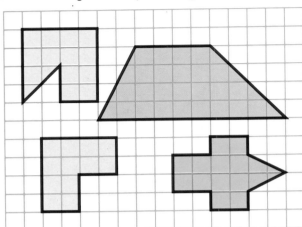

1 Draw each shape on $\frac{1}{2}$ cm squared paper with:

(a) a scale factor of 2 (b) a scale factor of $\frac{1}{2}$.

> A shape and its enlargement are similar to each other. The letter k is used for scale factor.

2 Find the scale factor, k, for each pair of similar shapes.

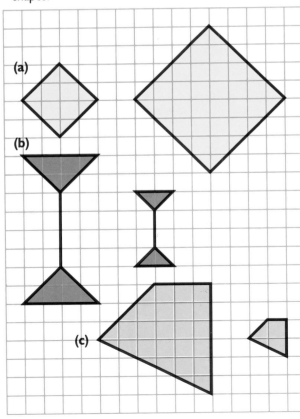

3 For each pair of similar shapes find the length of the named side.

Scale factor $k = 2$

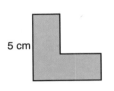
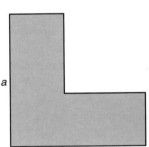

Scale factor $k = \frac{1}{3}$

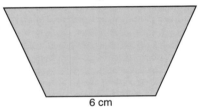

Scale factor $k = \frac{1}{4}$

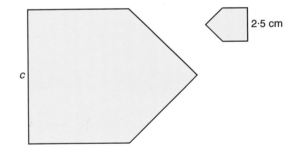

Scale factor $k = 1\frac{1}{2}$

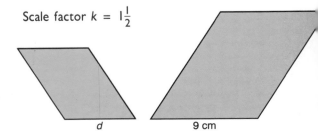

You need 1 cm squared paper.

1 (a) Copy the shapes.

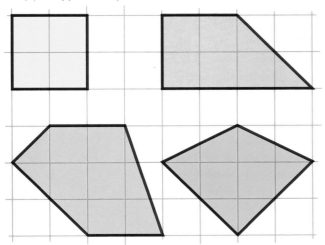

(b) For each shape draw a similar shape of:
  • scale factor 2   • scale factor 3.
(c) Measure the angles in each set of similar shapes.
(d) Write about the angles of similar shapes.

Shapes that are similar contain the same angles.

2 Find the missing angles in each pair of similar shapes.

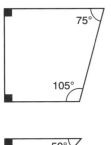

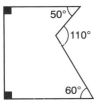

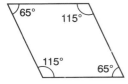

3 For each pair of similar shapes find:
  • the sizes of the named angles
  • the scale factor, *k*
  • the lengths of the named sides.

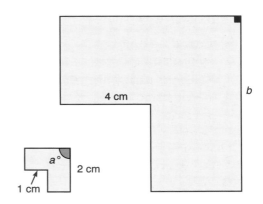

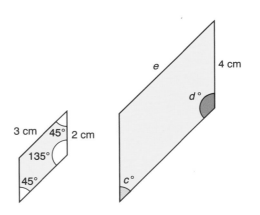

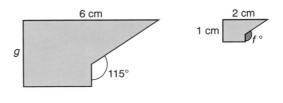

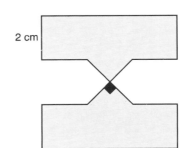

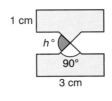

Up and down the scales

● **Remember**

Two shapes are similar when one is an enlargement of the other.

You need 1 cm squared paper.

1 **(a)** Copy these triangles.
For each triangle draw:
- a similar triangle of scale factor 2
- a similar triangle of scale factor 3.

(b) Measure the angles in each set of triangles.

(c) Write about what you find.

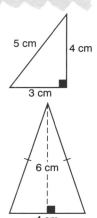

Triangles which are **similar** contain the same angles.

2 **(a)** Sketch each triangle and fill in the sizes of **all** angles.

(b) Find pairs of triangles which are **similar** to each other.

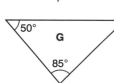

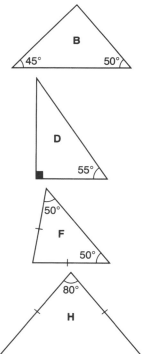

To find the scale factor look at one pair of corresponding sides.

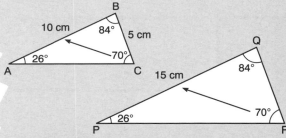

Sides AB and PQ correspond.
They are both opposite the 70° angle.
Triangle PQR is an enlargement.
The scale factor, k, is greater than 1.

$k = 15 \div 10 = \mathbf{1 \cdot 5}$

Sides BC and QR correspond.
They are both opposite the 26° angle.

$QR = 5 \times 1 \cdot 5 = \mathbf{7 \cdot 5 \ cm}$

3 For each pair of similar triangles find:
- the scale factor, k
- the length of the named side.

(a) Find EF.

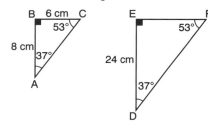

(b) Find JK.

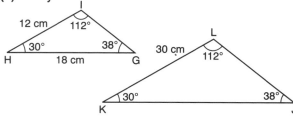

(c) Find PR.

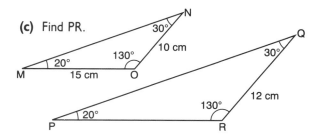

To find the scale factor, *k*, look at one pair of corresponding sides.

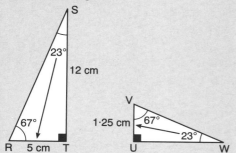

Sides RT and UV correspond.
They are both opposite the 23° angle.
Triangle UVW is a reduction.
The scale factor is less than 1.

k = 1·25 ÷ 5 = **0·25**

Sides ST and UW correspond.
They are both opposite the 67° angle.

QR = 12 × 0·25 = **3 cm**

4 For each pair of similar triangles:
• find the scale factor, *k*
• find the length of the named side.

(a) Find EF.

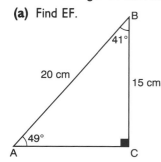

(b) Find JK.

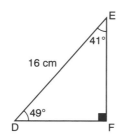
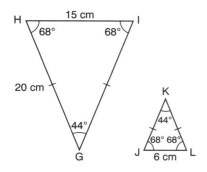

5 Find the length of PR.

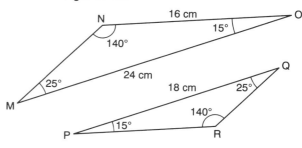

To solve problems 6, 7 and 8:
• sketch the similar triangles
• mark known sides and angles
• find the scale factor
• answer the question.

6 A post 3 m high casts a shadow 4 m long. At the same time a tree casts a shadow 20 m long. How high is the tree?

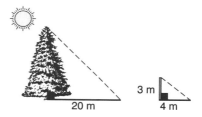

7 Peter, who is 1·8 m tall, and his son Billy are standing under a spotlight.

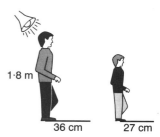

Peter's shadow is 36 cm long. Billy's shadow is 27 cm long. How tall is Billy?

� Challenge

8 This advertising board is held open by a horizontal wooden support.
How long is the support?

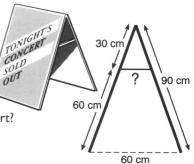

The scale factor for area is the square of the scale factor for length. If the scale factor for length is k, the scale factor for area is k^2.

This sail has an area of 5·6 m². It has been enlarged by a scale factor of 1·5.

Scale factor for length $k = 1·5$
Scale factor for area $k^2 = 1·5^2 = 2·25$
Area of the enlarged sail = 5·6 × 2·25 = **12·6 m²**

Sabine and Andy make sails. These are their sketches of a series of similar sails they have made.

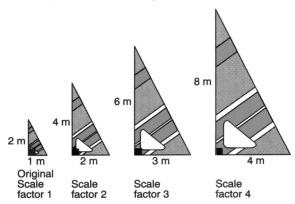

2 m

4 m

6 m

8 m

1 m
Original
Scale
factor 1

2 m
Scale
factor 2

3 m
Scale
factor 3

4 m
Scale
factor 4

1 (a) Calculate the area of each sail.
 (b) Copy and complete the table.

Scale factor for length	Area (m²)	Scale factor for area
1	1	$1 = 1^2$
2	4	$4 = 2^2$
3		
4		

 (c) What do you think will be the area of a sail enlarged by scale factor 5?
 (d) Make a sketch of the sail and check.
 (e) What do you think will be the area of a sail enlarged by scale factor $\frac{1}{2}$?
 (f) Make a sketch of the sail and check.

2 A sail has an area of 4·2 m². An enlargement is made of scale factor 2. Find the area of the enlarged sail.

3 The main sail of Andy's boat has an area of 8 m². A half-size model is being made. Find the area of the sail in the model.

4 This photograph of Sabine's boat has been enlarged. Find the area of the enlargement.

60 cm²

10 cm

14 cm

▼ Challenge

5 Andy has two similar sails for his boat. Their areas are 5·2 m² and 11·7 m². The length of the small sail is 1·3 metres. Find the length of the large sail.

Duddingston School U-16 football team scored this number of goals in a cup competition.

The average number of goals can be found in three different ways. These averages are called the mean, median and mode.

Mean

$$\frac{5+2+3+3+6+7+4}{7} = \frac{30}{7} = 4 \cdot 285\ldots$$

The **mean** number of goals is **4·3** to one dp.

1 The other teams in the cup competition scored the following goals.

Prestonhouse	1, 4, 3, 5, 3, 2
Malbury	3, 0, 2, 7, 6, 1, 2
Castleton	2, 3, 0, 1
Mertham	7, 3, 2, 2, 5, 2, 1, 3

Calculate the mean number of goals scored by each team.

Median

To find the median, arrange the data in order. The **median** is the **middle** value. There are an equal number of values above and below the median.

2, 3, 3, 4, 5, 6, 7   23, 28, 32, 33, 43, 60

The **median** is **4**.   The **median** is **32·5**.

2 Find the median for each set of data:
   (a) 23, 16, 26, 31, 19, 42, 36
   (b) 8, 5, 6, 10, 7, 8, 5, 5, 7, 2, 7, 9
   (c) 3·2, 4·3, 3·6, 2·8, 5·7, 2·9, 4·5, 3·1

3 These are the times of the runners in a 100 m race.
   11·3 s, 12·6 s, 11·5 s, 12·7 s, 11·9 s
   Find: (a) the median   (b) the mean time taken.

Mode

To find the mode, arrange the data in order. The **mode** is the **most common** or frequent value.

2, 3, 3, 4, 5, 6, 7

The **mode** is **3**.
This is sometimes called the **modal** number.

4 Find the mode for each set of data:
   (a) 5, 7, 3, 4, 5, 6, 2, 3, 2, 6, 4, 2
   (b) 2·3, 4·1, 2·4, 4·7, 2·3, 5·4, 4·1, 2·3,
   (c) 67, 86, 54, 62, 71, 54, 53, 59, 62
       54, 86, 74, 62, 54, 67, 69, 87, 54

5 Members of the Portobello Swimming Club took part in a charity swim. These are the number of lengths completed by the swimmers.

16	23	14	25	23	18	9	25
17	25	19	25	22	19	15	20

For the number of lengths completed, find:
   (a) the mean   (b) the median   (c) the mode.

6 Francis collected the following number of eggs each day from her hens during one fortnight:

Find the mean, median and modal number of eggs.

7 Cricketers use the mean when calculating their averages.
   (a) Mike scored a total of 215 runs in 5 innings. Find his average number of runs per innings.
   (b) Mike scored 31 runs in his next innings. What was his average number of runs for the 6 innings?

8 After 7 games in the football league, United had a mean score of 3 goals per game.
   (a) How many goals had they scored altogether?
   (b) United scored 5 goals in their next game. After this game, what was the mean number of goals scored?

Tally-Ho!

The Portobello Scouts are taking part in a competition. They have formed 2 teams, the *Badgers* and the *Foxes*.

Basketball Shoot		Badgers		
3	1	3	5	4
4	4	1	2	4
1	2	4	0	3
2	3	4	4	4

Jeremy and Harriet are keeping a record of the number of points scored by the *Badgers* team in the Basketball Shoot.

Jeremy calculates the mean like this:

$$\frac{3+1+3+5+4+4+4+1+2+4+1+2+4+0+3+2+3+4+4+4}{20}$$

$$= 2 \cdot 9$$

There is a large amount of data so Harriet uses a frequency table to calculate the mean.

Points	Tally marks	Frequency	Frequency × points
0	I	1	0
1	III	3	3
2	III	3	6
3	IIII	4	12
4	HHH III	8	32
5	I	1	5
Total		20	58

3 scouts each scored 2 points. 6 altogether

Total points scored

Number taking part in Basketball Shoot

The **mean** number of points scored is $\frac{58}{20}$ = **2·9**.

1 Jeremy recorded these points scored by the *Foxes* in the Basketball Shoot.

Basketball Shoot				Foxes		
5	1	3	4	5	0	3	5
4	0	2	3	4	5	1	2
1	3	4	2	4	2	5	2

(a) Copy and complete this frequency table for the scores.

Points	Tally marks	Frequency	Frequency x points
0			
1			

(b) Calculate the mean number of points scored.

2 These are the scores for the two teams in the Throwing the Horseshoe event.

Horseshoe		Badgers		
5	3	6	1	3
6	2	5	0	4
5	1	4	3	5
3	5	8	5	1

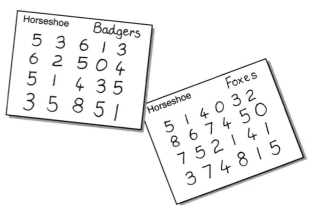

Horseshoe		Foxes		
5	1	4	0	3	2
8	6	7	4	5	0
7	5	2	1	4	1
3	7	4	8	1	5

(a) Make a frequency table for each set of scores.
(b) Which team had the better mean score?

Harriet can also find the median and mode of the Basketball scores from the frequency table.

Points	Tally marks	Frequency
0	I	1
1	III	3
2	III	3
3	IIII	4
4	HHt III	8
5	I	1
	Total	20

There are 20 scores. The middle score will be between the 10th and 11th ordered score.
The median is 3.

The most frequent score is 4.
The **mode** is 4

3 This frequency table shows the points scored by the *Badgers* in the Target competition.

Points	Frequency	Frequency × points
10	1	
11	0	
12	5	
13	2	
14	1	
15	2	
16	4	
17	3	
18	2	
Total		

(a) Copy and complete the frequency table.
(b) Find the mean, median and modal score.

4 These are the points scored by the *Foxes* in the Target competition.

Target						Foxes	
13	17	14	10	15	11	12	18
11	14	10	16	18	18	14	17
16	10	16	10	14	16	15	16

(a) Calculate the mean, median and modal score for the *Foxes*.
(b) Which team had the better average? Explain.

5 These frequency tables show the number of points scored by each team in the Power Press-ups event.

Power Press-ups						Badgers	
Number of points	0	1	2	3	4	5	6
Frequency	2	0	5	2	4	3	4

Power Press-ups						Foxes	
Number of points	0	1	2	3	4	5	6
Frequency	2	4	5	4	6	1	2

(a) For each team calculate:
  • the mean   • the median
  • the modal score.
(b) Which team had the better average? Explain.

6 The graph shows the scores of the teams in the Keepie Uppie competition.

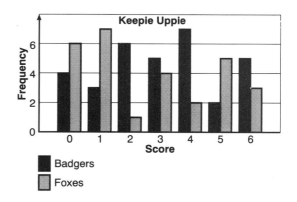

(a) Find the mean, median and mode for each team.
(b) Which team had the better average? Explain.

Scouts mean business

The frequency table shows the distances thrown by the *Foxes* in the Chuck the Welly competition.

Distance (m)	Frequency
10 – 14	2
15 – 19	7
20 – 24	10
25 – 29	3
30 – 34	2

This frequency table can be used to calculate the average distance thrown.

Distance (m)	Frequency	Midpoint	Frequency × midpoint
10 – 14	2	12	24
15 – 19	7	17	119
20 – 24	10	22	220
25 – 29	3	27	81
30 – 34	2	32	64
Total	24		508

There are 10 values in this class interval. We assume they are evenly spread and use the middle value or midpoint when calculating the mean.

These are the middle values of the class intervals.

The mean distance thrown is $\frac{508}{24}$ = 21·166 . . .
= 21 m to the nearest metre.

The modal class interval is **20 – 24**.
The median lies in the class interval **20 – 24**.

1 This frequency table shows the points scored by the *Badgers* in the Chuck the Welly competition.

Distance (m)	Frequency
10 – 14	2
15 – 19	6
20 – 24	8
25 – 29	1
30 – 34	2
35 – 39	1

(a) Calculate the mean distance thrown.
(b) Find the modal class interval.
(c) In which class interval does the median lie?

2 These are the distances, in feet, jumped in the Long Jump.

Long Jump

13	11	15	17	16	13	8	17	9	15
10	14	9	16	12	8	13	15	10	9
8	11	14	15	12	15	13	11	13	14
16	14	13	11	9	12	16	15	13	15

(a) Copy and complete this frequency table of these distances.

Distance (feet)	Tally marks	Frequency	Midpoint	Frequency × midpoint
8 – 10				

(b) Calculate the mean distance jumped.
(c) Find the modal class interval.
(d) In which class interval does the median lie?

3 The frequency table shows the times taken by some scouts to peel one potato in the Potato Peeling competition.

Time in seconds	Frequency
0 – 14	3
15 – 29	1
30 – 44	5
45 – 59	9
60 – 74	6
75 – 89	0
90 – 104	4

(a) Calculate the mean time taken to peel one potato.

(b) What is the modal class interval?

(c) In which class interval does the median lie?

4 These are the times, in seconds, run in the Three-Legged Race.

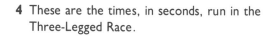

Three-Legged Race

```
35 52 32 38 39 47 50 35 35 48
40 36 38 42 39 35 54 47 36 44
53 38 49 41 36 46 30 48 32 36
37 38 47 51 39 45 38 47 33 43
```

(a) Make a frequency table for these times using the class intervals
30 – 34, 35 – 39 . . .

(b) Find:
  • the mean time taken
  • the modal class interval
  • the class interval in which the median lies.

5 These are the times, in seconds, run in the Sack Race.

Sack Race

```
33 27 29 22 30 24 34 30 24 28 32
24 34 31 29 26 31 35 29 32 35 22
31 29 25 31 35 28 23 27 25 30 27
21 32 27 32 29 34 31 33 35 32 32
28 35 21 30 26 30 28 25 29 22 34
```

(a) Make a frequency table for these times using the class intervals
21 – 23, 24 – 26. . .

(b) Find:
  • the mean time taken
  • the modal class interval
  • the class interval where the median lies.

What's the average?

1 This frequency table shows the ages of teachers in a secondary school.

Age in years	Frequency
20 – 29	8
30 – 39	18
40 – 49	29
50 – 59	22
60 – 69	3

(a) What is the most common age range for teachers?

(b) Calculate the mean age.

(c) In which class interval does the median lie?

2 The graph shows the weights of 50 new-born babies.

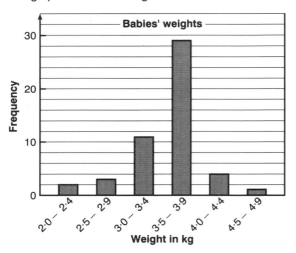

(a) What is the modal class interval?

(b) In which class interval does the median lie?

(c) Calculate the mean weight.

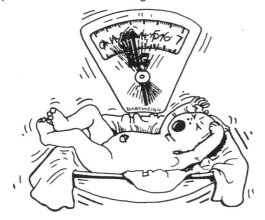

3 The graph shows the marks gained in a French test by Class 4A and Class 4B.

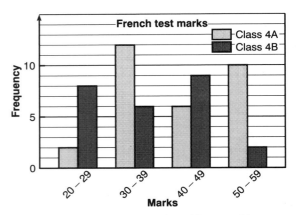

(a) How many students in class 4A scored between 30 and 39?

(b) How many students are there in class 4B?

(c) For each class find:
  • the mean test mark
  • the modal class interval
  • the class interval in which the median lies.

(d) Which class had the better average? Explain your answer.

4 In an experiment fifty plants were fed with a new nutrient and fifty plants were given no nutrient. The heights of the plants were recorded after 4 weeks.

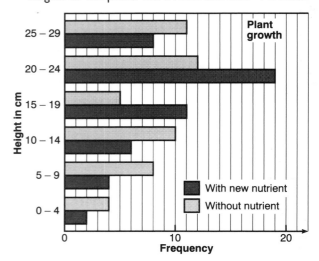

(a) Find the mean height of a plant:
  • fed with the new nutrient
  • not fed with the new nutrient.

(b) What difference does using a nutrient make? Explain your answer.

Write any two numbers less than 10.
8,6

Add the numbers and write the units digit.
8,6,4

Repeat this for the 6 and 4.
8,6,4,0

Continue like this until the two
starting numbers appear again –

(8,6,) 4,0,4,4,8,2,0,2,2,4,6,0,6,6,2,8,0,8, (8,6)

You can write this as a number chain.

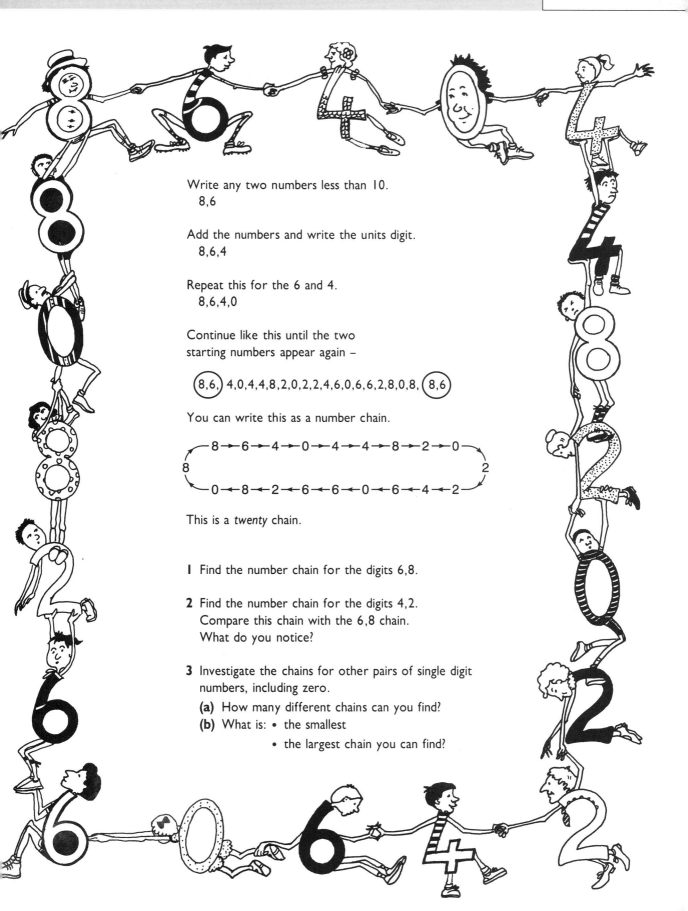

This is a *twenty* chain.

1 Find the number chain for the digits 6,8.

2 Find the number chain for the digits 4,2.
Compare this chain with the 6,8 chain.
What do you notice?

3 Investigate the chains for other pairs of single digit
numbers, including zero.
  (a) How many different chains can you find?
  (b) What is: • the smallest
      • the largest chain you can find?

1 Each diagram shows a right-angled triangle with squares drawn on each of its sides. The lengths of the sides are in centimetres. Copy and complete the table.

Triangle	A	B
Area of smallest square in cm^2	3 × 3 = 9	
Area of middle-sized square in cm^2	4 × 4 = 16	
Sum of the areas of the 2 smallest squares in cm^2	25	
Area of largest square in cm^2		

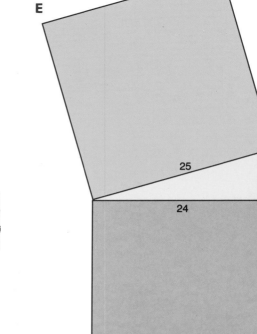

E

25
24
7

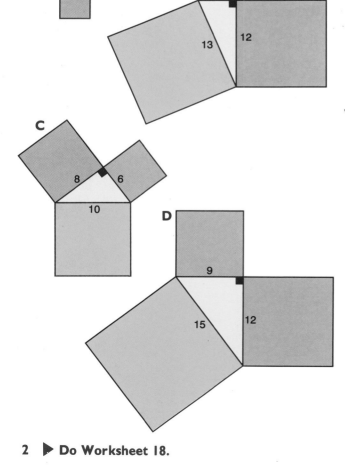

A

5
3
4

B

5
13
12

C

8
6
10

D

9
15
12

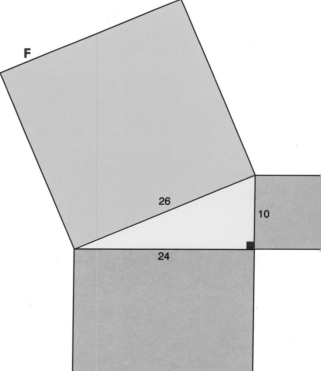

F

26
10
24

Over 2500 years ago a Greek mathematician called
Pythagoras claimed that for every right-angled triangle

the area of the square on the
longest side

=

the area of the square on
the shortest side

+

the area of the square on the
middle side

You should see from the work you have done that
Pythagoras was correct.
This result is known as **Pythagoras' Theorem**.

3 For each diagram:
- calculate the areas of the blank squares
- find the area of the green square.

(a)

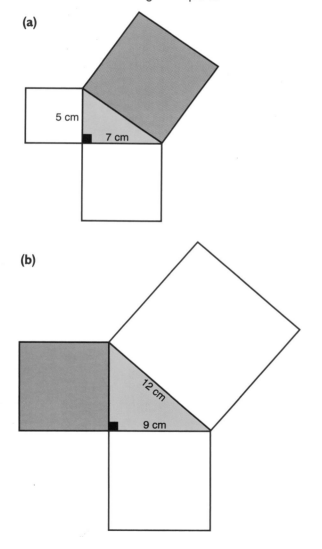

5 cm

7 cm

(b)

12 cm

9 cm

(c)

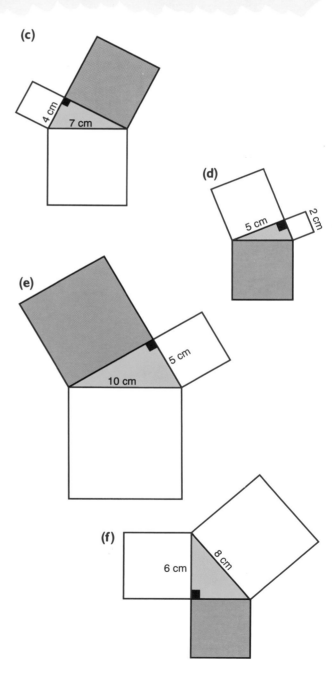

4 cm

7 cm

(d)

5 cm

2 cm

(e)

5 cm

10 cm

(f)

6 cm

8 cm

Siding with Pythagoras

The area of a square is 81 cm². What is the length of each side?

Area of square = 81 cm²
Length of side = √81
= 9 cm

Each side of the square is **9 cm**.

1 Calculate the lengths of the sides of each of these squares.

(a)
Area = 25 cm²

(b)
Area = 49 cm²

(c)
Area = 121 cm²

(d)
Area = 144 cm²

Calculate the length of the side marked x in this right-angled triangle.

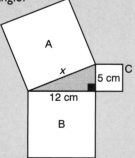

A

x

C
5 cm

12 cm

B

Area of square B = 12² = 144 cm²
Area of square C = 5² = 25 cm²

By Pythagoras' Theorem
Area of square A = 144 + 25 = 169 cm²
Length of the side marked x = √169
= **13 cm**

2 Calculate the length of the side marked x in each of these right-angled triangles.

(a)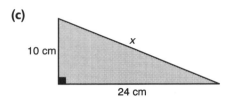
x
4 cm
3 cm

(b)
x
8 cm
15 cm

(c)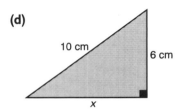
10 cm
x
24 cm

(d)
10 cm
6 cm
x

(e)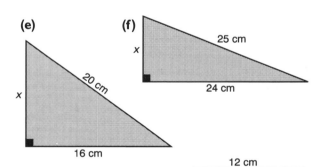
x
20 cm
x
16 cm

(f)
25 cm
x
24 cm

(g)
12 cm
9 cm
x

(h)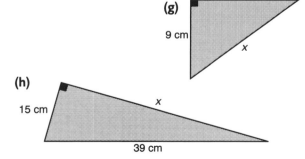
15 cm
x
39 cm

(i)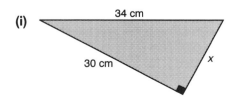
34 cm
30 cm
x

In a right-angled triangle the longest
side is called the **hypotenuse**.
The hypotenuse is the side
opposite the right angle.
In this triangle **c** is the hypotenuse.

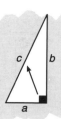

3 Name the hypotenuse in each of these triangles.

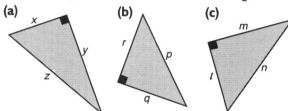

(a) **(b)** **(c)**

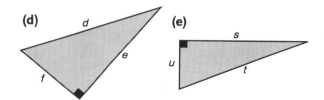

(d) **(e)**

Pythagoras' Theorem can be stated as:

$$(\text{hypotenuse})^2 = (\text{shortest side})^2 + (\text{middle side})^2$$

For any right-angled triangle with
sides **a, b** and hypotenuse **c**
$c^2 = a^2 + b^2$

Use Pythagoras' Theorem like this:

$c^2 = 4^2 + 5^2$
$\quad = 16 + 25$
$\quad = 41$
$c = \sqrt{41}$
$\quad = 6 \cdot 403 \ldots$
$\quad = \textbf{6·4 cm}$ to one dp.

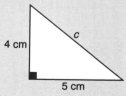

$11^2 = a^2 + 8^2$
$121 = a^2 + 64$
$a^2 = 57$
$a = \sqrt{57}$
$\quad = 7 \cdot 549 \ldots$
$\quad = \textbf{7·5 cm}$ to one dp.

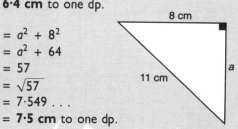

4 Calculate the length of the unknown side, correct
to one decimal place, in each of these triangles.

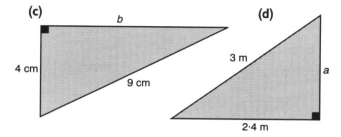

(a) **(b)**

(c) **(d)**

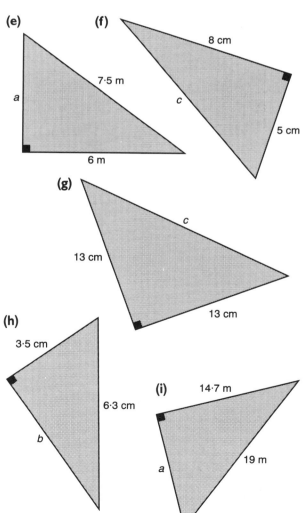

(e) **(f)**

(g)

(h)

(i)

Jim is a design engineer with Atlas Constructions Ltd. He often has to work out the lengths of sides of right-angled triangles. When working on the slipway for a lifeboat station Jim calculates the length of the slope.

He looks at a sketch of the slipway.

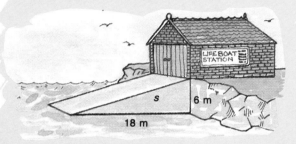

He draws a right-angled triangle.

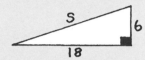

He uses Pythagoras' Theorem to find the length, s metres, of the slope.

$$s^2 = 6^2 + 18^2$$
$$= 36 + 324$$
$$= 360$$
$$s = \sqrt{360}$$
$$= 18 \cdot 973 \ldots$$

The length of the slope is **19·0 m** rounded to one dp.

1 Jim has also worked on these projects. Use Pythagoras' Theorem to calculate the marked lengths. Round your answers to one decimal place.

(a) Buttress supporting an old building

(b) Support carrying a railway's overhead power line

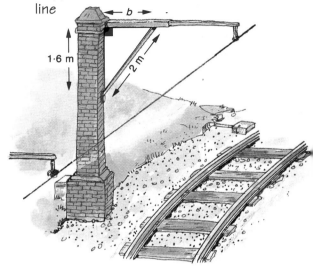

(c) Television transmitter with support cables two heights

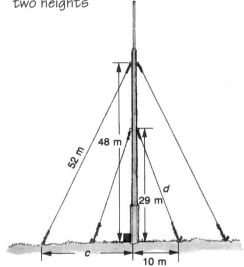

(d) Footbridge over a stream

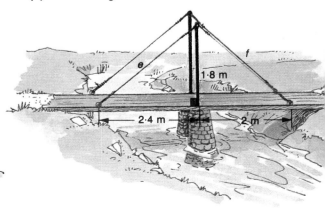

(e) Frame for a coal wagon

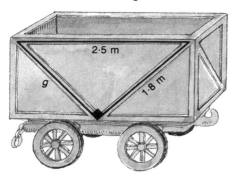

2·5 m

g

1·8 m

(f) Support beams for a barn roof

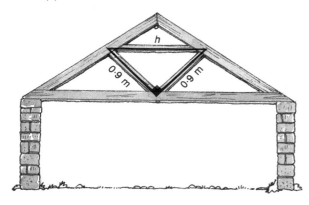

h

0·9 m

0·9 m

(g) Roof girders for a factory

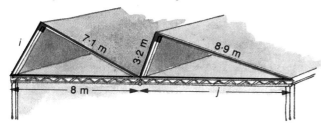

i

7·1 m

3·2 m

8·9 m

8 m

j

(h) Straps holding an attic floor

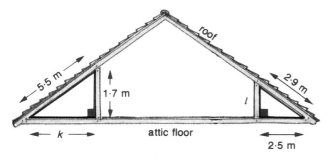

roof

5·5 m

2·9 m

1·7 m

l

k

attic floor

2·5 m

(i) Crane on a building site

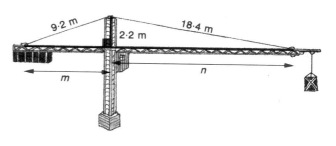

9·2 m

2·2 m

18·4 m

m

n

(j) Girders of a railway bridge

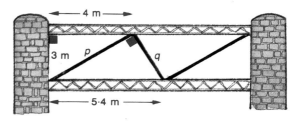

4 m

3 m

p

q

5·4 m

(k) Triangular bracket on the end of a
semi-circular gutter

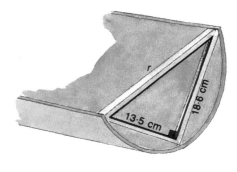

r

18·6 cm

13·5 cm

(l) Girders holding a semi-circular bridge under
repair

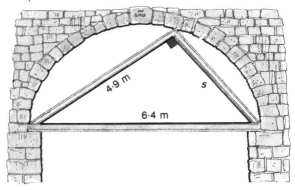

4·9 m

s

6·4 m

Up, up and across

To find the distance between two points, A and B, on a coordinate diagram:

- join A to B
- make AB the hypotenuse of a right-angled triangle
- mark in the lengths of the other two sides
- use Pythagoras' Theorem.

To find the distance between A(2, 3) and B(6, 6):

$$\begin{aligned} AB^2 &= 3^2 + 4^2 \\ &= 9 + 16 \\ &= 25 \\ AB &= \sqrt{25} \\ &= 5 \end{aligned}$$

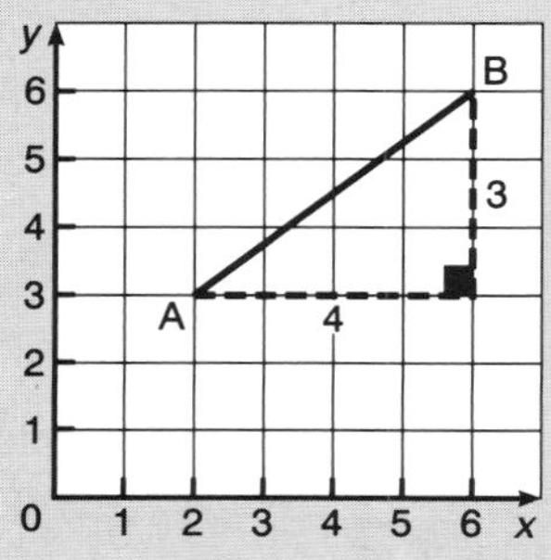

The distance between A and B is **5·0 units** correct to one dp.

1 Plot these pairs of points on coordinate diagrams and calculate the distance between each pair correct to one decimal place.

(a) P(1, 2) and Q(7, 10) **(b)** S(1, 0) and T(9, 5)
(c) V(3, 7) and W(9, 2) **(d)** C(0, 10) and D(9, 2)
(e) E(9, 9) and F(2, 3) **(f)** K(8, 0) and L(0, 8)

2 Plot the points P(1, 7), Q(4, 7), R(6, 2) and S(1, 4) on a coordinate diagram. Join the points.

(a) What type of quadrilateral have you drawn?
(b) Calculate the length of the diagonal SQ.
(c) Calculate the length of the diagonal PR.

3 The vertices of a triangle are A(0, 6), B(6, 7) and C(5, 1). Calculate the length of each side of the triangle. What type of triangle is ABC?

4 A ship leaves port and sails 10 km east. It then sails 7 km north. How far would it sail if it returned directly to port?

5 Daveston lies 9 miles due south of Johnston. Clarkston lies 11 miles due west of Johnston. How far northwest is Clarkston from Daveston?

6 Each tile on a kitchen wall is a square of side 15 cm. A fly crawls in a straight line from the corner of the light switch marked A to the corner of the socket marked B. How far did it crawl?

Challenge

7 Show that the points (3, 2), (10, 3), (11, 6), (9, 10) and (2, 9) all lie on a circle with centre (6, 6). (Hint: all the points on the circumference of a circle are the same distance from the centre.)

Work on an egg

Detour:
Circle patterns,
ellipses and egg
shapes

152

You need compasses and a ruler.

1 Draw these diagrams using compasses.

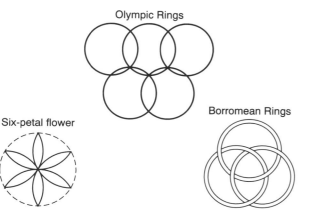

Olympic Rings

Six-petal flower

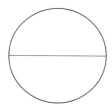

Borromean Rings

2 Follow these instructions to draw an **ellipse**.
  - Draw a circle, with a radius of 5 cm.
  - Draw a diameter.

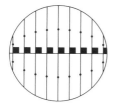

  - Draw lines perpendicular to the diameter.
  - Mark the mid-point of each section of line above and below the diameter.
  - Mark the ends of the diameter.

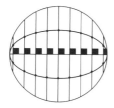

  - Join all the marked points with a smooth curve. This curve is an ellipse.

3 Draw another ellipse by joining the points one third of the way up and one third of the way down each perpendicular line.

4 Follow these instructions to draw an **egg shape**.
  - Draw a semicircle with a radius of 3 cm.
  - Draw the diameter joining the ends and extend it in both directions by about 1 cm.

Fat end

  - Set your compasses to a radius bigger than 3 cm.
  - With the end of the extended diameter as centre, draw an arc about 4 cm long from one end of the semicircle.
  - With the same radius draw an arc of the same length from the other end of the semicircle.

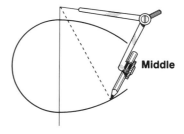

Middle

  - Draw straight lines joining the ends of these arcs to their centres.
  - With the point where the two straight lines meet, draw an arc to complete the egg shape.

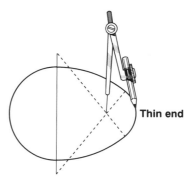

Thin end

5 Draw other egg shapes by starting with semicircles of different sizes.

This is the new Aquabeach leisure centre in Highborough.

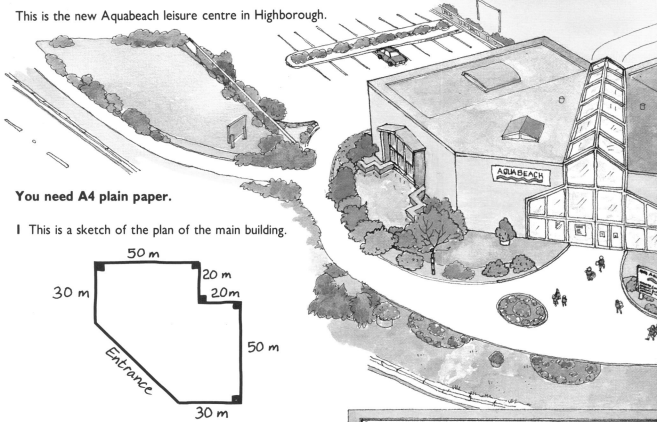

You need A4 plain paper.

1 This is a sketch of the plan of the main building.

50 m

30 m

20 m

20 m

50 m

Entrance

30 m

(a) Make a scale drawing of the plan using a scale of 1 cm to 5 m.

(b) Calculate the floor area of the building.

2 Amongst the facilities at Aquabeach are the Tropicana Pool, squash courts and the Pump Room, a multi-gym. These are their measurements. Show how you would arrange them inside the centre. Give reasons for choosing this arrangement.

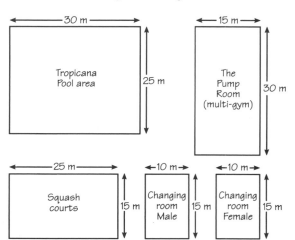

Welcome to **AQUABEACH** Leisure Centre

	Adults	Children
Swimming (per session)	£1·65	£0·90
Multi-gym (for 40 mins)	£2·80	—
Squash (for 30 mins)	£0·80	£0·80
Leisure access card	10% discount	

3 Find the cost of entry to Aquabeach for each of these groups.

(a) 2 adults and 1 child for a swimming session.

(b) 3 adults and 2 children for a swimming session. The children and one adult have leisure access cards.

(c) 3 adults for 40 mins in the multi-gym and 2 adults for one hour of squash. Two of the adults for the multi-gym have leisure access cards.

4 The Clark family paid £7·80 for swimming. No one had a leisure access card. How many adults and children are in the family?

5 The centre has a group discount scheme.

AQUABEACH *Leisure Centre*

School parties of 8 or more

Swimming 33⅓ % *discount*
(*1 teacher goes free with each group of 10*)

Other groups of 10 or more
Swimming 20% *discount*
Multi-gym 15% *discount*

Find the cost for each of these groups.

(a) Greenside School have booked a swimming session for 22 pupils and 2 teachers.

(b) 14 members of the Blackford Rugby Club have booked 2 hours in The Pump Room.

6 The table gives the annual salaries of the permanent staff at Aquabeach.

Position	No of people	Annual salary
manager	1	£19 000
secretaries	2	£14 000
receptionists	2	£10 000
pool attendants	10	£7 000
instructors	5	£12 000
groundsmen	2	£13 000
cleaners	4	£6 000

Calculate:

(a) the total monthly wage bill for the centre

(b) the average monthly wage for the staff.

7 All staff are given an increase of 5% pa on their existing salaries. What is the new salary for:

(a) the manager   **(b)** an instructor
(c) a cleaner?

8 Jane, the manager, carries out a survey to check whether the centre is being fully used.

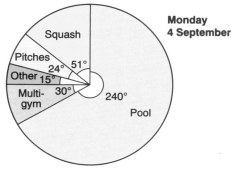

Monday
4 September

On Monday 4 September the total number of people using the centre was 1200. How many people used:

(a) the pool   **(b)** the pitches   **(c)** the multi-gym
(d) squash courts   **(e)** other facilities?

9 The table gives the number of people using the centre on Saturday 9 September. Draw a pie-chart to show the information.

Facility	Number of people on Sat 9 Sept
swimming pool	1470
squash courts	216
outdoor facilities	312
multi-gym	96
other activities	66

10 This table shows the ages and numbers of people using the multi-gym during one week.

Age	Number of people
0 – 9	0
10 – 19	52
20 – 29	158
30 – 39	231
40 – 49	175
50 – 59	48
60 – 69	14

Find: **(a)** the mean age   **(b)** the modal age group
(c) the class interval in which the median lies.

1 Students from Greenside School use the facilities at Aquabeach. Every Wednesday Louise, Brenda, Hayley and Nicola use the fitness training equipment. Today they will be using the cycle, treadmill, rowing-machine and steppers. Use the clues to find who is using each piece of equipment.

- The girls are 14, 15, 16 and 17 years old.
- Louise is wearing the striped leotard.
- The girl with the striped leotard is next in age to the oldest girl, who is wearing a plain leotard.
- Brenda is the youngest girl.
- The rower is next in age to the cyclist.
- Hayley is two years older than the girl in the flowered leotard.
- The girl with the spotted leotard is on the cycle.
- The girl on the steppers is not the oldest.

Nicola calculates her **maximum heart rate** in beats per minute using the formula $M = 220 - a$ where M is the maximum heart rate and a is the age in years.
Nicola is 15 years old so $a = 15$.

$$M = 220 - 15$$
$$M = 205$$

Her maximum heart rate is **205 beats per minute**.

2 (a) Copy and complete the table:

Age, a	15	20	45	50
Maximum heart rate, M	205	200		

(b) Use the information in your table to draw a graph.

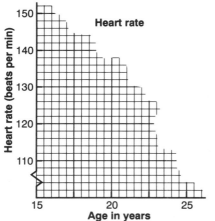

To improve her level of aerobic fitness, Nicola must train hard enough to keep her heart beating at between 70% and 85% of her maximum heart rate. This is called the **training zone**.

To the nearest whole number:
70% of 205 is 144 beats per minute.
85% of 205 is 174 beats per minute.
Nicola's training zone is
between 144 and 174 beats per minute.

3 (a) Extend and complete your table.

Age, a	15	20	25
Maximum heart rate, M	205	200	
70% of maximum heart rate	144		
85% of maximum heart rate	174		

(b) Plot and shade the training zone on your graph.

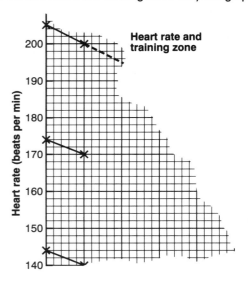

Heart rate and training zone

4 Six boys from the school competed against each other to find out how many press-ups they could do in one minute.

	Tom	Ian	Rob	Sam	Jim	Guy
Weight (kg)	60	56	52	70	64	62
Press-ups	30	26	24	38	34	32

(a) Draw a scatter graph to show the information in the table.

(b) Describe the correlation between the boys' weights and the number of press-ups they did.

5 The boys took part in a mini-competition with four events. Points were awarded for each event:

first – 4 points, second – 2 points, third – 1 point.
The table shows the results of the first three events.

	Squat thrusts	Sit-ups	Press-ups	Dips
First	Tom	Ian	Jim	
Second	Jim	Jim	Ian	
Third	Ian	Tom	Rob	

(a) Who is winning the competition at this stage?
(b) Find two possible results of the Dips event so that Ian is the overall winner.

Weights are made up of a bar, some weight discs and collars to hold the discs in place. The total weight of the bar and collars is 5 kg. The same weight discs must be on each end of the bar. There are weight discs of $2\frac{1}{2}$ kg, 5 kg, 10 kg and 20 kg.

Jim wants to lift 65 kg.
He makes up the weight
as follows:
Bar and collars = 5 kg.
Weight discs = 65 – 5 = 60 kg.
Weight discs on each end = 60 ÷ 2 = 30 kg

To use the **minimum** number of discs, Jim will make up the bar using 2 × 20 kg and 2 × 10 kg discs.

6 Find the minimum number of weight discs needed to make each lifting weight.

(a) 35 kg   **(b)** 55 kg   **(c)** 75 kg
(d) 40 kg   **(e)** 80 kg   **(f)** 120 kg

■ Investigation

7 What is the minimum number of weight discs you would need in a set to allow you to make every weight from 20 kg to 100 kg in steps of 5 kg?

1 At the pool, locker number 8 is in the middle row. In which row is locker number:

(a) 27   (b) 56   (c) 253?

2 At the poolside Alex starts issuing red bands to the bathers at 10 am and changes the colour every 20 minutes. At 11 am the bathers with the red bands are called out. Swimmers are then called out by colour every 20 minutes.

(a) What is the maximum length of time a bather can be in the pool?

(b) Copy and complete the table to show the session times.

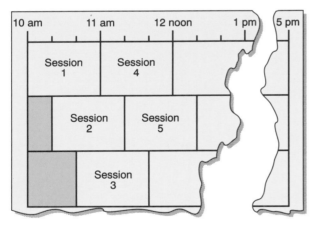

3 What is the minimum number of colours of bands Alex needs? Add this information to your table.

4 For each person, find:
- the time at which their session ends
- the maximum time he/she can be in the pool.

(a) Jim collects his band at 10.12 am
(b) Sharon collects her band at 11.45 am
(c) Paul collects his band at 1335 hours
(d) Jan collects her band at 3.40 pm

5 For the tyre ride, which colour of tyre should each person use?

(a) Tom, 125 cm   (b) Clare, 0·88 m
(c) Dave, 2·1 m   (d) Sheila, 1·21 m
(e) John, 1·05 m   (f) Rob, 0·9 m
(g) Gordon, 0·41 m taller than Clare
(h) Rona, 0·41 m shorter than Tom

6 The tyre ride is 80 metres long with a whirlpool one third of this distance from the end. To 2 decimal places, find the distance from the top of the ride to the whirlpool.

7 Douglas services the water pumps in the Tropicana Pool. He uses this table of information about them.

Area of use	Number of pumps	Capacity of pump, m^3 per hour
Pool	2	111
Water cannons	1	240
Tyre ride	2	34·2
Geysers	1	60
Wild water channel	2	500

(a) How many pumps are in use?
(b) Where is the most powerful pump used?
(c) How many cubic metres of water are pumped every hour?
(d) A new pump for the tyre ride has a capacity of 4000 cm^3 per second. What is its capacity in m^3 per hour?

8 It takes 40 minutes for all the water in the pool to be filtered. At this rate how long would it take to filter a pool of capacity 75 000 litres?

9 1 gallon is about 4·55 litres. Write the capacity of the pool in gallons.

Pool capacity 30 000 litres

10 A balance tank holds the water which is displaced by people entering the pool. On average one person displaces 0·48 gallons of water.
(a) How much water will be displaced by:
  • 6 people • 15 people • 140 people?
(b) How many people will it take to displace:
  • 96 gallons • 19·2 gallons
  • 3·84 gallons of water?

11 On the coldest night of the year the water in the outdoor section was at 29°C, and the air temperature was ⁻4°C. What was the difference between the temperature of the water and the air?

12 The diagram shows a plan of the outdoor section of the Tropicana Pool.
Find its area.

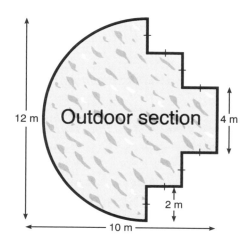

12 m — Outdoor section — 4 m — 2 m — 10 m

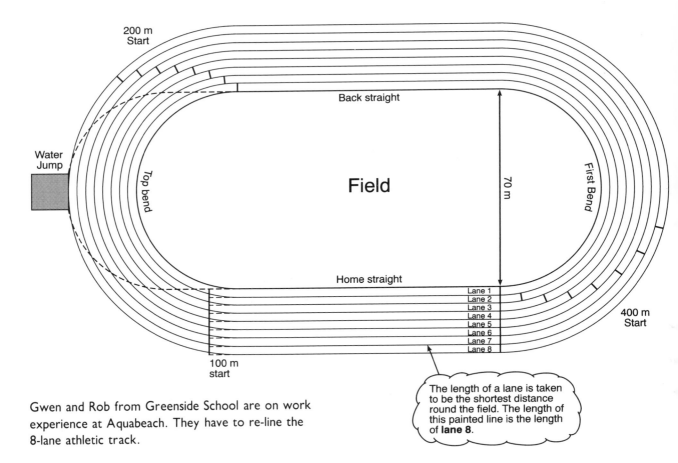

200 m
Start

Back straight

Water
Jump

Top bend

Field

70 m

First Bend

Home straight

Lane 1
Lane 2
Lane 3
Lane 4
Lane 5
Lane 6
Lane 7
Lane 8

400 m
Start

100 m
start

> The length of a lane is taken to be the shortest distance round the field. The length of this painted line is the length of **lane 8**.

Gwen and Rob from Greenside School are on work experience at Aquabeach. They have to re-line the 8-lane athletic track.

Answer to one decimal place.

1 Rob paints the inside line of lane 1 which has a length of 400 m.
Find: • the length round each bend
  • the length of each straight.

2 Each lane is 1·2 m wide. Gwen paints the lines which separate the lanes. For each line find:
  • the length round each bend
  • the total length.

3 Write the lengths of the lanes in order, starting with lane 1.

4 A 400 m race is one lap of the track and the runners must stay in their own lanes. They start at different positions which is known as a "staggered start".
  (a) What is the length of the "stagger" between the first and the second lanes?
  (b) At the start how much further ahead of the runner in lane 1 is the runner in lane 6?

5 A 200 m race starts at the beginning of the top bend and is run in lanes.
  (a) What is the length of the "stagger" between the first and second lanes?
  (b) How much further ahead of the runner in lane 1 is the runner in lane 8?

6 In an 800 m race only the first bend is run in lanes then the runners "break" into the inside lane and run as near to the kerb as possible. To have a clear run Tom stays in lane 2 for the whole race. How far does he run?

7 The same finishing line is used for all races. Races longer than 800 m are not run in lanes. For each of these races:
  • find how many laps are needed
  • describe where it starts.
  (a) 1500 m race   (b) 3000 m race
  (c) 5000 m race

The outdoor sports area is rectangular, with the athletics track in one corner.

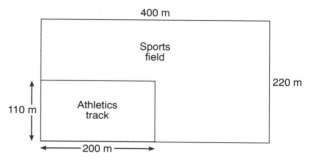

Gwen and Rob have to try to fit 3 football pitches, 2 hockey pitches and 2 rugby pitches into the available space.

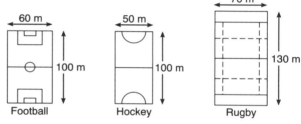

10 (a) Calculate the area available for the pitches.

(b) Calculate the area to be covered by the 7 pitches.

(c) Can the pitches be fitted into the available area? Explain.

11 Jane, the Centre manager, tells Gwen and Rob that there must be **at least 5 m**

• between touchlines
• between touchlines and the perimeter of the sports field.

Draw a scale diagram to show where Gwen and Rob could position the pitches.

8 In the 3000 m steeplechase, runners have to jump barriers which include a water jump. The water jump is outside the track at the top bend. This makes one lap in a steeplechase 16 metres longer than in other races.

(a) How many laps are there in this race?
(b) Describe where this race starts.

▼ **Challenge**

9 Gwen and Rob have an accurate scale diagram of the running track to help them. On a sheet of A3 paper make a scale drawing of the running track using a scale of 1 cm to 5 m. Mark the starts of all the races.

Just one problem after another!

1 A cable car is used to transport people to the top of Vertigo Mountain.

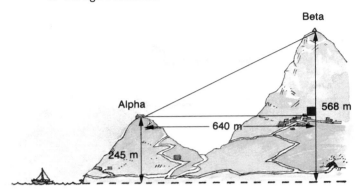

Station Alpha is 245 m above sea level and Station Beta is at the top of the mountain which is 568 m high.
The cable between the stations is in need of repair.
The engineers have 1400 m of cable. Do they have enough cable to go from Alpha to Beta and back again?

2 The table gives the costs for staying at the Hotel Allegro.

Hotel Allegro - Half Board Prices

Number of nights	7	11	14
13 Apr – 7 May	284	367	425
8 May – 11 Jun	369	451	512
12 Jun – 9 Jul	370	486	548
10 Jul – 30 Jul	423	549	615
31 Jul – 20 Aug	417	530	595
21 Aug – 1 Oct	398	492	554
2 Oct – 24 Oct	338	424	485

Supplements per person per night
Single room £5·65
Full board £6·75

SPECIAL OFFER
depart during May or October and children under 12 go free

(a) Find the cost of a holiday to the Hotel Allegro for Jane and Martin Jackman for one week, starting on 4th August.

(b) Margaret Hawkins has £1150 to take her children Julie, aged 8, and Darren, aged 14, for a fortnight from 1st May, to the Hotel Allegro.
If Julie and her mum share a room and Darren has a single room, will Margaret have enough money to cover the hotel bill?

3 After 10 games of football, Bathgate Thistle have an average score of 2·7 goals. These are the goals scored so far by Harburn City.

How many goals would Harburn need to score in their next game to have the same average as Bathgate Thistle?

4 David is on holiday in Greece. He has £45 of his spending money left. Does he have enough money to buy this jug if the exchange rate is £1 = 320 drachmae?

14 200 drachmae

5 (a) The frame for this photograph costs £3·80 per metre. How much did the frame cost?

25 cm

50 cm

(b) This enlargement has the same type of frame. How much did this frame cost?

80 cm

6 This is the gable end of Jacob's house.

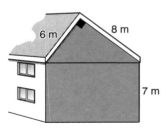

6 m   8 m

7 m

Calculate the area of the gable end.

7 Class 4W took part in a games competition.

- In the first round the class formed 4 teams to play mini-hockey and the remaining 21 students took part in athletics.
- In the second round the class formed 8 mini-hockey teams and the remaining 9 students took part in athletics.

(a) How many students were in each mini-hockey team?

(b) How many students were there altogether in the class?

8 Super Oil is sold in 2 litre cans costing £4·25 each. Lubi-Oil is sold in 1·5 litre cans costing £3·25.

(a) The engine of Libby's car requires 5 litres of oil each time it is serviced. What is the cheapest way of filling the engine with oil if only whole cans can be bought and the oils must not be mixed?

(b) If Super Oil is used, it is recommended that it is replaced after 5000 miles. If Lubi-Oil is used, it is recommended that it is replaced after 6000 miles. Which oil is the better value? Explain.

9 Jean is making a lampshade with a circular base of radius 35 centimetres.

She wants to attach a fringe around the edge of the base. The fringe costs £1·75 per metre and is only sold in complete metres. How much will the fringe cost?

10 Stephanie and Khalid play squash at a local club.

(a) Stephanie pays an annual membership fee of £50. In addition, each time she plays it costs her £1 for the court.

Copy and complete the table below to show the cost for different numbers of games.

Number of games	0	5	10	15	20
Cost for Stephanie					

(b) Using the scale shown, draw a graph to show the cost for Stephanie to play squash.

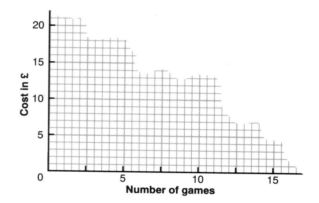

(c) Khalid does not pay an annual membership. He has to pay £3 entrance fee and £2 to hire the court each time he plays.

Copy and complete the table below to show the cost for different numbers of games.

Number of games	0	5	10	15	20
Cost for Khalid					

(d) On the same diagram as before show the cost for Khalid to play squash.

(e) What advice would you give to someone who wants to play squash in this club?

Answers for textbook

Page 1 Kieran House Garden

1 (a) $P = 36$ m $A = 81$ m^2 (b) $P = 16$ m $A = 12$ m^2
  (c) $P = 12$ m $A = 6$ m^2 (d) $P = 36$ m $A = 60$ m^2
2 (a) 21 m (b) 20·5 m (c) 20 m (d) 80 m
3 Meadow grass (a) 25 m^2 (b) £35
  Rye grass (a) 10·5 m^2 (b) £16·80
  Lesser timothy (a) 3·36 m^2 (b) £5·88
4 (a) 32 m (b) Various answers possible. For example,
  24 m, 26 m, 30 m, 40 m

Page 2 Kieran House Garden

1 (a), (b) Practical work. (c) 18 cm^2 (d) 36 cm^2
  (e) The area of the kite is half that of the surrounding rectangle.
2 (a), (b) Practical work. (c) 20 cm^2 (d) 40 cm^2
  (e) The area of the rhombus is half that of the surrounding rectangle.
3 (a) 300 m^2 (b) 144 m^2 (c) 132 m^2 (d) 125 m^2
4 (a) 60 m (b) 32 m (c) 38 m (d) 52 m

Page 3 The Walled Garden

1 (a), (b), (c) Practical work. (d) 28 cm^2
2 (a) 12 m^2 (b) 192 m^2 (c) 30 m^2
3 (a) 16 m (b) 23 m (c) 54 m 4 $A = 112$ m^2 $P = 50$ m
5 • ACDF $A = 160$ m^2 $P = 60$ m • BCEF $A = 64$ m^2 $P = 36$ m

Page 4 The Walled Garden

1 (a) Practical work. (b) 54 cm^2 (c) 30 cm^2 (d) 42 cm^2 (e) 42 cm^2
  (f) Answers using each method are the same.
2 Practical work. 3 (a) 5·5 m^2 (b) 39 m^2 (c) 84 m^2
4 (a) 5·8 m (b) 13·5 m (c) 7·5 m

Page 5 The Old Orchard

1 (a) P 18 m^2 Q 48 m^2 R 12 m^2 (b) 78 m^2
2 (a) 66 m^2 (b) 198 m^2
3 (a) Flower bed 30 m^2 Lawn 334 m^2
  (b) Flower bed 37·5 m^2 Lawn 322·5 m^2
4 (a) 31·6 m (b) 17·6 m^2 (c) 1·76 kg

Page 6 The Old Orchard

1 A rectangle B kite C trapezium
  D rhombus E parallelogram F trapezium
2 (a) J $P = 16$ units (b) K $P = 26$ units (c) L $P = 16$ units
      $A = 15$ units^2 $A = 36$ units^2 $A = 16$ units^2
3 (a) P 24 units^2 (b) Q 14 units^2 (c) R 16 units^2 (d) S 24 units^2
4 (a) $P = 14$ units $A = 10$ units^2
  (b) $P = 28$ units $A = 26$ units^2
5 (a) M 14 units^2 (b) N 11 units^2
6 (a) (2,1) (8,5) (b) 24 units^2 7 (1,3) (⁻5, ⁻2)

Page 7 Paper trail

1 (a) Yes (b) Yes
2 (a) (b) No (c) No

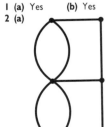

3, (a) 4 (a)

Network	Traversable (Yes/No)	Number of odd nodes	Number of even nodes
A	Yes	2	0
B	Yes	0	3
C	Yes	2	1
D	No	4	0
E	Yes	0	4
F	Yes	2	1
G	No	4	1
H	Yes	2	2
I	No	4	4
Student's own networks.			

3 (b) Student's own networks.
4 (b) Yes. Student's explanation.
  (c) P Not traversable Q Traversable R Traversable

Page 8 Inverearn Games

1 (a) Scott 1·17 m Bruce 1·31 m Fergus 1·10 m Dougal 0·98 m
  Angus 1·07 m
  (b) Bruce, Scott, Fergus, Angus, Hugh, Dougal
  (c) 33 cm or 0·33 m (d) 1 metre 11 centimetres
2 (a) Angus 3·45 m Pat 2·90 m Hugh 3·08 m Willie 3·04 m
  Scott 3·27 m Fergus 3·40 m
  (b) Angus, Fergus, Scott, Hugh, Willie, Pat
  (c) 55 cm or 0·55 m (d) 3 m 19 cm
3 (a) Scott 9·97 m Hugh 10·09 m Walter 9·98 m Blair 9·90 m
  Callum 10·10 m Hamish 9·09 m Torquil 10·00 m Lorne 9·99 m
  (b) Callum, Hugh, Torquil, Lorne, Walter, Scott, Blair, Hamish
  (c) 1 m 1cm or 1·01 m (d) 9 m 89 cm
4 (a) Willie 3·35 m Ian 2·99 m Duncan 3·08 m Colin 2·90 m
  Jamie 2·89 m Corrin 3·03 m Stewart 3·04 m
  (b) Willie, Duncan, Stewart, Corrin, Ian, Colin, Jamie
  (c) 46 cm or 0·46 m (d) 3 m 4 cm

Page 9 Inverearn Games

1 (a) Donald, Angus, Jamie, Torquil, Fergus, Callum, Geoff, Bryan
  (b) 2·975 seconds (c) 13·445 seconds
2 (a) Moray, Colin, Scott, Graeme, Ian, Simon, Hamish, Marcus, Stewart
  (b) 1·775 seconds (c) 27·667 seconds
3 (a) 355·605 seconds (b) 450·433 seconds
  (c) 237·07 seconds (d) 59·268 seconds or 59·267 seconds

4 (a) $\frac{6}{10}$, 0·6 (b) $\frac{3}{10}$, 0·3

5 (a) £18 (b) £42 (c) £9 (d) £26·40 (e) £16·20 (f) £36·60
6 (a) £0·60 (b) £3·00 (c) £4·20 (d) £1·80 (e) £5·40 (f) £3·60
7 Multiplying £6 by a number greater than one gives an answer greater than £6.
  Multiplying £6 by a number less than one gives an answer less than £6.
8 Student's own examples to show:
  • dividing by a number less than one has an increasing effect
  • dividing by a number greater than one has a decreasing effect

Page 10 F. R. Action Ltd

1 (a) $3\frac{3}{4}$ m (b) $\frac{1}{4}$ m

2 (a) $4\frac{3}{4}$ (b) $8\frac{1}{4}$ (c) 8 (d) $3\frac{1}{4}$ (e) $\frac{1}{4}$ (f) $1\frac{1}{2}$

3 (a) $1\frac{3}{4}$ m (b) $1\frac{3}{4}$ m (c) $\frac{1}{2}$ m 4 (a) $3\frac{3}{4}$ (b) $4\frac{1}{2}$ (c) $1\frac{3}{4}$

5 $4\frac{7}{8}$ m 6 $10\frac{7}{8}$ m 7 (a) $5\frac{5}{8}$ (b) $5\frac{5}{8}$ (c) $11\frac{7}{8}$

8 $8\frac{1}{8}$ m 9 $6\frac{5}{8}$ m

10 (a) $4\frac{1}{4}$ (b) 4 (c) $8\frac{1}{8}$ (d) $6\frac{1}{8}$ (e) $9\frac{3}{8}$ (f) $8\frac{5}{8}$

Page 11 F. R. Action Ltd

1 $5\frac{23}{30}$ litres 2 $5\frac{3}{4}$ litres 3 $12\frac{5}{18}$ metres

4 (a) $6\frac{1}{2}$ (b) $12\frac{7}{10}$ (c) $10\frac{7}{12}$ (d) $6\frac{49}{72}$ (e) $5\frac{23}{24}$ (f) $11\frac{1}{18}$

(g) $5\frac{17}{21}$ (h) $9\frac{29}{35}$ (i) $12\frac{37}{60}$

5 $2\frac{17}{40}$ metres 6 $1\frac{1}{2}$ metres 7 $1\frac{1}{24}$ litres

8 (a) $2\frac{5}{12}$ (b) $2\frac{11}{20}$ (c) $3\frac{5}{18}$ (d) $2\frac{19}{40}$ (e) $3\frac{4}{21}$ (f) $2\frac{19}{60}$

9 $1\frac{9}{20}$ litres

10 (a) $1\frac{5}{6}$ (b) $2\frac{13}{20}$ (c) $1\frac{17}{30}$ (d) $2\frac{61}{72}$ (e) $2\frac{47}{70}$ (f) $\frac{17}{40}$

11 (a) $3\frac{5}{6}$, $1\frac{1}{6}$ (b) $6\frac{7}{15}$, $1\frac{2}{15}$ (c) $10\frac{5}{24}$, $1\frac{11}{24}$

(d) $4\frac{31}{35}$, $1\frac{24}{35}$ (e) $7\frac{13}{90}$, $2\frac{23}{90}$ (f) $11\frac{49}{60}$, $4\frac{1}{60}$

Page 12 F. R. Action Ltd

1 (a) $\frac{1}{2}$ hour (b) $\frac{1}{4}$ hour (c) $\frac{3}{4}$ hour (d) $\frac{1}{6}$ hour (e) $\frac{2}{3}$ hour

(f) $\frac{1}{3}$ hour (g) $\frac{5}{12}$ hour (h) $\frac{7}{12}$ hour (i) $\frac{4}{5}$ hour (j) $\frac{2}{5}$ hour

(k) $\frac{7}{20}$ hour (l) $\frac{17}{20}$ hour

2 (a) $\frac{3}{5}$ (b) $\frac{2}{5}$ (c) $\frac{7}{8}$ (d) $\frac{3}{7}$ (e) $\frac{2}{5}$ (f) $\frac{2}{3}$ (g) $\frac{2}{3}$ (h) $\frac{7}{8}$

3 Sajid £3·60, Frank £3·90, Joyce £4·95, Jackie £4·00, Dave £4·68

4 (a) £47·85 (b) £19·20 (c) £35

5 $1\frac{1}{2}$ litres 6 (a) $3\frac{1}{5}$ litres (b) $1\frac{7}{9}$ litres 7 $2\frac{1}{2}$ bags

Page 13 Oatfield College Farm

1 (a) 84 acres (b) 147 acres (c) 56 acres (d) 17·5 acres
2 (a) 78 (b) 42 (c) 9 (d) 111 (e) 39 (f) 81 (g) 57 (h) 63

3 (a) 35% (b) $92\frac{1}{2}$% (c) $67\frac{1}{2}$% (d) $52\frac{1}{2}$%

4 (a) • 75 cows • 177 sheep • 30 goats • 27 pigs
(b) • 91 hens • 22·75%
5 (a) 126·6 acres (b) 110·7 acres (c) 53·4 acres
(d) 56·4 acres (e) 26·7 acres (f) 21·8 acres
6 (a) 79·2 kg (b) 100·8 kg (c) 133·2 kg (d) 46·8 kg
7 (a) 25·2 acres (b) 6·72 acres (c) 15·12 acres (d) 8·96 acres

Page 14 Oatfield College Farm

1 18 2 (a) 112 acres (b) 812 acres
3 (a) £18 975 (b) £363 975 4 60·9 acres 5 388 kg
6 (a) £38·25 (b) £10·88 (c) £8·67 (d) £1·02
(e) £0·68 (f) £15·26 (g) £4·78 (h) £0·54
7 12·25 hours 8 3·9 tonnes 9 237 litres

Page 15 Oatfield statistics

1

	(a)	(b)
oats	$\frac{1}{4}$	25%
fruit	$\frac{5}{42}$	11·9%
potatoes	$\frac{2}{21}$	9·5%
carrots	$\frac{1}{12}$	8·3%
barley	$\frac{1}{6}$	16·7%

2 (a) $\frac{10}{203}$ (b) 4·9% 3 (a) $\frac{5}{16}$ (b) 31·25%

4 (a) table tennis 27% snooker 21%
badminton 15% squash 37%
(b) football 43% hockey 20%
running 12% tennis 25%
(c) cola 51% orange 16%
lemon 7% blackcurrant 27%
(d) salted 16% bacon 23%
cheese 32% prawn 29%
5 Student's report.

Page 16 Double vision

1 (a) 3 cm³ (b) 8 cm³ (c) 6 cm³
2 (a) 8 cm³ (b) 9 cm³ (c) 5 cm³ (d) 10 cm³ (e) 8 cm³ (f) 11 cm³
3 (a) 10 cm³ (b) 12 cm³ (c) 9 cm³

Page 17 Dot-to-dot

1, 2 Practical work. 3 10 4 17

Page 18 Boxed in

1 (a) 14·8 m (b) 13·2 m (c) 17·6 m
(d) 16·8 m (e) 14·4 m (f) 13·4 m
2 (a) 180 cm (b) 200 cm (c) 248 cm
(d) 252 cm (e) 330 cm (f) 390 cm
3 Hamster 320 cm Rabbit 345 cm Cat 780 cm

Page 19 Made to measure

1 (a) Total edge length 480 cm (b) Total edge length 600 cm
Volume 64 000 cm³ Volume 90 000 cm³
Total surface area 9600 cm² Total surface area 13 450 cm²
(c) Total edge length 624 cm
Volume 124 416 cm³
Total surface area 15 552 cm²
2 (a) 120 cm³ (b) 840 cm³ (c) 480 cm³
3 (a) Area of base 24 cm² (b) Area of base 30 cm²
Volume 360 cm³ Volume 840 cm³
(c) Area of base 12 cm²
Volume 108 cm³
4 (a) Total edge length 93 cm (b) Total edge length 135·2 cm
Total surface area 408 cm² Total surface area 776·8 cm²
(c) Total edge length 63 cm
Total surface area 186 cm²
5 (a) 68 cm, 72 cm (b) 144 cm³, 144 cm³

Page 20 Measuring up

1 (a) 1573 cm³ (b) 1·5 litres
2 (a) 110 075 cm³ (b) 108 000 cm³ 3 3000 cm²
4 (a) 44·8 m (b) 40 m² 5 4225 kg
6 (a) 353 cm² (b) 101 cm (c) 414 cm³
7 (a) 36 000 cm³ (b) 20 cm × 30 cm × 60 cm

Page 21 La Patisserie

1 (a) 3e (b) 5p (c) 2d (d) 4m (e) 6t (f) 3r
(g) 8f (h) 12s (i) 2z (j) 6b (k) 7c (l) 24n
(m) 16q (n) 22c (o) 32y (p) 15k
2 (a) 6a (b) 12d (c) 10f (d) 24t
(e) 40u (f) 35r (g) 121k (h) 60n
3 (a) 11p (b) 10k (c) 13t (d) 14s (e) 20d (f) 23m
(g) 16q (h) 12n (i) 14x (j) 7t (k) 11w (l) 31r
4 (a) 5g (b) f (c) 2m (d) 11t (e) 13d (f) 7r
(g) h (h) 25s (i) 12y (j) 8x (k) 9b (l) 2p
(m) 5k (n) 8d (o) 12w (p) 0 (q) 9d (r) 0

Page 21 La Patisserie (ctd)

5 (a) $9e$ (b) $3t$ (c) $11s$ (d) $13m$ (e) d (f) $2b$
(g) $3x$ (h) $32p$ (i) $7u$ (j) $15r$ (k) $14t$ (l) $15y$
(m) $20w$ (n) $26a$ (o) m (p) 0

Page 22 La Patisserie

1 (a) $11c + 13e$ (b) $17p + 5c$ (c) $13t + 11s$ (d) $14x + 15y$
(e) $11u + 10v$ (f) $11m + 8n$ (g) $6a + 10b$ (h) $15w + 20z$
(i) $11d + 8f$
2 (a) $2s + 10t$ (b) $2y + 11x$ (c) $11q + 2r$ (d) $10w + 3v$
(e) $4m + 9n$ (f) $t + 18y$ (g) $10a + 6b$ (h) $6d + 6c$
(i) $4k + 2b$ (j) $10u + 15v + 3w$ (k) $10a + 6b + 15c$
3 (a) $11w + 9$ (b) $9j + 3$ (c) $5p + 24$ (d) $4x + 1$
(e) $13r$ (f) $9f + 16$ (g) $8m + 21$ (h) $8h + 14$
(i) $t + 1$ (j) $10a + 17b$ (k) $15x + 23y$ (l) $18k$
(m) $21u + 10v$ (n) $3s + 9t + 9$ (o) $6p + 5q + 6$ (p) $6g + 3h + 3$
(q) $10a + 6b + 22$

Page 23 La Patisserie

1 (a) $10r + 8s$ (b) $30y + 10x$ (c) $40f + 16g$ (d) $16m + 12n$
(e) $28h + 35j$ (f) $60u + 10v$ (g) $48a + 18b$ (h) $44x + 22z$
(i) $80s + 40t$ (j) $40w + 100v$ (k) $49p + 21q$ (l) $88a + 96b$
2 (a) $12a + 20b + 28$ (b) $30r + 42s + 18$ (c) $72x + 24y + 8$
(d) $24u + 3v + 33$ (e) $48d + 40f + 32$ (f) $30w + 40z + 100$
(g) $14m + 35n + 49$ (h) $55x + 60y + 75$ (i) $120g + 100h + 400$
(j) $18p + 63q + 72$
3 (a) $10a - 15b$ (b) $42x - 18y$ (c) $36m - 4n$ (d) $40f + 30g$
(e) $42r + 48s - 24$ (f) $45t - 15s + 10$ (g) $90x - 99y - 81$
(h) $50h - 10g + 70$ (i) $24d + 27e - 24$ (j) $22u - 77v - 121$
4 (a) $21a + 33b$ (b) $36s + 38t$ (c) $37x + 36y$ (d) $100f + 60g$
(e) $27u + 6v$ (f) $68m + 14n$ (g) $94h + 13j$ (h) $23c + 58d$
5 (a) $17x + 18y + 37$ (b) $41x + 44y + 12$ (c) $37p + 22q + 78$
(d) $48m + 25n + 19$ (e) $80r + 30s + 68$ (f) $48f + 13g + 43$

Page 24 An orderly approach

1 (a) 23   (b) 22   (c) 3   (d) 4
2 (a) 16   (b) 8   (c) 35   (d) 13   (e) 13   (f) 7   (g) 19   (h) 12
3 (a) $5 - 2 \times 2 = 1$ or $5 - 2 - 2 = 1$
(b) $6 + 3 \times 1 = 9$ or $6 + 3 \div 1 = 9$
(c) $4 \times 10 - 2 = 38$ (d) $5 + 3 \times 2 = 11$
4 One answer is given for each number. Others are possible.
$2 + 3 - 4 \times 1 = 1$
$2 \times 3 - 4 \times 1 = 2$
$3 \times 2 + 1 - 4 = 3$
$4 + 3 - 1 - 2 = 4$
$4 \times 2 - 3 \times 1 = 5$
$3 + 1 + 4 \div 2 = 6$
$4 \div 2 \times 3 + 1 = 7$
$2 + 3 + 4 - 1 = 8$
$2 \times 3 + 4 - 1 = 9$
$1 + 2 + 3 + 4 = 10$
5 (a) 24   (b) 18   (c) 12   (d) 40   (e) 25   (f) 5   (g) 3   (h) 0
6 (a) 25   (b) 60   (c) 15   (d) 140
(e) 40   (f) 26   (g) 125   (h) 90
7 (a) 49   (b) 19   (c) 100   (d) 2   (e) 81   (f) 3
8 (a) $3 \times (2 + 4) = 18$ (b) $(6 - 2) \times 7 = 28$
(c) $(12 - 8) \times 5 = 20$ (d) $(8 + 4) \div 3 = 4$

Page 25 Weathering the storm

1

Beaufort Scale	Description	Average speed at 10 m above ground level
0	Calm	0
1	Light air	1·875
2	Light breeze	5·625
3	Gentle breeze	10·625
4	Moderate breeze	15
5	Fresh breeze	21·875
6	Strong breeze	27·5
7	Near gale	35
8	Gale	43·125
9	Strong gale	51·25
10	Storm	58·75

2 (a) $50°F$ (b) $68°F$ (c) $41°F$ (d) $66·2°F$
(e) $32°F$ (f) $34·7°F$ (g) $92·3°F$ (h) $155·3°F$
3 (a) $50°C$ (b) $30°C$ (c) $0°C$ (d) $70·5°C$
(e) $36·5°C$ (f) $0·5°C$

Page 26 Words and symbols

1 (a) 182·7   (b) 96·6   (c) 455   (d) 65
(e) 50   (f) 16   (g) 12·5   (h) 3·468
2 (a) 100   (b) 51   (c) 12·75
3 (a) 30·625   (b) 1064·7   (c) 1800   (d) 16·49
(e) 0·81   (f) 9·1   (g) 2   (h) 0·075
4 (a) 1 hours 20 min   (b) 2 hours 5 min   (c) 1 hour 10 min
5 (a) 3 hr 30 min   (b) 4 hr 40 min   (c) 4 hr 29 min   (d) 4 hr 5 min

Pages 27 and 28 Press round-up

1 (a) • 7   • 6   • 4   • 2   (b) Student checks total.
2 (a) Sport 48°   Home news 96°   Entertainment 120°   Foreign news 24°
Politics 72°
(b) • 8   • 2   • 4   • 10   • 6
3 Foreign news 14   Entertainment 30   Politics 16   Sport 12   Home news 18
4 Student's pie chart showing: Foreign news 84°   Home news 96°
Sport 48°   Entertainment 72°   Politics 60°
5 Student's pie chart showing: Sport 80°   Home news 60°
Entertainment 120°   Politics 40°   Foreign news 60°
6 Investigation.

Pages 29, 30 and 31 Going for Gold

1 (a) 3 men   (b) Mike   (c) 14 m   (d) Ben   (e) 5   (f) Ali
(g) Bob weighs 75 kg and threw 18 m   (h) 20 m   (i) 9·5 m
2 As the men's weights increased the distance the shot was thrown increased.
3 (a) Graph.   (b) Sue   (c) Cath   (d) Ann   (e) Ann's jump
(f) As the women's heights increased the distance they jumped increased.
4 (a) 2 men   (b) Mike   (c) Mike   (d) 22 laps
(e) As the men's weights increased the number of laps they ran decreased.
5 (a) Graph.
(b) As the men's weights increased their times for the hurdles increased.
6 (a) Graph.
(b) As the women's heights increased their swim times decreased.
7 (a) Graph.
(b) As the women's weights increased the distances they threw the javelin increased.
8 (a) Graph.
(b) As the men's heights increased the distances they jumped increased.
9 (a) Graph.
(b) As the women's heights increased their times for the sprint decreased.
10 (a) Graph.
(b) There is no correlation between the men's weights and their snooker breaks.

Page 32 Lining them up

1 (a) 0·2 m (b) 0·1 m 2 (a) 1·4 m (b) 2·1 m (c) 3·3 m
3 (a) 1·7 m (b) 4·2 m (c) 5·9 m 4 Worksheet 1, question 1.
5 (a) 2 g (b) 2 mm
6 (a) 12 mm (b) 30 mm (c) 43 mm
7 (a) 25 g (b) 45 g (c) 54 g
8 Worksheet 1, question 3.
9 (a) Graph.
(b) Accuracy of answers depends on graph • about 18 cm³ • about 78 cm³

Page 33 The balancing game

1 (a) $3x + 5 = 11$ [−5][−5] $3x = 6$, $x = 2$
(b) $2 + 4y = 22$ [−2][−2] $4y = 20$, $y = 5$
(c) $41 = 5c + 6$ [−6][−6] $35 = 5c$, $7 = c$
(d) $8 + 2f = 8$ [−8][−8] $2f = 0$, $f = 0$

2 (a) $t = 11$ (b) $w = 3$ (c) $t = 8$ (d) $r = 2$
(e) $y = 4$ (f) $p = 15$ (g) $c = 5$ (h) $a = 3$

3 (a) $3v + 4 = 2v + 7$ [−2v][−2v] $v + 4 = 7$ [−4][−4] $v = 3$
(b) $6 + 7f = 5f + 16$ [−5f][−5f] $6 + 2f = 16$ [−6][−6] $2f = 10$, $f = 5$
(c) $10w = w + 9$ [−w][−w] $9w = 9$, $w = 1$
(d) $3r + 10 = 5r + 6$ [−3r][−3r] $10 = 2r + 6$ [−6][−6] $4 = 2r$, $2 = r$
(e) $6t + 10 = 7t$ [−6t][−6t] $10 = t$
(f) $8 + 2y = 4y + 2$ [−2y][−2y] $8 = 2y + 2$ [−2][−2] $6 = 2y$, $3 = y$

4 (a) $t = 12$ (b) $k = 6$ (c) $x = 5$ (d) $d = 2$ (e) $p = 0$ (f) $n = 6$

Page 34 The unbalancing game

1 (a) $5d + 7 \geq 22$ [−7][−7] $5d \geq 15$, $d \geq 3$
(b) $6 + 4v < 30$ [−6][−6] $4v < 24$, $v < 6$
(c) $24 \geq 3k + 12$ [−12][−12] $12 \geq 3k$, $4 \geq k$
(d) $20 > 8w + 4$ [−4][−4] $16 > 8w$, $2 > w$

2 (a) $x \leq 10$ (b) $f \geq 6$ (c) $4 > r$ (d) $c \leq 12$
(e) $g \geq 2$ (f) $b > 8$ (g) $5 < p$ (h) $n \geq 1$

3 (a) $4t + 4 \leq t + 13$ [−t][−t] $3t + 4 \leq 13$ [−4][−4] $3t \leq 9$, $t \leq 3$
(b) $7 + 2w \geq 2 + 3w$ [−2w][−2w] $7 \geq 2 + w$ [−2][−2] $5 \geq w$, $w \leq 5$
(c) $2r + 7 > 3r$ [−2r][−2r] $7 > r$, $r < 7$
(d) $9p < 3p + 6$ [−3p][−3p] $6p < 6$, $p < 1$

4 (a) $k \geq 10$ (b) $y \geq 7$ (c) $v < 3$ (d) $w \leq 5$ (e) $r > 0$ (f) $h \geq 9$

Page 35 The Sweet Tooth

1 (a) $6p - 5 = 13$ [+5][+5] $6p = 18$, $p = 3$
(b) $1 = 4w - 3$ [+3][+3] $4 = 4w$, $w = 1$
(c) $5w - 1 \leq 24$ [+1][+1] $5w \leq 25$, $w \leq 5$
(d) $3 < 2k - 7$ [+7][+7] $10 < 2k$, $k > 5$
(e) $12 - 2m = 4m$ [+2m][+2m] $12 = 6m$, $m = 2$
(f) $50 - 3a = 2a$ [+3a][+3a] $50 = 5a$, $a = 10$
(g) $3x < 49 - 4x$ [+4x][+4x] $7x < 49$, $x < 7$
(h) $60 - 7x \geq 8x$ [+7x][+7x] $60 \geq 15x$, $x \leq 4$
(i) $35 - 2r = 5r$ [+2r][+2r] $35 = 7r$, $r = 5$
(j) $15x - 20 \leq 5x$ [−5x][−5x] $10x - 20 \leq 0$ [20][−20] $10x \leq 20$, $x \leq 2$
(k) $14 - 2f > 5f$ [+2f][+2f] $14 > 7f$, $2 > f$, $f > 2$
(l) $8p - 12 < 6p$ [−6p][−6p] $2p - 12 < 0$ [+12][+12] $2p < 12$, $p < 6$

2 (a) $d = 5$ (b) $x = 6$ (c) $t > 9$ (d) $m > 11$ (e) $c = 5$
(f) $a = 30$ (g) $b < 13$ (h) $y < 8$ (i) $p > 3$ (j) $k \geq 9$
3 (a) $v = 13$ (b) $r \leq 4$ (c) $f = 2$ (d) $v \geq 18$ (e) $y > 0$ (f) $t = 8$

Page 36 The Sweet Tooth

1 (a) $x = 6$ (b) $k = 27$ (c) $p = 40$ (d) $w = 128$
(e) $n = 35$ (f) $m = 108$ (g) $y = 9$ (h) $a = 12$
(i) $r = 36$ (j) $b = 96$ (k) $f = 20$ (l) $n = 11$
(m) $w = 70$ (n) $c = 40$ (o) $y = 80$ (p) $v = 280$
(q) $d = 240$ (r) $x = 120$ (s) $y = 50$ (t) $p = 300$
(u) $a = 14$ (v) $b = 80$ (w) $r = 15$ (x) $k = 35$
2 (a) $y = 30$ (b) $p = 25$ (c) $x = 336$ (d) $b = 130$
(e) $y = 176$ (f) $a = 30$ (g) $b = 55$ (h) $v = 72$
(i) $m = 80$ (j) $w = 36$
3 (a) $x = 5$ (b) $t = 5$ (c) $p = 21$ (d) $v = 7$

Page 37 Sweet secrets

1 (a) $4t + 20$, $8t + 40$ (b) $5t + 20$, $15t + 60$
(c) $2t + 20$, $4t + 40$ (d) $4t + 20$, $16t + 80$

Page 37 Sweet secrets (ctd)

2 (a) $6c + 12$ (b) $20y + 12$ (c) $12 + 42p$ (d) $20 + 10t$
  (e) $15d - 40$ (f) $35k - 7$ (g) $36 - 45w$ (h) $72 - 120m$
  (i) $10 + 16y$ (j) $63 - 21r$ (k) $20f + 40$ (l) $42b + 18$
3 (a) 75p   (b) 60p
4 (a) $k = 6$ (b) $p = 3$ (c) $y = 5$ (d) $n = 10$
  (e) $r = 1$ (f) $m = 6$ (g) $w = 10$ (h) $r = 4$
  (i) $x = 20$ (j) $v = 12$ (k) $a = 38$ (l) $b = 15$

Page 38 Find the unknown

1 (a) 25 mints   (b) 50 mints   (c) 56 mints   (d) 66 mints
2 (a) 18 creams   (b) 12 toffees   (c) 40 truffles
3 Friday – 2 hours, Saturday – 8 hours, Sunday – 5 hours
4 (a) 1 metre   (b) 4 metres
5 (a) • 12 small tubs   • 16 small tubs (b) $l = 15$ (c) $s = 2$

Page 39 Pieces of seven

1

	Number of pieces						
	1	2	3	4	5	6	7
Triangle	✓	✓	✓	✓	✓		✓
Square	✓	✓	✓	✓	✓		✓
Rectangle	✓	✓	✓	✓	✓	✓	✓
Parallelogram	✓	✓	✓	✓	✓	✓	✓
Trapezium		✓	✓	✓	✓	✓	✓

2 Triangle using 6 pieces
  Square using 6 pieces
  Trapezium using 1 piece

Page 40 A la Carte

1 (a) £2400   (b) £20 000
2 (a) Nevis £470   Lomond £1125   Ochil £2090   Pentland £1990
  (b) $P = s - c$
3 (a) $7s + 21r + 14d$ (b) 4 units
4 (a) 324 000 cm³   (b) 840 cm
5 (a) 924 cm², 144 cm, £186·96   (b) 798 cm², 134 cm, £161·61

Pages 41 and 42 Wheeler's Garage

1 (a)

No of litres	5	10	15	20	25
Cost (£)	2·40	4·80	7·20	9·60	12·00

  (b) Graph.
2 (a) • £14·40   • £10·56   • £15·84
  (b) • 35 litres   • 17·5 litres   • 21 litres   • 31 litres
3 (a) 9 litres   (b) 18 litres   (c) 23 litres
  (d) 2 litres   (e) 31 litres   (f) 20 litres
4 (a) 2 gallons   (b) 2·4 gallons   (c) 4 gallons   (d) 3·4 gallons
  (e) 4·6 gallons   (f) 6·6 gallons
5 (a) £57·92   (b) £101·36   (c) £7·24   (d) £65·16
6 24 minutes
7 (a) • £6·50   • £13·00   • £26·00   • £32·50   (b) Graph
  (c) • £15·60   • £23·40   • £27·30   (d) £71·50
8 (a) • 36 minutes   • 48 minutes   • 12 minutes   • 18 minutes
  (b) • 9   • 5   • 15
9 (a) • 7500 litres   • 2500 litres   • 11 250 litres   • 16 875 litres
  (b) • 2 hours 40 minutes   • 2 hours 20 minutes
      • 24 minutes   • 6 minutes

Pages 43 and 44 Road up!

1 (a)

Length	1	2	3	4	5	6	8	10
Number	120	60	40	30	24	20	15	12

  (b) The number of sections is halved.   (c) Graph.

2 (a)

Length	1	2	3	4	5	6	10	12
Number	180	90	60	45	36	30	18	15

  (b) The number of sections is halved.   (c) Graph.

3 (a)

Length of stone (m)	0·5	1·0	2·0
Number of stones	400	200	100

  (b) The number of stones is doubled.
4 (a) 144   (b) 72   (c) 36
5 (a) When one quantity is doubled the other is halved.
  (b) When one quantity is halved the other is doubled.
  (c) The graph of two quantities in inverse proportion is not a straight line.

6 $1\frac{1}{2}$ hours   7 (a) 60 minutes   (b) 15 minutes

8 (a) 20 seconds   (b) 80 seconds
9

Speed of the machine in mph	0·5	1	2	4
Time taken in minutes	48	24	12	6

10 (a)

Number of cones on each trip	1	2	3	4	6	8	12	16
Number of trips	48	24	16	12	8	6	4	3

  (b) The number of trips is divided by 3.
11 (a) 18 hours   (b) • 6 trucks   • 9 trucks
12 (a) When one quantity is trebled, the other is divided by 3.
  (b) When one quantity is divided by 3, the other is trebled.

Page 45 Pumped dry

1 (a) 10 days   (b) 12 days   (c) 24 days   2 15 hours

3 (a) 15 hours   (b) 12 hours   (c) 10 hours   (d) $7\frac{1}{2}$ hours

4 (a) 18 hours   (b) 9 hours   (c) 6 hours   (d) $4\frac{1}{2}$ hours
5 (a) 40 hours   (b) 6 lorries   (c) 5 lorries

Page 46 Chunk's

1 • Direct proportion   (a) 112   (b) 168   (c) 420   (d) 1680
2 • Direct proportion   (a) 16   (b) 40   (c) 88   (d) 140

3 • Inverse proportion   (a) 12 hours   (b) 2·4 hours   (c) $1\frac{1}{2}$ hours

4 • Inverse proportion   (a) 48 hours   (b) 8 hours   (c) 3 hours
5 Quantities are not in proportion.
6 (a)

Weight of bar (g)	Cost of bar (p)
20	8
40	16
60	24
80	32
100	40

  (b) Graph.   (c) • 20 p   • 38 p   • 66 p
7 No. Student's explanation.

Page 47 Trying triangles

1 Missing numbers are:
  (a) 19, 13   (b) 20, 11, 9   (c) 17, 13, 3   (d) 52, 25, 10, 15, 12, 4
2 (a) $n = 2$ (b) $n = 2$ (c) $n = 5$ (d) $n = 8$
3 Missing numbers are: (a) 12, 10, 3   (b) 19, 23, 10, 13, 4, 6
  (c) 85, 38, 47, 20, 8, 12, 15, 6, 2, 10.

4 (a) Missing numbers are: 24, 11, 13 and 40, 19, 21
  (b) Student's triangle. The number at the top is 4 times the middle consecutive number.
  (c) Student's triangle.
5 Missing numbers for four ways are:
  • 5, 2, 4, 1   • 4, 3, 2, 2   • 6, 1, 6, 0   • 3, 4, 0, 3
6 There are 5 ways of completing the triangle. The missing numbers are:
  • 6, 4, 4, 0   • 5, 5, 3, 2   • 4, 6, 2, 4   • 3, 7, 1, 6   • 2, 8, 0, 8

Page 48   True size

Answers depend on the accuracy of student's measurements.
1 B 2·40 m   C 4·08 m   D 1·62 m   E 1·92 m
2 (a) 1:200   **(b)** • 21·2 m   • 8 m   • 3 m
  (c) Yes, width of the gate is 4 m   **(d)** 11 posts

Page 49   Mapping it out

Answers depend on the accuracy of student's measurements.
1

From	To	Map distance	True distance
Golf course	Carn Beag Dearg	8·4 cm	4·2 km
Carn Beag Dearg	Carn Mor Dearg	3·2 cm	1·6 km
Carn Mor Dearg	Col	2 cm	1 km
Col	Ben Nevis	1·7 cm	0·85 km
Ben Nevis	Achintee House	9·2 cm	4·6 km

2 5·4 km   **3** 0·75 km or 750 m

Page 50   Which way?

Answers depend on the accuracy of student's measurements.
1 (a) 045°   **(b)** 135°   **(c)** 180°   **(d)** 315°
2 (a), (b)

Stage	Bearing
Start ➡ 1	060°
1 ➡ 2	125°
2 ➡ 3	242°
3 ➡ 4	118°
4 ➡ 5	245°
5 ➡ Finish	252°

3 Practical work. Drawing bearings.   **4** Practical work. Drawing bearings.

Page 51   Getting to the point

Answers depend on the accuracy of student's measurements.
1 Worksheet 2
2 (a) Practical work. Scale drawings.   **(b)** • 7 km   • 7 km   **(c)** 325°
3 (a) Practical work. Scale drawings.   **(b)** • 69 km   • 19 km

Page 52   Going to the top

Student should produce a scale drawing for each question.
Answers depend on the accuracy of student's measurements.
1 (b) 25 m   **2 (a)** 92 m   **(b)** 160 m   **(c)** 300 m   **(d)** 380 m
3 (b) 23 m   **(c)** 43 m   **4** 97 m

Page 53   Tor Cliff

Student should produce a scale drawing for each question.
Answers depend on the accuracy of student's measurements.
1 56 m   **2** 100 m   **3** 33 m   **4** 39 m
5 (a) • 24°   • 24°   **(b)** They are equal.   **6 (a)** 14 m   **(b)** 2·7 m

Page 54   Common ground

1

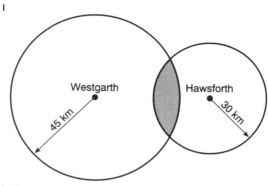

2 (a) Worksheet 3   **(b)** St Lucinda, Malbatu, Imtipo
  (c) Bofata, Imtipo   **(d)** Imtipo   **(e)** Tintomi
3

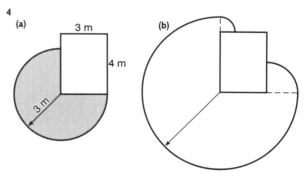

4

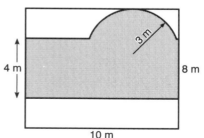

Pages 55 and 56   The scale of the problem. . .

Students should produce a scale drawing for each question.
Answers depend on the accuracy of student's measurements.
1 Yes. The tree is 10·7 m high.
2 (a) Student's scale drawing.

3 (a) 23 km   **(b)** 25 km   **(c)** 25 km/h   **(d)** 024°
4 • 21 km   • 7 km   **5** Bearing 028°, distance 3·5 km   **6** 46 km
7 (b) 273°   **(c)** 41 km   **8 (a)** 1·3 km   **(b)** 4·5 km
9 Practical work.

Pages 57 and 58   Ocean Park

1 (a), (e)

Section size (s)	1	2	3	4	5
Number of pontoons (p)	3	5	7	9	11

(b) The increase in the number of pontoons each time is 2.

(c) • The number of pontoons is two times the section size then add 1.
   • $p = 2s + 1$

(d) 11   (e) Students check.   (f) 21

2 (a) 5

(b) • The hire cost is five times the number of hours then add 3.
   • $c = 5h + 3$

(c) £33. Student's check.   (b) £63

3 (a), (d)

Number of yachts (y)	1	2	3	4	5
Number of dinghies (d)	4	6	8	10	12

(b) 2   (c) $d = 2y + 2$ (d) Student's check, 14   (e) 32

4 (a)

Number of bouys (b)	1	2	3	4	5
Number of ropes (r)	0	3	6	9	12

(b) 3   (c) $r = 3b - 3$ (d) Student's check, 15   (e) 87

5 (a) $c = 6r - 2$ (b) Student's check, 28   (c) 88

Page 59   Mosaic patterns

1 Worksheets 4 and 5.

2 (a)

Size (s)	2	3	4	5	6
Number of tiles (n)	3	8	15	24	35

(b)

Size (s)	2	3	4	5	6
Number of tiles (n)	3	8	15	24	35
First difference		5	7	9	11
Second difference			2	2	2

(c) The second difference is 2 so the formula begins with s^2.

(d)

Size^2 (s^2)	4	9	16	25	36
Number of tiles (n)	3	8	15	24	35

(e) Number of tiles = Size^2 − 1 or $n = s^2 - 1$ (f) 99

3 (a)

Size (s)	2	3	4	5	6
Number of tiles (n)	2	7	14	23	34
First difference		5	7	9	11
Second difference			2	2	2

Size^2 (s^2)	4	9	16	25	36
Number of tiles (n)	2	7	14	23	34

• $n = s^2 - 2$ • Student check using the formula and by drawing.
• 47

(b)

Size (s)	2	3	4	5	6
Number of tiles (n)	1	6	13	22	33
First difference		5	7	9	11
Second difference			2	2	2

Size^2 (s^2)	4	9	16	25	36
Number of tiles (n)	1	6	13	22	33

• $n = s^2 - 3$ • Student check using the formula and by drawing.
• 46

Page 60   Number sequences

1 (a) 11   (b) 15   (c) 1   (d) 13

2 (a) add 3   (b) add 7   (c) subtract 4   (d) subtract 12
   (e) multiply by 3   (f) divide by 2

3 (a) 3, 8, 13, 18, 23, 28, 33, 38   (b) 8, 17, 26, 35, 44, 53, 62, 71
   (c) 50, 44, 38, 32, 26, 20, 14, 8   (d) 92, 81, 70, 59, 48, 37, 26, 15

4 (a) 2, 4, 8, 16, 32, 64   (b) 729, 243, 81, 27, 9, 3
   (c) 1, 9, 17, 25, 33, 41   (d) 120, 105, 90, 75, 60, 45
   (e) 1, 10, 100, 1000, 10 000, 100 000   (f) 42, 37, 32, 27, 22, 17

5 (a) • 5   • 35   • 41   (b) • 13   • 28   • 31
   (c) • 56   • 31   • 26   (d) • 2   • 33   • 65
   (e) • 3   • 96   • 192   (f) • 1   • 3125   • 15 625
   (g) • 10 000   • $\frac{1}{10}$ • $\frac{1}{100}$

6 (a) 6   (b) 15   (c) 18   (d) 21   (e) 24   (f) 30

Page 61   Number sequences

1 (a)

Term Number	Term
1	2
2	4
3	6
4	8
5	10
6	12
7	14
8	16

(b)

Term Number	Term
1	5
2	10
3	15
4	20
5	25
6	30
7	35
8	40

(c)

Term Number	Term
1	11
2	17
3	23
4	29
5	35
6	41
7	47
8	53

(d)

Term Number	Term
1	4
2	11
3	18
4	25
5	32
6	39
7	46
8	53

(e)

Term Number	Term
1	1
2	4
3	9
4	16
5	25
6	36
7	49
8	64

(f)

Term Number	Term
1	4
2	7
3	12
4	19
5	28
6	39
7	52
8	67

2 (a) multiply by 4   **(b)** multiply by 7   **(c)** multiply by 6
  (d) multiply by 10   **(e)** multipy by 3 then add 1
  (f) multiply by 4 then add 3   **(g)** multiply by 5 then subtract 1
  (h) multiply by 8 then subtract 3

3 (a)

Term Number	Term
1	2
2	4
3	6
4	8
5	10
n	2n

- $U_n = 2n$

(b)

Term Number	Term
1	2
2	6
3	10
4	14
5	18
n	4n − 2

- $U_n = 4n - 2$

(c)

Term Number	Term
1	2
2	5
3	8
4	11
5	14
n	3n − 1

- $U_n = 3n - 1$

(d)

Term Number	Term
1	1
2	4
3	9
4	16
5	25
n	n^2

- $U_n = n^2$

(e)

Term Number	Term
1	3
2	6
3	11
4	18
5	27
n	$n^2 + 2$

- $U_n = n^2 + 2$

(f)

Term Number	Term
1	0
2	3
3	8
4	15
5	24
n	$n^2 − 1$

- $U_n = n^2 - 1$

4 (a)

Term Number	Term
1	2
2	3
3	4
4	5
5	6

- 2, 3, 4, 5, 6

(b)

Term Number	Term
1	8
2	11
3	14
4	17
5	20

- 8, 11, 14, 17, 20

(c)

Term Number	Term
1	1
2	3
3	5
4	7
5	9

- 1, 3, 5, 7, 9

Page 61 Number sequences (ctd)

4 (d)

Term Number	Term
1	$3\frac{1}{2}$
2	4
3	$4\frac{1}{2}$
4	5
5	$5\frac{1}{2}$

  • $3\frac{1}{2}$, 4, $4\frac{1}{2}$, 5, $5\frac{1}{2}$

(e)

Term Number	Term
1	1
2	4
3	9
4	16
5	25

  • 1, 4, 9, 16, 25

(f)

Term Number	Term
1	8
2	11
3	16
4	23
5	32

  • 8, 11, 16, 23, 32

5 (a) $U_n = \frac{1}{n}$ **(b)** $U_n = \frac{1}{n+1}$ **(c)** $U_n = \frac{1}{n^2}$ **(d)** $U_n = \frac{n}{n+1}$

Page 62 Fly-High Kites

1 (a) • $a = 40°$, $b = 100°$ • isosceles, obtuse-angled
(b) • $a = 60°$, $x = y = 1·3$ m • equilateral (acute-angled)
(c) • $a = b = 54°$ • isosceles, acute-angled
(d) • $a = 45°$, $b = 90°$ • isosceles, right-angled
(e) • $a = 80°$, $x = 50$ cm • isosceles, acute-angled
(f) • $a = b = c = 60°$ • equilateral

Pages 63 and 64 Flying high

1 (a) square **(b)** rhombus **(c)** kite **(d)** rectangle **(e)** square
(f) rhombus **(g)** V-kite **(h)** square
2 (a) $x = 0·9$ m, $y = 1·2$ m, $z = 1·5$ m
(b) $a = 22°$, $b = 266°$, $x = 2·4$ m, $y = 1·4$ m
(c) $a = 106°$, $b = 74°$, $c = 106°$, $d = 90°$, $v = w = x = 0·5$ m, $y = 0·4$ m, $z = 0·3$ m
(d) $a = 125°$, $b = 46°$, $x = 94$ cm, $y = 130$ cm, $z = 50$ cm
(e) $a = 125°$, $b = c = 55°$, $w = 0·6$ m, $x = 1·0$ m, $y = 0·7$ m, $z = 1·5$ m
3 Student draws diagrams.
(a) (7, 2) **(b)** (9, 2) **(c)** (⁻3, 2) **(d)** (⁻1, 2) and (3, 2)
4 (a) square **(b)** parallelogram **(c)** kite and V-kite **(d)** rhombus & square
(e) rhombus & square **(f)** parallelogram, rhombus, kite & V-kite
(g) parallelogram, rectangle, square & rhombus

Page 65 Lines and points

1 A kite must be balanced otherwise it will twist and spiral to the ground.
2 Worksheet 6

3 (a) 4 **(b)** 3 **(c)** 2(half-turn) **(d)** 6
(e) 2(half-turn) **(f)** 5 **(g)** 8 **(h)** 6
4 Worksheet 7

Page 66 Making shapes

Practical work. Accurate drawing of quadrilaterals.

Pages 67 and 68 What's the angle?

1 (a) $a = 40°$ **(b)** $a = 65°$ **(c)** $a = 58°$, $b = 37°$
(d) $a = 50°$, $b = 130°$
(e) $a = 100°$, $b = 80°$, $c = 80°$, $d = 100°$
(f) $a = 124°$, $b = 56°$, $c = 34°$, $d = 146°$
(g) $a = 130°$, $b = 50°$, $c = 28°$, $d = 152°$ **(h)** $a = 70°$, $b = 140°$
2 (a) $a = b = c = 28°$, $d = 62°$ **(b)** $a = 240°$, $b = 35°$, $c = 50°$
(c) $a = 40°$, $b = c = d = 70°$
(d) $a = 90°$, $b = 34°$, $c = 56°$, $d = e = 34°$
(e) $a = 90°$, $b = c = 45°$ **(f)** $a = 40°$, $b = c = 70°$, $d = 110°$, $e = 28°$
(g) $a = 46°$, $b = 88°$, $c = 272°$, $d = 22°$, $e = 44°$
(h) $a = 65°$, $b = 50°$, $c = 25°$, $d = 65°$
(i) $a = 90°$, $b = c = 40°$, $d = 50°$, $e = 70°$
(j) $a = 40°$, $b = c = 70°$, $d = 40°$, $e = 50°$
(k) $a = 150°$, $b = c = 30°$, $d = 75°$ **(l)** $a = 135°$, $b = 25°$, $c = 65°$
(m) $a = 35°$, $b = 120°$, $c = 30°$, $d = 25°$, $e = 65°$
(n) $a = b = 50°$, $c = d = e = 80°$, $f = 50°$

Page 69 The Fly-High catalogue

1 (a) square **(b)** equilateral triangle
2

Kite	Geometric name
Sanjo Rokkaku	hexagon
Li Special	pentagon
Bermudan	regular octagon
Bow Three-stick	regular pentagon
Levitor	hexagon
Diagonal Four-stick	octagon
Barn-door	hexagon
Diagonal Three-stick	regular hexagon
V-form Three-stick	pentagon

Page 70 Polygon stars

1 Practical work. Accurate drawing of a regular hexagon.
2 (a) 45° **(b)** 72° **(c)** 90° **(d)** 120°
Practical work. Accurate drawings of regular polygons.
3 (a) • 120° • 108° • 135° **(b)** Student checks by measuring angles.
4 Practical work. Drawing regular star hexagon.
5 Practical work. Drawing regular star polygons.

Page 71 Decimal Place

1 (a) 2 **(b)** 1 **(c)** 2 **(d)** 3 **(e)** 2 **(f)** 3
2 a = 7·32 b = 7·35 c = 7·38 d = 7·43 e = 7·47 f = 12·463
g = 12·466 h = 12·468 i = 12·474 j = 12·475 k = 12·479
l = 0·9671 m = 0·9675 n = 0·9677 o = 0·9679 p = 0·9682
q = 0·9687 r = 0·9688
3 Practical work. Number lines.
4 (a) 2·4 **(b)** 13·3 **(c)** 8·24 **(d)** 10·40 **(e)** 5·357 **(f)** 6·71
(g) 93·144 **(h)** 0·2 **(i)** 14·0 **(j)** 1·00
5 (a) 6·7 or 6·8 **(b)** 9·31 or 9·32 **(c)** 18·820 or 18·821
(d) 189·4 or 189·5 **(e)** 78·9 or 79·0 **(f)** 5·49 or 5·50
(g) 7·68 **(h)** 10·899 or 10·900 **(i)** 1·107 **(j)** 5·00

Page 72 The solar system

	(a)	(b)	(c)
Mercury	60 000 000 km	58 000 000 km	57 900 000 km
Venus	100 000 000 km	110 000 000 km	108 000 000 km
Jupiter	800 000 000 km	780 000 000 km	778 000 000 km
Uranus	3 000 000 000 km	2 900 000 000 km	2 880 000 000 km

2

	(a)	(b)	(c)
Mars	4 min	4·3 min	4·33 min
Jupiter	30 min	35 min	34·9 min
Uranus	3 min	2·5 min	2·52 min
Neptune	4 min	4·0 min	4·03 min

3 (a) 2 Earth years   (b) 1·9 Earth years   (c) 1·88 Earth years

4

	(a)	(b)	(c)
Jupiter	10 Earth years	12 Earth years	11·9 Earth years
Saturn	30 Earth years	29 Earth years	29·5 Earth years
Uranus	80 Earth years	84 Earth years	84·0 Earth years
Pluto	200 Earth years	250 Earth years	249 Earth years

Page 73 Beetling about

1

	(a)	(b)
Blister	0·01 m	0·015 m
Colorado	0·03 m	0·025 m
Golden	0·03 m	0·027 m
Great Water	0·03 m	0·031 m
Rhinoceros	0·09 m	0·090 m
Rove	0·02 m	0·023 or 0·024 m
Stag	0·08 m	0·075 m

2 0·007 m

3 A 0·003 m, B 0·003 m, C 0·006 m, D 0·006 or 0·007 m,
E 0·004 m, F 0·004 or 0·005 m

4

	(a)	(b)	(c)
U	0·2 m	0·15 m	0·153 m
V	0·2 m	0·17 m	0·170 m
W	0·1 m	0·15 m	0·147 m
X	0·2 m	0·19 m	0·185 m
Y	0·1 m	0·13 or 0·14 m	0·135 m
Z	0·1 m	0·12 m	0·123 or 0·124 m

5 Practical work.

Page 74 Simon says. . .

1 (a) • 20, 40   • 60   • 58
(b) • 300, 800   • 1100   • 1052
(c) • 7, 10   • 17   • 19·98
(d) • 0·5, 0·3   • 0·8   • 0·77
(e) • 500, 200   • 300   • 331
(f) • 7, 2 or 3   • 4 or 5   • 4·89
(g) • 20, 3   • 17   • 15·855
(h) • 1000, 500   • 500   • 825
(i) • 2, 3   • 6   • 7·2974
(j) • 20, 4   • 80   • 63·92
(k) • 0·4, 0·2   • 0·08   • 0·0819
(l) • 0·06, 0·9   • 0·054   • 0·05336
(m) • 20, 5   • 4   • 3·3826. . .
(n) • 200, 80   • 2·5   • 2·187. . .
(o) • 8, 0·2   • 40   • 43·44. . .
(p) • 0·1, 10   • 0·01   • 0·01263. . .

2 (a) • 120 m   • 109·6 m
3 (a) • 5000 m²   • 5341 m²
(b) • 18 900 m²   • 19 688 m²
(c) • 30 m   • 23·87 m
4 (a) C (b) B (c) B (d) B (e) B

Page 75 Unavoidable errors

1 (a) 10 cm   (b) 10·1 cm   (c) 10·11 cm

2

	Lower bound	Upper bound
Bore	71·5 mm	72·5 mm
Stroke	60·5 mm	61·5 mm
Capacity	992·5 cm³	993·5 cm³
Power output	3·25 kW	3·35 kW
Valve seat width	1·35 mm	1·45 mm
Camshaft endfloat	0·25 mm	0·35 mm
Valve spring length	23·95 mm	24·05 mm
Oil capacity	2·245 litre	2·255 litre
Valve guide diameter	7·025 mm	7·035 mm
Piston diameter	78·865 mm	78·875 mm
Main bearing play	0·0225 mm	0·0235 mm
Bearing diameter	40·9675 mm	40·9685 mm

Page 76 A perfect fit!

1 (a) • 17·9 mm   • 18·1 mm   • 0·2 mm
(b) • 5·5 cm   • 5·9 cm   • 0·4 cm
(c) • 2·75 kg   • 3·25 kg   • 0·5 kg
(d) • 133·5 kg   • 136·5 kg   • 3 kg
(e) • 0·49 litre   • 0·51 litre   • 0·02 litre
(f) • 5·238 litre   • 5·242 litre   • 0·004 litre
(g) • 0·137 m   • 0·143 m   • 0·006 m
(h) • 0·0139 m   • 0·0141 m   • 0·0002 m

2 (a) 6·52 cm, 6·31 cm, 6·78 cm   (b) 1·201, 1·198, 1·199
3 (a) (5 ± 1) cm   (b) 17·5 ± 0·5) mm   (c) (5·4 ± 0·2) kg
(d) (135·7 ± 0·3) kg   (e) (4·25 ± 0·25) m   (f) (1375 ± 25) cm³
(g) (0·125 ± 0·001) m   (h) (0·083 ± 0·003) l
4 (a) 46 (b) 0·9 (c) 2·28   5 (a) 47 (b) 0·94 (c) 2·27
6 The answers are not exactly the same.   7 (a) 990 cm³ (b) 0·01 mm

Page 77 Keep it simple

1 (a) 6 (b) 20   2 (a) 5 (b) 13 (c) Student's table. (d) 69
3 (a) 55 (b) 385

Page 78 Fair Game

Student's conjectures and appropriate tests.

Pages 79 and 80 Sunningdale

1 – 4 Practical work. Answers depend on student's scale drawings.
5 21 tents, 4 caravans or 11 caravans and 9 tents.
6 Booking Chart on Worksheet 11.
7 Sheila, Ann, Maurice, Joan, Helen, Paul.
8 (a) 30 m
(b) p = 240 m   q = 10p   r = 12   s = £18   t = 17   u = 7p
9 (a) 12 (b) 24

Pages 81 and 82 Problems, problems . . .

1 (a) RIGHT 110
    FORWARD 10
(b) FORWARD 10
    RIGHT 90
    FORWARD 10
    RIGHT 70
    FORWARD 11
    RIGHT 130
    FORWARD 11
2 (a) • 45 lb   • 450 lb   (b) 12 days

Pages 81 and 82 Problems, problems... (ctd)

3 (a)
```
      H   H   H   H   H
      |   |   |   |   |
H  —  C — C — C — C — C — H
      |   |   |   |   |
      H   H   H   H   H


    H   H   H   H   H   H
    |   |   |   |   |   |
H — C — C — C — C — C — C — H
    |   |   |   |   |   |
    H   H   H   H   H   H
```
(b) 18 (c) 16 (d) $h = 2c + 2$

4 Scale drawing. Answers depend on the accuracy of student's measurements.
(a) 245 cm (b) £36·75
5 (a) $P = 26t$ (b) $t = 2·5$ cm   6 (a) 12 tins (b) 19 cm
7 (a) 16 pillars
(b)

Number of floors	1	2	3	4	5	6
Number of pillars	0	8	16	24	32	40

(c) $P = 8(x - 1)$ or $P = 8x - 8$ (d) 64 pillars
8 (a) Several answers possible. (b) Rachel £26, Morven £15, Alasdair £9

Page 83 Don't be so negative!

1 (a) 13 (b) $^-1$ (c) $^-5$ (d) 2 (e) $^-2$
(f) $^-16$ (g) $^-11$ (h) $^-8$
2 (a) 2 (b) $^-4$ (c) $^-5$ (d) 5 (e) $^-13$ (f) $^-16$
(g) 2 (h) $^-12$ (i) 0 (j) $^-9$ (k) $^-12$ (l) 7
(m) 11 (n) $^-6$ (o) $^-14$ (p) 1 (q) $^-15$ (r) $^-2$
3 (a) 20 (b) 56 (c) $^-36$ (d) $^-30$
4 (a) $^-18$ (b) $^-20$ (c) $^-16$ (d) $^-21$ (e) $^-12$
(f) $^-5$ (g) 0 (h) $^-27$ (i) $^-70$
5 (a) 4 (b) $^-5$
6 (a) $^-2$ (b) $^-3$ (c) $^-25$ (d) $^-3$ (e) $^-3$ (f) $^-5$
(g) $^-12$ (h) $^-6$ (i) $^-13$
7 (a) $^-5$ (b) $^-11$ (c) 3 (d) $^-3$ (e) $^-20$ (f) $^-42$
(g) 9 (h) 14 (i) 8 (j) 0 (k) $^-4$ (l) $^-16$

Page 84 Don't be so negative!

1 (a) $7 - {}^-2 = 9$ Sally's score goes up 9 points
(b) $9 - {}^-4 = 13$ Katy's score goes up 13 points
(c) $^-4 - {}^-9 = 5$ Paul's score goes up 5 points
(d) $^-7 - {}^-1 = {}^-6$ Pierre's score goes down 6 points
2 (a) $2 - {}^-5 = 7$ (b) $1 - {}^-6 = 7$ (c) $^-9 - {}^-4 = {}^-5$
(d) $^-3 - {}^-6 = 3$ (e) $0 - 4 = {}^-4$ (f) $0 - {}^-5 = 5$
3 (a) $6 - {}^-1$ (b) $4 - {}^-5$ (c) $^-1 - {}^-4$ (d) $^-5 - {}^-3$
  $= 6 + 1$ $= 4 + 5$ $= {}^-1 + 4$ $= {}^-5 + 3$
  $= 7$ $= 9$ $= 3$ $= {}^-2$
(e) $^-8 - {}^-7$ (f) $^-7 - {}^-3$ (g) $5 - {}^-6$ (h) $^-7 - {}^-7$
  $= {}^-8 + 7$ $= {}^-7 + 3$ $= 5 + 6$ $= {}^-7 + 7$
  $= {}^-1$ $= {}^-4$ $= 11$ $= 0$
4 (a) 8 (b) 8 (c) $^-2$ (d) 2 (e) 0
(f) 8 (g) 8 (h) 2 (i) $^-2$ (j) 0
5 (a) 3 (b) $^-1$ (c) $^-4$ (d) 4 (e) $^-5$ (f) 2
(g) $^-1$ (h) 4 (i) 0 (j) 4 (k) 9 (l) $^-13$

Page 85 Number patterns

1 (a)
$2 \times 3 = 6$ (b) $4 \times {}^-3 = {}^-12$
$2 \times 2 = 4$ $3 \times {}^-3 = {}^-9$
$2 \times 1 = 2$ $2 \times {}^-3 = {}^-6$
$2 \times 0 = 0$ $1 \times {}^-3 = {}^-3$
$2 \times {}^-1 = {}^-2$ $0 \times {}^-3 = 0$
$2 \times {}^-2 = {}^-4$ $^-1 \times {}^-3 = 3$
$2 \times {}^-3 = {}^-6$ $^-2 \times {}^-3 = 6$

(c)
$^-5 \times 2 = {}^-10$ (d) $^-3 \times {}^-7 = 21$
$^-5 \times 1 = {}^-5$ $^-2 \times {}^-7 = 14$
$^-5 \times 0 = 0$ $^-1 \times {}^-7 = 7$
$^-5 \times {}^-1 = 5$ $0 \times {}^-7 = 0$
$^-5 \times {}^-2 = 10$ $1 \times {}^-7 = {}^-7$
$^-5 \times {}^-3 = 15$ $2 \times {}^-7 = {}^-14$
$^-5 \times {}^-4 = 20$ $3 \times {}^-7 = {}^-21$

2 (a) $^-12$ (b) $^-42$ (c) 24 (d) $^-16$ (e) 45 (f) 36 (g) $^-28$
(h) $^-35$ (i) 9 (j) 81 (k) 25 (l) 400
3 (a) $^-2 \times 3 \times 4$ (b) $5 \times {}^-4 \times {}^-7$
  $= {}^-6 \times 4$ $= {}^-20 \times {}^-7$
  $= {}^-24$ $= 140$
(c) $3 \times {}^-2 \times {}^-1$
  $= {}^-6 \times {}^-1$
  $= 6$
4 (a) $^-24$ (b) 10 (c) $^-30$ (d) $^-64$
(e) 0 (f) $^-40$ (g) 120 (h) $^-125$
5 (a) $^-4$ (b) $^-4$ (c) 5 (d) $^-8$ (e) 6
(f) $^-5$ (g) 7 (h) 21 (i) $^-7$
6 (a) $\dfrac{5 \times {}^-6}{^-2}$ (b) $\dfrac{5 \times {}^-8}{2 \times {}^-4}$ (c) $\dfrac{^-8 \times {}^-3}{4 \times {}^-2}$ (d) $\dfrac{^-36}{(^-3)^2}$
  $= \dfrac{^-30}{^-2}$ $= \dfrac{^-40}{^-8}$ $= \dfrac{24}{^-8}$ $= \dfrac{^-36}{9}$
  $= 15$ $= 5$ $= {}^-3$ $= {}^-4$
7 (a) $^-8$ (b) $^-5$ (c) $^-7$
8 $(^-1)^2 = 1$ $(^-1)^3 = {}^-1$
$^-1$ to an even power is 1 and $^-1$ to an odd power is $^-1$.

Page 86 What an expression!

1 (a) $5a + 15$ (b) $6b + 3$ (c) $4c - 28$ (d) $10d - 6p$
2 (a) $^-2(3 + 4)$ or $^-2 \times 3 + {}^-2 \times 4$
  $= {}^-2 \times 7$ $= {}^-6 + {}^-8$
  $= {}^-14$ $= {}^-14$
(b) $^-3(5 - 1)$ or $^-3 \times 5 - {}^-3 \times 1$
  $= {}^-3 \times 4$ $= {}^-15 - {}^-3$
  $= {}^-12$ $= {}^-15 + 3$
                      $= {}^-12$
3 (a) $^-3(a + 5)$ (b) $^-2(5b + 7)$
  $= {}^-3a + {}^-15$ $= {}^-10b + {}^-14$
  $= {}^-3a - 15$ $= {}^-10b - 14$
(c) $^-5(c - 2)$ (d) $^-4(3f - 8)$
  $= {}^-5c - {}^-10$ $= {}^-12f - {}^-32$
  $= {}^-5c + 10$ $= {}^-12f + 32$
4 (a) $^-4p - 12$ (b) $^-6q - 21$ (c) $^-15r - 35s$
(d) $^-7x + 21$ (e) $^-3w + 2z$ (f) $^-28 + 35j$
(g) $^-2t - 4u - 6$ (h) $^-12n + 28m - 20$
5 (a) $5 - (a + 1)$ (b) $7b - (2b + 1)$
  $= 5 + {}^-1(a + 4)$ $= 7b + {}^-1(2b + 1)$
  $= 5 - a - 4$ $= 7b - 2b - 1$
  $= 1 - a$ $= 5b - 1$
(c) $^-2d - (7 - 3d)$
  $= {}^-2d + {}^-1(7 - 3d)$
  $= {}^-2d - 7 + 3d$
  $= d - 7$
6 (a) $3a - 5$ (b) $7f + 8$ (c) $^-3c - 3$ (d) $^-2h - 7$
7 (a) $a - 1$ (b) $2b + 9$ (c) $12 - 16c$ (d) $15d - 64$
(e) $6 - 13e$ (f) $4h + 12$

Page 87 Up and down

1 (a) Struan $^-40$ m, Duncan $^-20$ m
(b) Freezing point is $^-32°C$
2 (a) $p = {}^-2$ (b) $p = {}^-5$ (c) $f = {}^-2$ (d) $v = {}^-1$
(e) $y = {}^-8$ (f) $r = {}^-10$ (g) $k = {}^-6$ (h) $c = {}^-5$
3 (a) $c = {}^-2$ (b) $x = {}^-7$ (c) $p = {}^-5$
(d) $k = {}^-3$ (e) $y = {}^-5$ (f) $a = {}^-12$
4 (a) $m = {}^-4$ (b) $t = {}^-16$ (c) $f = 6$ (d) $b = 20$
(e) $m = {}^-1$ (f) $r = {}^-2$ (g) $y = 11$ (h) $p = 11$
(i) $d = 2$ (j) $x = {}^-3$

5 (a) $t = {}^-25$ (b) $y = {}^-42$ (c) $x = {}^-18$ (d) $y = {}^-12$
  (e) $c = 24$ (f) $v = 35$ (g) $h = 81$ (h) $w = 66$
6 (a) $n = {}^-4$ (b) $b = {}^-1$ (c) $t = {}^-3$ (d) $m = {}^-4$
  (e) $y = {}^-2$ (f) $w = {}^-10$ (g) $s = 3$ (h) $a = {}^-7$
  (i) $f = 5$ (j) $x = 2$

Page 88 Probably the Best

1

	Rock	Easy listening	Classical	Total
Instrumental	2	6	2	10
Vocal	9	3	3	15
Total	11	9	5	25

2 (a) $\frac{9}{25}$ or 0·36 (b) $\frac{2}{25}$ or 0·08 (c) $\frac{6}{25}$ or 0·24

3 (a) $\frac{11}{25}$ or 0·44 (b) $\frac{9}{25}$ or 0·36 (c) $\frac{5}{25}$ or $\frac{1}{5}$ or 0·2 (d) $\frac{10}{25}$ or $\frac{2}{5}$ or 0·4

4 (a) $\frac{16}{25}$ or 0·64 (b) $\frac{20}{25}$ or $\frac{4}{5}$ or 0·8 (c) $\frac{25}{25}$ or 1

5 (a) $\frac{20}{25}$ or $\frac{4}{5}$ or 0·8 (b) $\frac{15}{25}$ or $\frac{3}{5}$ or 0·6 (c) $\frac{10}{25}$ or $\frac{2}{5}$ or 0·4
  (d) $\frac{22}{25}$ or 0·88

6 (a) $\frac{2}{24}$ or $\frac{1}{12}$ or 0·08 (b) $\frac{11}{24}$ or 0·46 (c) $\frac{8}{24}$ or $\frac{1}{3}$ or 0·33
  (d) $\frac{14}{24}$ or $\frac{7}{12}$ or 0·58 (e) $\frac{14}{24}$ or $\frac{7}{12}$ or 0·58 (f) $\frac{20}{24}$ or $\frac{5}{6}$ or 0·83

7 (a) $\frac{3}{23}$ or 0·13 (b) $\frac{6}{23}$ or 0·26 (c) $\frac{8}{23}$ or 0·35 (d) $\frac{11}{23}$ or 0·48
  (e) $\frac{14}{23}$ or 0·61 (f) $\frac{18}{23}$ or 0·78

Page 89 Face the music

1 No. Barbara appears to assume that the customer will select a format at random. This is not true.
2 Worksheets 12 and 13.

3 (a) $\frac{99}{250}$ or 0·40 (b) $\frac{56}{250}$ or $\frac{28}{125}$ or 0·22
  (c) $\frac{38}{250}$ or $\frac{19}{125}$ or 0·15 (d) $\frac{134}{250}$ or $\frac{67}{125}$ or 0·54
  (e) $\frac{4}{250}$ or $\frac{2}{125}$ or 0·02 (f) $\frac{23}{250}$ or 0·09

4 (a) method 1 (b) method 3 (c) method 3 (d) method 2
  (e) method 1 (f) method 2 (g) method 1 (h) method 2

Page 90 Great expectations

1 (a) 40 (b) 100 (c) 60
2

	Rock	Jazz	Easy listening	Classical
(a)	120	12	52	16
(b)	210	21	91	28
(c)	108	10·8	46·8	14·4
(d)	157·8	15·8	68·4	21·0

3

	Under £10	£10 – £20	Over £20
(a)	240	100	60
(b)	210	87 or 88	52 or 53
(c)	255	106	64
(d)	185	77	46

4

	(a)	(b)
• Peters	$\frac{20}{200}$ or $\frac{1}{10}$ or 0·1	4·5
• DMR	$\frac{30}{150}$ or $\frac{1}{5}$ or 0·2	2
• Epsilon	$\frac{7}{217}$ or 0·03	1·3

5

	Jazz	Easy listening	Rock	Classical
(a)	3	6	6	3
(b)	4	8	8	4
(c)	2·5	5	5	2·5
(d)	2·8	5·7	5·7	2·8

6

Week beginning	Jazz	Easy listening	Rock	Classical
15 Aug	22	31	146	16
22 Aug	25	36	52	18
29 Aug	38	54	79	28
5 Sept	32	45	66	23

Page 91 The questionnaire

1

Q1	Q2	Q3	Q4	Q5
Closed	Open	Open	Closed	1st part closed 2nd part open

Q6	Q7	Q8	Q9	Q10
1st part closed 2nd part open	Closed	Open	Closed	Open

2 (a) Student's list should include an indication that the responses are easy to analyse.
  (b) Student's list should include an indication that the person answering may not be able to answer the question as (s)he would like.
3 (a) Student's list should include an indication that there are no restrictions on how the question can be answered.
  (b) Student's list should include an indication that the responses may be difficult to analyse.
4 Student's answer. For example:
How many items did you buy today? Please tick one.
☐ 0 ☐ 1 ☐ 2
☐ 3 ☐ 4 ☐ More than 4
5 Q1 and Q2. Most people usually listen to music which they prefer. The 1st choice in Q2 will normally be the one chosen in Q1.
or
Q6 and Q8. If someone answers 'No' to Q6 (s)he will reply '0' to Q8.
6 Student's explanations. Note: all methods are biased because they will not produce a random selection of people who are likely to use the shop.
7 Student's suggestions.

Page 92 The questionnaire

1 Worksheet 14
2 (a) Classical
  (b) • $\frac{8}{20}$ or $\frac{2}{5}$ or 0·4 • $\frac{5}{20}$ or $\frac{1}{4}$ or 0·25 • $\frac{5}{20}$ or $\frac{1}{4}$ or 0·25
    • $\frac{2}{20}$ or $\frac{1}{10}$ or 0·1
  (c) Cassette (d) • 40% • 50% • 10% (e) 35% (f) $\frac{6}{20}$ or $\frac{3}{10}$ or 0·3
3 Student's choice of graph. 4 £9·50

Page 92 The questionnaire (ctd)

5 Student's analysis. For example, allocating 4 points to the 1st choice, 3 to the second, 2 to the third and 1 to the fourth and calculating the total number of points for each type produces

Type of music	Total points
Pop	52
Easy listening	55
Jazz	46
Classical	31

Pop is the most popular type in Q1 but Easy listening appears to be more popular by this analysis of Q2.

One explanation is that although fewer people chose Easy listening as their 1st choice a large number put it 2nd.

6 (a) $\frac{7}{20}$ or 0·35   (b) $\frac{7}{20}$ or 0·35   (c) $\frac{9}{20}$ or 0·45

(d) $\frac{2}{20}$ or $\frac{1}{10}$ or 0·1   (e) $\frac{16}{20}$ or $\frac{4}{5}$ or 0·8   (f) $\frac{5}{20}$ or $\frac{1}{4}$ or 0·25   (g) 0

7 (a) 245   (b) 245   (c) 315   (d) 70

8 Student's survey and report about musical tastes.

9 Student's survey and report.

Page 93 Tied in Celtic Knots

Practical work. Compass design.

Page 94 Harrison's Hypermarket

1 (a) £800   (b) £484   (c) £439·50   (d) £287·90

2 (a) • £496   • £36   (b) • £196   • £40

(c) • £911·40   • £91·40   (d) • £286·35   • £26·35

Page 95 Harrison's Hypermarket

1 Yes

2 (a) £450   (b) £97·75   (c) £84·20   (d) £165

3 (a) £5704   (b) £9073·50   (c) £14 812

4 (a) £232·96   (b) £207·36   (c) £445·50

5 (a) £8405·80   (b) £1378   (c) £351·39

6 £980

Page 96 Harrison's Hypermarket

1 (a) • £90 • 25% • $\frac{1}{4}$ (b) • £36 • 15% • $\frac{3}{20}$

(c) • £62·40 • 12% • $\frac{3}{25}$ (d) • £96 • 20% • $\frac{1}{5}$

(e) • £55 • $12\frac{1}{2}$% • $\frac{1}{8}$ (f) • £204 • 30% • $\frac{3}{10}$

2 (a) • £8·60 • 10% • $\frac{1}{10}$ (b) • £42 • 15% • $\frac{3}{20}$

(c) • £77 • 20% • $\frac{1}{5}$ (d) • £49·50 • 20% • $\frac{1}{4}$

(e) • £17·30 • 20% • $\frac{1}{5}$ (f) • 0·60 • $12\frac{1}{2}$% • $\frac{1}{8}$

Page 97 Ellerman Electrical

1 Worksheet 15

2 (a) £372   (b) £197·40   (c) £431·22 or £431·23

(d) £1045·56   (e) £325·92

3 (a) £187·53   (b) £119·92 or £119·93   (c) £411·82

Page 98 Ellerman Electrical

1 (a) £98·58   (b) £35·91   (c) £42·20

(d) £66·50   (e) £94·15   (f) £150·77

2 Worksheet 16

Pages 99 and 100 High Finance

1 Student's reasons.

2 (a) Interest for 1 year = 8% of £2500 = £200

     Interest for 4 years = £200 × 4 = £800

     Total amount due = £2500 + £800 = £3300

(b) Interest for 1 year = $9\frac{1}{2}$% of £3200 = £304

     Interest for 6 years = £304 × 6 = £1824

     Total amount due = £3200 + £1824 = £5024

(c) Interest for 1 year = 6% of £980 = £58·80

     Interest for 3 years = £58·80 × 3 = £176·40

     Total amount due = £980 + £176·40 = £1156·40

(d) Interest for 1 year = 13·25% of £8400 = £1113

     Interest for 9 years = £1113 × 9 = £10 017

     Total amount due = £8400 + £10 017 = £18 417

3 (a) £40, £840   (b) £80, £880   (c) £120, £920   (d) £280, £1080

4 (a) £2365   (b) £213·40   (c) £5588

5 (a) £792   (b) £17 700   (c) £38   (d) £5652·50

6 (a) £1890   (b) £8190   (c) £227·50

7 (a) £80·25   (b) £227   (c) £435   (d) £116·25

8 Interest for 1 year = 15% of £470 = £70·50

     Interest for $\frac{1}{2}$ year = £70·50 × $\frac{1}{2}$ = £35·25

     Total amount due = £470 + £35·25 = £505·25

9 (a) $\frac{1}{3}$ (b) $\frac{1}{4}$ (c) $\frac{3}{4}$ (d) $\frac{5}{12}$ (e) $\frac{1}{6}$ (f) $\frac{1}{12}$

10 (a) Interest for 1 year = 3% of £3500 = £105

     Interest for $\frac{7}{12}$ years = £105 × $\frac{7}{12}$ = £61·25

     Total amount due = £3500 + £61·25 = £3561·25

(b) Interest for 1 year = $4\frac{1}{4}$% of £1600 = £68

     Interest for $2\frac{3}{4}$ years = £68 × $2\frac{3}{4}$ = £187

     Total amount due = £1600 + £187 = £1787

11 (a) £36, £2436   (b) £90, £2490   (c) £756, £3156   (d) £918, £3318

12 (a) £90·80   (b) £112·50   (c) £233·75   (d) £179·75

Pages 101 and 102 Insure with Smartsure

1 Student's reasons.

2 (a) 38p   (b) £273·60

3 (a) £257·04   (b) £260·40   (c) £493·44

(d) £137·88   (e) £136·08   (f) £189·84

4 (a) £21·42   (b) £21·70   (c) £41·12

(d) £11·49   (e) £11·34   (f) £15·82

5 (a) £111·60   (b) £10·23

6 (a) Student's list.   (b) Student's explanation.

7 (a) £84   (b) £42·50   (c) £52·80   (d) £24·15

8 (a) £128   (b) £16·25   (c) £144·25

9 (a) £97   (b) £235·20   (c) £177·70

10 £379·80   11 (a) £385·85   (b) £264·10

12 (a) £384·20   (b) £244·16   13 Investigation.

Page 103 Quinn's Mini-market

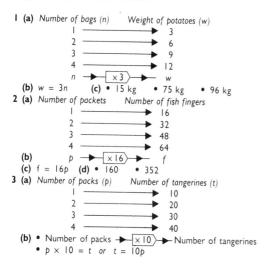

1 (a)
Number of bags (n)	Weight of potatoes (w)
1	3
2	6
3	9
4	12
n $\rightarrow$ $\boxed{\times 3}$ $\rightarrow$	w

(b) $w = 3n$ (c) • 15 kg • 75 kg • 96 kg

2 (a)
Number of packets	Number of fish fingers
1	16
2	32
3	48
4	64

(b) $p \rightarrow \boxed{\times 16} \rightarrow f$

(c) $f = 16p$ (d) • 160 • 352

3 (a)
Number of packs (p)	Number of tangerines (t)
1	10
2	20
3	30
4	40

(b) • Number of packs $\rightarrow \boxed{\times 10} \rightarrow$ Number of tangerines

  • $p \times 10 = t$ or $t = 10p$

(c) • 90 • 140

4 (a)
Number of bags	Number of mini-chocs
1	25
2	50
3	75
4	100

(b) Number of bags $\rightarrow \boxed{\times 25} \rightarrow$ Number of mini-chocs

(c) $c = 25b$ where c is the number of mini-chocs
    and b is the number of bags.

(d) • 150 • 250 • 625

Page 104 Life with the Bains

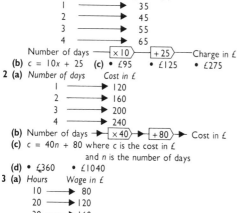

1 (a)
Number of days (x)	Charge in £ (c)
1	35
2	45
3	55
4	65

Number of days $\rightarrow \boxed{\times 10} \rightarrow \boxed{+25} \rightarrow$ Charge in £

(b) $c = 10x + 25$ (c) • £95 • £125 • £275

2 (a)
Number of days	Cost in £
1	120
2	160
3	200
4	240

(b) Number of days $\rightarrow \boxed{\times 40} \rightarrow \boxed{+80} \rightarrow$ Cost in £

(c) $c = 40n + 80$ where c is the cost in £
    and n is the number of days

(d) • £360 • £1040

3 (a)
Hours	Wage in £
10	80
20	120
30	160
40	200

(b) Number of hours $\rightarrow \boxed{\times 4} \rightarrow \boxed{+40} \rightarrow$ Wage in £

(c) $w = 4n + 40$ where w is the wage in £
    and n is the number of hours.

(d) • £88 • £220

4 (a)
Number of computers	Wage in £
0	100
1	150
2	200
3	250

(b) Number of computers $\rightarrow \boxed{\times 50} \rightarrow \boxed{+100} \rightarrow$ Wage in £

  $w = 50n + 100$ where w is the wage in £
    and n is the number of computers.

(c) • £350 • £450

Page 105 Bargain basement

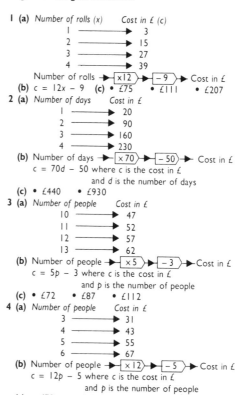

1 (a)
Number of rolls (x)	Cost in £ (c)
1	3
2	15
3	27
4	39

Number of rolls $\rightarrow \boxed{\times 12} \rightarrow \boxed{-9} \rightarrow$ Cost in £

(b) $c = 12x - 9$ (c) • £75 • £111 • £207

2 (a)
Number of days	Cost in £
1	20
2	90
3	160
4	230

(b) Number of days $\rightarrow \boxed{\times 70} \rightarrow \boxed{-50} \rightarrow$ Cost in £
    $c = 70d - 50$ where c is the cost in £
        and d is the number of days

(c) • £440 • £930

3 (a)
Number of people	Cost in £
10	47
11	52
12	57
13	62

(b) Number of people $\rightarrow \boxed{\times 5} \rightarrow \boxed{-3} \rightarrow$ Cost in £
    $c = 5p - 3$ where c is the cost in £
        and p is the number of people

(c) • £72 • £87 • £112

4 (a)
Number of people	Cost in £
3	31
4	43
5	55
6	67

(b) Number of people $\rightarrow \boxed{\times 12} \rightarrow \boxed{-5} \rightarrow$ Cost in £
    $c = 12p - 5$ where c is the cost in £
        and p is the number of people

(c) • £79 • £139

Page 106 From squares to curves

1 (a)
Length of side in cm	Area in cm²
0	0
1	1
2	4
3	9
4	16
5	25

(b)
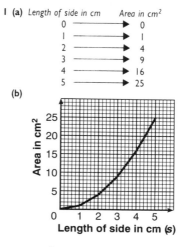

(c) $A = s^2$ (d) • 81 cm² • 144 cm² • 10·24 cm²

2 (a) Graph. (b) $h = 5t^2$

3 (a) Graph. (b) $A = 3r^2$

4 (a) Graph. (b) $l = d^2 + 5$

Page 107 Every picture tells a story

1 B

2 A Graph 4, B Graph 5, C Graph 2, D Graph 1, E Graph 8,
  F Graph 3, G Graph 7, H Graph 6

Page 108 A graphic description

1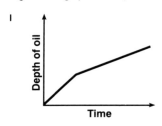

2

3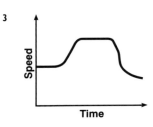

4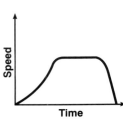

5 One graph is shown for each. Others are possible.

(a)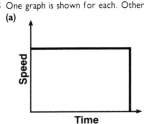

(b)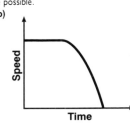

6 (a)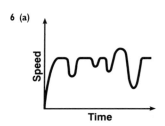

(b)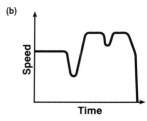

Page 109 Going places

1 (a) Section 4 (b) Section 5 (c) Sections 2, 4 and 6
 (d) Section 1 (e) Section 3
2 (a) 150 miles (b) 4 hours (c) 37·5 mph
3 (a) They passed each other. (b) Sally
 (c) She took less time for lunch.
4 (a) 50 miles
 (b) • Sam travelled at a steady speed (50 mph) all the way without stopping.
  • Bill travelled at a steady speed (about 75 mph) for 2 hours and
   36 minutes, stopped for 30 minutes, then completed his journey at a
   steady speed (about 83 mph).
 (c) Bill overtakes Sam.
 (d) While Bill is stopped Sam overtakes him. Then Bill starts again and soon
  overtakes Sam.
 (e) Speeding.

Page 110 A tale of two graphs

1 (a)

Number of copies	Cost in pence
10	180
20	260
30	340
40	420
50	500
60	580
70	660
80	740
90	820
100	900

 (b) Graph (c) • £7 • £21
2 (a)

Number of copies	Cost in pence
10	120
20	240
30	360
40	480
50	600
60	650
70	700
80	750
90	800
100	850

 (b) Graph. (c) • 420p • 725p • 1600p
3 (a) • Speedprint £19·20 • Fastprint £4·60
  • Fastprint £6·04 • Speedprint £8·40
 (b) Students memo should include: for up to 25 copies use Speedprint.
  for between 25 and 83 copies use Fastprint.
  for more than 83 copies use Speedprint.

Page 111 Catch the Hare

Board game.

Page 112 Coining it!

1 (a) 7·22 cm (b) 10·05 cm (c) 6·28 cm (d) 5·65 cm (e) 7·54 cm
2 (a) 34·54 cm (b) 14·76 cm (c) 210·38 cm
 (d) 50·24 cm (e) 989·10 mm (f) 13·50 m
3 (a) 69·1 mm (b) 62·8 mm (c) 74·1 mm (d) 59·7 mm (e) 82·3 mm
4 (a) 72·8 cm (b) 14·4 cm (c) 213·5 mm
 (d) 75·4 cm (e) 147·0 cm (f) 27·0 m

Page 113 Revolution!

1 (a) 2·826 m (b) 56·52 m (c) 106 revolutions
2 (a) 2·2608 m
 (b) • 221 revolutions • 442 revolutions • 22 116 revolutions
3 (a) 612 revolutions (b) 212 revolutions (c) 227 revolutions
4 (a) 243·35 m (b) 203 revolutions 5 (a) 15·072 m (b) 8 revolutions

Page 114 Around and about

1 (a) 22·0 cm (b) 36·6 cm (c) 56·7 cm
2 (a) 14·3 cm (b) 7·3 mm (c) 20·7 m (d) 1·8 cm (e) 31·8 km
 (f) 3·1 mm (g) 1·5 cm (h) 783·4 mm (i) 7·4 cm
3 (a) 103·2 cm (b) 215·3 cm (c) 133·4 cm
4 (a) 3·98 m (b) 0·16 m (c) 15·61 m
5 (a) 1·91 cm (b) 3·74 m (c) 0·17 km

Page 115 Squaring the circle

1 (a) Practical work. Drawing circles.
 (b) (c)

Radius, r	r²	Area, A
2 cm	4 cm²	about 12 cm²
3 cm	9 cm²	about 28 cm²
4 cm	16 cm²	about 50 cm²
5 cm	25 cm²	about 78 cm²
6 cm	36 cm²	about 113 cm²

 (d) The area of a circle is about $3 \times r^2$
2 (a) 6·2 m² (b) 2·3 m² (c) 2·0 m²
3 (a) 379·9 cm² (b) 1962·5 km² (c) 314 m²
 (d) 15·9 mm² (e) 145·2 m² (f) 1·2 cm²
 (g) 34 618·5 m² (h) 39·9 m² (i) 0·3 cm²
4 (a) 4·5 m² (b) 1·3 m² (c) 3·3 m²

Page 116 Piecing it together

1 (a) 49·6 cm² (b) 52·1 cm² (c) 33·3 cm²
2 (a) 9·3 cm² (b) 1 510·3 mm² (c) 11·8 cm² (d) 14·8 cm²
3 (a) 218·3 cm² (b) 63·1 m²

Page 117 Problems, problems . . .

1 471 cm
2 (a) 2·5 m² (b) 5·65 m (c) £7·35
3 (a) 29·7 m (b) 51·4 m² (c) • £43·69 • £10·15
4 Yes. The area sprayed in Ken's garden is 26·4 m² which is greater than 25 m².
5 (a) 270 cm (b) 105 cm 6 (a) 182·8 m (b) 4 tins of paint

Page 118 Point of contact

1 (a) Worksheet 17.
 (b) The angle between a tangent and the radius drawn to its point of
 contact is 90 degrees.
 (c) Student's diagrams to test statement.
2 a = 90°, b = 67°, c = 48°, d = 33°, e = 64°, f = 15°,
 g = 45°, h = 45°, i = 90°, j = 60°

Page 119 Angles, all right!

1 (a) Worksheet 17. (b) The angle in a semi-circle is 90 degrees.
 (c) Student's diagrams to test statement.
2 a = 62°, b = 18°, c = 55°, d = 45°, e = 45°, f = 25°
3 a = 80°, b = 50°, c = 40°, d = 100°, e = 40°, g = 55°,
 h = 55°, i = 35°, j = 110°, k = 35°, l = 60°, m = 60°,
 n = 60°, o = 120°, p = 30°, q = 30°, r = 60°

Page 120 Active angles

1 55° 2 a = 28°, b = 15° 3 (a) 90° (b) 90° (c) 60°
4 a = 30°, b = 45°, c = 45°, d = 65°, e = 9°, f = 5°
5 34°
6 (a) • 10° • 20° • 30° • 40° • 50° • 60°
 (b) They are equal. (c) Student tests statement.

Pages 121 and 122 Solve it!

1 33°C 2 £7000
3 (a) 600 cards (b) Machine A (c) 2400 cards 4 4 months

5 (a)
 (b) $\frac{3}{8}$

6 80% 7 13·76 cm² 8 Gavin £185 Sandy £200 Heather £225
9 (a) Yes. (b) Q. The sum of 7 and 3 is less than 11. (c) 5 cm and 25 cm
10 (a) 6 (b) 11 (c) 16 11 185·04 cm 12 £1 and 4 shillings
13 (a)

Number of copies	Cost (p)
6	60
12	120
18	138
24	156
30	174
36	192
42	210
48	228

 (b) Graph. (c) 4·4p

14 (a) 81 cm² (b) $\frac{18}{81}$ or $\frac{2}{9}$

Pages 123 and 124 The Gullivers' travels

1 £214, £228, £409, £342, £304, £99, £114, £209, £299, £114
2 La Solara is the cheapest whichever dates are chosen.
3 16th July – 1st August. Height of the tourist season.
4 No. Student's explanation 5 (a) £792·30 (b) £1790·35
6 £243, £1248·90, £1009·80, £1112·65, £1054·10, £662·46,
 £605·20
7 Tent at Campesi since it costs £851·80 which is less than £1000.
 La Solara costs £1592·85 which is too expensive.
8 (a) £650·20 (b) £130·04 (c) £520·16 (d) 28th June
9 (a) £1281·40 (b) £1378 (c) £778·26 10 £753·80

Page 125 The sunshine factor

1 (a) 79°F (b) 79°F 2 (a) 8 hours (b) 9 hours
3 (a) 4 hours (b) 5 hours 4 (a) 13°F (b) 12°F
5 Student's choice of resort with explanation.
6 Bar chart. 7 Line graph.

Page 126 All change

1 (a) 216 500 lire (b) 324 750 lire (c) 541 250 lire (d) 270 625 lire
2 (a) • 409 fr • 613·50 fr • 736·20 fr • 818 fr
 (b) • 85·80 Sfr • 171·60 Sfr • 214·50 Sfr • 289·58 Sfr
3 (a) 1017 sch (b) 363 Dm (c) $369·68 (d) 29 925 pes
 (e) 150·45 punts
4 (a) £303 (b) £252·50 (c) £126·25 (d) 378·75
5 £803·50 6 Investigation.

Page 127 Planning the trip

1 (a) 250 miles (b) 319 miles (c) 378 miles (d) 327 miles
 (e) 215 miles (f) 432 miles (g) 193 miles

Page 127   Planning the trip (ctd)

2 155 miles
3 (a) 1 hour   **(b)** 5 hours   **(c)** 8 hours   **(d)** 8 hours 30 min
4 (a) 1745   **(b)** 0114   **(c)** 1725   **(d)** 0445   **(e)** 0430
5 (a) 5 hr 55 min   **(b)** 0705   **6 (a)** 1445   **(b)** 1830

Page 128   En route

1 (a) £6·11   **(b)** £8·82   **(c)** £10·42
2 (a) £10·33   **(b)** £1·75   **(c)** £6·06   **(d)** £121·73
3 £116·62
4 (a) £11·00   **(b)** £9·17   **(c)** £1·83
5 (a) 653 km   **(b)** 52·24 litres   **(c)** • 352·62 fr   • £43·11

Page 129   Francly speaking

1 (a) 40 km/h   **(b)** 64 km/h   **(c)** 137·6 km/h
2 (a) 20 mph   **(b)** 25 mph   **(c)** 77·5 mph
3

Road	Maximum speed limit
motorways	112 km/h
dual carriageways	112 km/h
other roads	96 km/h
built-up areas	48 km/h

Motorways and built-up areas since British speed limits are: motorway 112 km/h,
built-up areas 48 km/h
4 65 mph is 104 km/h. So Bob would be breaking the speed limit on other
roads and in built-up areas
5 (a) 155·09 Sfr   **(b)** £72·30   **6 (a)** 121·30 Sfr   **(b)** £56·55

Page 130   Chequing in

1 (a) • 39 500 lire   • £18·24   **(b)** • 97 200 lire   • £44·90
   (c) • 78 580 lire   • £36·30
2 (a) 44 400 lire (£20·51)   **(b)** 1815
3 (a) 318 401 lire   **(b)** • 159 201 lire   • 212 268 lire   • 447 602 lire
4 (a) Bag 7233 lire   T-shirt 8775 lire   Bracelet 5593 lire
   (b) Total cost is 21 601 lire and £25 = 530 667. Yes she has enough.
5 Investigation.

Page 131   Marking time

1 (a) 7 days   **(b)** 7 days   **(c)** 14
2 January 31, February 28, March 31, April 30, May 31, June 30, July 31,
August 31, September 30, October 31, November 30, December 31.
3 Student's answer.   **4 (a)** No.   **(b)** No.
5 Student's balanced calendar.   **6** Investigation, calendar with 13 months.

Page 132   Little and Large

1 to 4 Practical work. Similar shapes.
5 •

	Scale factor	Logo size
Leaflet	1	original
Box label	2	larger
Letter heading	$\frac{1}{2}$	smaller
Business card	$\frac{1}{4}$	smaller
Compliments slip	$\frac{3}{4}$	smaller
Carpeting	$3\frac{1}{2}$	larger

• When the scale factor is greater than 1 the logo becomes larger.
• When the scale factor is less than 1 the logo becomes smaller.

6 $4\frac{1}{2}$

Page 133   All shapes and sizes

1 Practical work. Similar shapes.   **2** 2, $\frac{1}{2}$, $\frac{1}{3}$
3 a = 10 cm, b = 2 cm, c = 10 cm, d = 6 cm

Page 134   Shapes from another angle

1 (a), (b) Practical work. Similar shapes.
   (c) The angles in each set are the same.   **(d)** Student's own conclusion.
2 a = 75°, b = 105°, c = 110°, d = 115°, e = 65°
3 a = 90, k = 4, b = 8 cm, c = 45°, d = 135°, k = 2, e = 6 cm,
   f = 115°, $k = \frac{1}{3}$, g = 3 cm, h = 90°, $k = \frac{1}{2}$, i = 6 cm

Pages 135 and 136   Up and down the scales

1 Practical work. Student should conclude that triangles which are similar
contain the same angles.
2 (a) Student's sketches with missing angles in triangle as:
   B 85°, C 30°, D 35°, E 70°, F 80°, G 45°, H 50°, 50°
   (b) A and D, B and G, C and E, F and H.
3 (a) k = 3   EF = 18 cm   **4 (a)** k = 0·8   EF = 12 cm
   (b) k = 2·5   JK = 45 cm   **(b)** k = 0·4   JK = 8 cm
   (c) k = 1·2   PR = 18 cm   PR = 12 cm
5 Student should have drawn sketches for questions 6 to 8.
6 15 m   **7** 1·35 m   **8** 20 cm

Page 137   Sail making

1 (a) 1 m², 4 m², 9 m², 16 m²
   (b)

Scale factor for length	Area (m²)	Scale factor for area
1	1	1 = 1²
2	4	4 = 2²
3	9	9 = 3²
4	16	16 = 4²

   (c) 25 m²   **(d)** Student's check.   **(e)** $\frac{1}{4}$ m²   **(f)** Student's check.

2 16·8 m²   **3** 2 m²   **4** 117·6 cm²   **5** 1·95 m

Page 138   Just average

1 Prestonhouse 3·0
   Malbury 3·0
   Castleton 1·5
   Mertham 3·1
2 (a) 26   **(b)** 7   **(c)** 3·4   **3 (a)** 11·9 s   **(b)** 12·0 s
4 (a) 2   **(b)** 2·3   **(c)** 54
5 (a) 19·7 lengths   **(b)** 19·5 lengths   **(c)** 25 lengths
6 mean 4·5 eggs   median 4·5 eggs   mode 4 eggs
7 (a) 43·0 runs   **(b)** 41·0 runs   **8 (a)** 21 goals   3·2 or 3·3

Pages 139 and 140 Tally-Ho!

1 (a)

Points		Frequency	Frequency × points
0		2	0
1		3	3
2		5	10
3		4	12
4		5	20
5		5	25
	Total	24	70

(b) 2·9

2 (a)

Badgers Score		Frequency	Frequency × score
0		1	0
1		3	3
2		1	2
3		4	12
4		2	8
5		6	30
6		2	12
7		0	0
8		1	8
	Total	20	75

Foxes Score		Frequency	Frequency × score
0		2	0
1		4	4
2		2	4
3		2	6
4		4	16
5		4	20
6		1	6
7		3	21
8		2	16
	Total	24	93

(b) Badgers mean = 3·8
Foxes mean = 3·9
The Foxes had the better mean score.

3 (a)

Points		Frequency	Frequency × points
10		1	10
11		0	0
12		5	60
13		2	26
14		1	14
15		2	30
16		4	64
17		3	51
18		2	36
	Total	20	291

(b) mean 14·5 or 14·6
median 15
modal score 12

4 (a) mean 14·2
median 14
modal score 16

(b) If the mean or modal score is used the Foxes have the better average. The Badgers have the better average if the median score is chosen.

5 (a)

Badgers	Foxes
• mean 3·5 or 3·6	• mean 2·8
• median 4	• median 3
• modal score 2	• modal score 4

(b) If the mean or median is used the Badgers have the better average. The Foxes have the better average if the mode is chosen.

6 (a)

Badgers	Foxes
mean 3·1	mean 2·6
median 3	median 2·5
modal score 4	modal score 1

(b) The Badgers have the better average using the mean, median or modal score.

Pages 141 and 142 Scouts mean business

1 (a) 21·5 **(b)** 20 – 24 **(c)** 20 – 24

2 (a)

Distance (feet)		Frequency	Midpoint	Frequency × midpoint
8 – 10		9	9	81
11 – 13		14	12	168
14 – 16		15	15	225
17 – 19		2	18	36
	Total	40		510

(b) 12·7 feet or 12·8 feet **(c)** 14 – 16 feet **(d)** 11 – 13 feet

3 (a) 53·1 s **(b)** 45 – 59 s **(c)** 45 – 59 s

4 (a)

Time (s)		Frequency	Midpoint	Frequency × midpoint
30 – 34		4	32	128
35 – 39		17	37	629
40 – 44		5	42	210
45 – 49		9	47	423
50 – 54		5	52	260
	Total	40		1650

(b) • 41·3s • 35 – 39 s • 35 –39 s

5 (a)

Time (s)		Frequency	Midpoint	Frequency × midpoint
21 – 23		6	22	132
24 – 26		8	25	200
27 – 29		14	28	392
30 – 32		16	31	496
33 – 35		11	34	374
	Total	55		1594

(b) • 29·0 s • 30 – 32 s • 27 – 29 s

Page 143 What's the average?

1 (a) 40 – 49 years **(b)** 43·8 years **(c)** 40 – 49 years

2 (a) 3·5 – 3·9 kg **(b)** 3·5 – 3·9 kg **(c)** 3·5 kg

3 (a) 12 **(b)** 25 **(c)** 4A • 42·5 • 30 – 39 • 30 – 39
4B • 36·5 • 40 – 49 • 30 – 39

(d) Using the mean or median Class 4A has the better average. Class 4B has the better average using the mode.

Page 143   What's the average? (ctd)

4 (a) • with new nutrient 18·5 cm   • without new nutrient 16·6 cm
  (b) Plants fed with the nutrient grow taller. They have a greater mean height.

Page 144   Numbers in chains

1 6, 8, 4, 2   **2** 4, 2, 6, 8   It is the same.
3 (a) Five different chains
  (b) • A three chain 0, 5, 5
    • A sixty chain
    0, 1, 1, 2, 3, 5, 8, 3, 1, 4, 5, 9, 4, 3, 7, 0, 7, 7, 4, 1, 5, 6, 1, 7, 8, 5,
    3, 8, 1, 9, 0, 9, 9, 8, 7, 5, 2, 7, 9, 6, 5, 1, 6, 7, 3, 0, 3, 3, 6, 9, 5, 4,
    9, 3, 2, 5, 7, 2, 9, 1

Pages 145 and 146   Right on, Pythagoras!

1

Triangle	A	B	C	D	E	F
Area of smallest square in cm²	9	25	36	81	49	100
Area of middle-sized square in cm²	16	144	64	144	576	576
Sum of the areas of the 2 smallest squares in cm²	25	169	100	225	625	676
Area of largest square in cm²	25	169	100	225	625	676

2 Worksheet 18
3 (a) • 25 cm², 49 cm²   • 74 cm²   **(b)** • 81 cm², 144 cm²   • 63 cm²
  (c) • 16 cm², 49 cm²   • 33 cm²   **(d)** • 4 cm², 25 cm²   • 29 cm²
  (e) • 25 cm², 100 cm²   • 75 cm²   **(f)** • 36 cm², 64 cm²   • 28 cm²

Pages 147 and 148   Siding with Pythagoras

1 (a) 5 cm **(b)** 7 cm **(c)** 11 cm **(d)** 12 cm
2 (a) $x = 5$ cm   **(b)** $x = 17$ cm   **(c)** $x = 26$ cm   **(d)** $x = 8$ cm
  (e) $x = 12$ cm   **(f)** $x = 7$ cm   **(g)** $x = 15$ cm   **(h)** $x = 36$ cm
  (i) $x = 16$ cm
3 (a) z **(b)** p **(c)** n **(d)** d **(e)** t
4 (a) $c = 6·7$ cm   **(b)** $a = 3·9$ cm   **(c)** $b = 8·1$ cm   **(d)** $a = 1·8$ m
  (e) $a = 4·5$ m   **(f)** $c = 9·4$ cm   **(g)** $c = 18·4$ cm   **(h)** $b = 5·2$ cm
  (i) $a = 12·0$ m

Pages 149 and 150   Pythagoras in action

1 (a) $a = 4·0$ m   **(b)** $b = 1·2$ m
  (c) $c = 20·0$ m $d = 30·7$ m   **(d)** $e = 3·0$ m $f = 2·7$ m
  (e) $g = 1·7$ m   **(f)** $h = 1·3$ m
  (g) $i = 3·7$ m $j = 9·5$ m   **(h)** $k = 5·2$ m $l = 1·5$ m
  (i) $m = 8·9$ m $n = 18·3$ m   **(j)** $p = 5$ m $q = 2·0$ m
  (k) $r = 23·0$ cm   **(l)** $s = 4·1$ m

Page 151   Up, up and across

1 (a) PQ = 10·0 units   **(b)** ST = 9·4 units   **(c)** VW = 7·8 units
  (d) CD = 12·0 units   **(e)** EF = 9·2 units   **(f)** KL = 11·3 units
2 (a) kite   **(b)** SQ = 4·2 units   **(c)** PR = 7·1 units
3 7·1 units, 6·1 units, 6·1 units. Isosceles triangle.
4 12·2 km   **5** 14·2 miles   **6** 214·8 cm
7 Student shows all points lie on a circle with radius 5 units.

Page 152   Work on an egg

Practical work. Drawing circle patterns, ellipses and egg shapes.

Pages 153 and 154   Aquabeach

1 (a) Practical work. Scale drawing of main building.   **(b)** 3700 m²
2 Practical work. Various arrangements are possible.
3 (a) £4·20   **(b)** £6·41   **(c)** £11·04   **4** 2 adults, 5 children
5 (a) £13·20   **(b)** £99·96   **6 (a)** £20 583·33   **(b)** £791·67
7 (a) £19 950   **(b)** £12 600   **(c)** £6300
8 (a) 800   **(b)** 80   **(c)** 100   **(d)** 170   **(e)** 50
9 Student's pie chart showing:
    swimming pool   245°
    squash courts   36°
    outdoor facilities   52°
    multi-gym   16°
    other facilities   11°
10 (a) 35·25 years   **(b)** 30 – 39 years   **(c)** 30 – 39 years

Pages 155 and 156   The Pump Room

1 Brenda – cycle,   Nicola – rowing-machine,   Louise – steppers,
  Hayley – treadmill
2 (a)

Age, a	15	20	25	30	35	40	45	50
Maximum heart rate, M	205	200	195	190	185	180	175	170

  (b) Graph.
3 (a)

a	15	20	25	30	35	40	45	50
M	205	200	195	190	185	180	175	170
70% of M	144	140	137	133	130	126	123	119
85% of M	174	170	166	162	157	153	149	145

  (b) Graph with shading to show training zone.
4 (a) Scatter graph.
  (b) As the boys' weights increased the number of press-ups they did
    increased.
5 (a) Jim   **(b)** Several answers possible.
6 (a) $2 \times 10 + 2 \times 5$ **(b)** $2 \times 20 + 2 \times 5$ **(c)** $2 \times 20 + 2 \times 10 + 2 \times 5$
  (d) $2 \times 10 + 2 \times 5 + 2 \times 2\frac{1}{2}$ **(e)** $2 \times 20 + 2 \times 10 + 2 \times 5 + 2 \times 2\frac{1}{2}$
  (f) $4 \times 20 + 2 \times 10 + 2 \times 5 + 2 \times 2\frac{1}{2}$
7 Investigation.

Pages 157 and 158   The Tropicana Pool

1 (a) bottom row   **(b)** middle row   **(c)** top row
2 (a) 1 hour
  (b)

10 am		11 am		12 noon		1 pm		2 pm		3 pm		4 pm		5 pm
	session 1		session 4		session 7		session 10		session 13		session 16		session 19	
	session 2		session 5		session 8		session 11		session 14		session 17			
		session 3		session 6		session 9		session 12		session 15		session 18		
col 1	col 2	col 3	col 4	col 1	col 2	col 3	col 4	col 1	col 2	col 3	col 4	col 1	col 2	col 3	col 4	col 1	col 2	col 3	col 4

3 4 colours. Colours added to table in question 4b.
4 (a) 11 am, 48 minutes **(b)** 12.40 pm, 55 minutes
  (c) 14.20, 45 minutes **(d)** 4.40 pm, 1 hour
5 (a) yellow **(b)** blue **(c)** yellow **(d)** yellow
  (e) blue **(f)** blue **(g)** yellow **(h)** blue
6 53·33 metres
7 (a) 8 **(b)** Wild water channel **(c)** 1590·4 m³ **(d)** 14·4 m³
8 100 minutes **9** 6593 gallons
10 (a) • 2·88 gallons • 7·2 gallons • 67·2 gallons
  (b) • 200 people • 40 people • 8 people
11 33°C **12** 80·52 m²

Pages 159 and 160 On the run

1 • 110 m • 90 m
2 (a) Lane 1 • 110 m • 400 m
  Lane 2 • 113·7 m • 407·4 m
  Lane 3 • 117·5 m • 415 m
  Lane 4 • 121·3 m • 422·6 m
  Lane 5 • 125 m • 430 m
  Lane 6 • 128·8 m • 437·6 m
  Lane 7 • 132·6 m • 445·2 m
  Lane 8 • 136·3 m • 452·7 m
3 400 m, 407·4 m, 415 m, 422·6 m, 430 m, 437·6 m, 445·2 m, 452·7 m
4 (a) 7·4 m **(b)** 37·6 m **5 (a)** 3·7 m **(b)** 26·3 m **6** 814·8 m

7 (a) • $3\frac{3}{4}$ laps • near start of back straight
  (b) • $7\frac{1}{2}$ laps • near start of top bend
  (c) • $12\frac{1}{2}$ laps • near start of top bend

8 (a) about $7\frac{1}{4}$ laps **(b)** near start of home straight

9 Practical work. Scale diagram of running track.
10 (a) 66 000 m² **(b)** 46 200 m² **(c)** Yes. Student's explanation.
11 Practical work. Scale diagram of sports field showing possible positions of pitches.

Pages 161 and 162 Just one problem after another!

1 Length of cable required is 1434 m.
  The engineers do not have enough cable since they only have 1400 m of cable.
2 (a) £834
  (b) The cost of the holiday is £929·10. Margaret has enough money since she has £1150 available.
3 5 goals.
4 £45 is worth 14 400 drachmae. He has enough money to buy the jug which costs 14 200 drachmae.
5 (a) £5·70 **(b)** £9·12 **6** 94 m² **7 (a)** 3 **(b)** 33
8 (a) Buy 3 cans of Super Oil, total cost £12·75
  (b) Lubi-Oil. Student's explanation.
9 £5·25
10 (a)

Number of games	0	5	10	15	20
Cost for Stephanie	50	55	60	65	70

  (b) Graph.
  (c)

Number of games	0	5	10	15	20
Cost for Khalid	0	25	50	75	100

  (d) Graph.
  (e) If they were going to play 12 or less games in a year, not to pay the annual membership fee.

Answers for worksheets

W1 Lining them up

1 (a) Graph completed.
  (b) Accuracy of answers depends on graph.

Drop height (m)	1·6	2·8	4·4	7·0	7·2
Bounce height (m)	0·8	1·4	2·2	3·5	3·6

2 (a) Graph completed.
  (b) Accuracy of answers depends on graph.

Weight (g)	15	30	35	45	65
Stretch (mm)	24	48	56	72	104

W2 Getting to the point

Practical work. Drawing bearings.

W3 Transmitters of Luandata

Practical work. Locus.

W4 and W5 Mosaic patterns

1 (a)

Size (s)	1	2	3	4	5
No of tiles (n)	1	4	9	16	25

  (b) 36 **(c)** Student checks by drawing.

2 (a)

Size (s)	1	2	3	4	5
Number of tiles (n)	1	4	9	16	25
First difference		3	5	7	9
Second difference			2	2	2

  (b) $n = s^2$
  $n = s^2$
  $n = 6^2$
  $n = 36$

3 (a)

Size (s)	1	2	3	4	5
No of tiles (n)	2	5	10	17	26

Size (s)	1	2	3	4	5
Number of tiles (n)	2	5	10	17	26
First difference		3	5	7	9
Second difference			2	2	2

The second difference is 2 so the formula begins with s^2

Size² (s²)	1	4	9	16	25
No of tiles (n)	2	5	10	17	26

Number of tiles = size² + 1 or $n = s^2 + 1$
  (b) Size 6 has 37 tiles. Student checks by drawing.
4 (a) $n = s^2 + 3$
  Size 6 has 39 tiles. Student checks by drawing.
  (b) $n = s^2 + 6$
  Size 6 has 42 tiles. Student checks by drawing.

W6 Lines and points

I Practical work. Number of axes of symmetry on shapes should be:
(a) I **(b)** 2 **(c)** I **(d)** 6 **(e)** 5 **(f)** 2
(g) I **(h)** 5 **(i)** I **(j)** 8 **(k)** 6 **(l)** 8

2 Practical work. Diagrams with axes of symmetry.

W7 About the point

I Table completed to show:

	Isosceles triangle	Equilateral triangle	Rectangle	Square	Rhombus	Kite	Parallelogram
No of axes of symmetry	I	3	2	4	2	I	0
Order of rotational symmetry	none	3	2	4	2	none	2

2 Practical work. Diagrams with rotational symmetry.

W8, W9 and W10 Hexagon, Square and Triangle Games

Board games.

W11 Sunningdale

	September Weekend Booking Form				
	Caravan I sleeps 3	Caravan 2 sleeps 3	Caravan 3 sleeps 5	Caravan 4 sleeps 5	Caravan 5 sleeps 6
Friday 28th	Burke		Clark	Dalton	Farren
Saturday 29th	Burke	Ford	Clark	Dalton	Farren
Sunday 30th	Jones	Ford	Clark	Dalton	Farren
Monday Ist	Jones	Ford		Pennel	
Tuesday 2nd				Pennel	

W12 and W13 Face the music

I (a)

Total no of albums sold	1	2	3	4	5	10	20	30	40	50	60	70	80	90	100
Relative frequency of cassette sales	$\frac{1}{1}$	$\frac{2}{2}$	$\frac{2}{3}$	$\frac{2}{4}$	$\frac{3}{5}$	$\frac{6}{10}$	$\frac{10}{20}$	$\frac{17}{30}$	$\frac{20}{40}$	$\frac{24}{50}$	$\frac{26}{60}$	$\frac{31}{70}$	$\frac{38}{80}$	$\frac{45}{90}$	$\frac{48}{100}$
Relative frequency to 2 dp	1·0	1·0	0·67	0·5	0·6	0·6	0·5	0·57	0·5	0·48	0·43	0·44	0·47 or 0·48	0·5	0·48

(b)

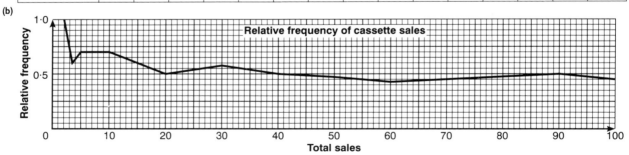

(c) • No   • It settles down to a value of 0·5   • 0·5

2 (a)

Total no of albums sold	1	2	3	4	5	10	20	30	40	50	60	70	80	90	100
Relative frequency of CD sales	0	0	$\frac{1}{3}$	$\frac{1}{4}$	$\frac{1}{5}$	$\frac{3}{10}$	$\frac{7}{20}$	$\frac{8}{30}$	$\frac{15}{40}$	$\frac{21}{50}$	$\frac{27}{60}$	$\frac{29}{70}$	$\frac{31}{80}$	$\frac{34}{90}$	$\frac{39}{100}$
Relative frequency to 2 dp	0	0	0·33	0·25	0·2	0·3	0·35	0·27	0·37	0·42	0·45	0·41	0·39	0·38	0·39

(b) Graph.
(c) • No • It settles down to a value of 0·4 • 0·4

3 (a)

Total no of albums sold	1	2	3	4	5	10	20	30	40	50	60	70	80	90	100
Relative frequency of record sales	0	0	0	$\frac{1}{4}$	$\frac{1}{5}$	$\frac{1}{10}$	$\frac{3}{20}$	$\frac{5}{30}$	$\frac{5}{40}$	$\frac{5}{50}$	$\frac{7}{60}$	$\frac{10}{70}$	$\frac{11}{80}$	$\frac{11}{90}$	$\frac{13}{100}$
Relative frequency to 2 dp	0	0	0	0·25	0·2	0·1	0·15	0·17	0·12	0·1	0·12	0·14	0·14	0·12	0·13

(b) Graph.
(c) • No • It settles down to a value of 0·1 • 0·1

W14 Questionnaire responses

1 Q1

Type of music	Tally marks	Frequency
Rock	ЖЖ |||	8
Easy listening	ЖЖ	5
Jazz	ЖЖ	5
Classical	||	2
	Total	20

Q4

Format	Tally marks	Frequency
CD	ЖЖ |||	8
Cassette	ЖЖ ЖЖ	10
Record	||	2
	Total	20

Q9

Age	Tally marks	Frequency
Under 17	|||	3
17 – 24	||||	4
25 – 32	||	2
33 – 40	ЖЖ |||	8
Over 40	|||	3
	Total	20

W15 Ellerman Electrical

1 (a) Cost in £
375
286
56
‾‾‾‾
717
25·80
129·99
‾‾‾‾
872·79

(b) Cost in £
138·24
169·20
120·96
‾‾‾‾
428·40
4·75
75·80
‾‾‾‾
508·95

(c)
Quantity	Cost in £
9	186·12
15	169·20
5	70·00
	‾‾‾‾
	425·32
	9·75
	76·14
	‾‾‾‾
	511·21

(d)
Quantity	Cost in £
30	138·00
36	353·28
	23·00
	‾‾‾‾
	514·28
	16·00
	92·80
	‾‾‾‾
	623·08

W16 Credit cards

1 (a) Present balance £119·61. Available credit £1380·39
(b) Present balance £44·32. Available credit £1955·68
(c) Payment £97·80 CR. Credit limit £1500

W17 Angling around

Tangents
Students drawings and measurements.
All angles are 90°

Angles in a semi-circle
Students drawings and measurements.
All angles are 90°

W18 A square fit!

Practical work. The area of square C is equal to the sum of the areas of square A and square B.

Heinemann Educational Publishers
Halley Court, Jordan Hill, Oxford OX2 8EJ
a division of Reed Educational & Professional Publishing Ltd

MELBOURNE AUCKLAND FLORENCE PRAGUE
MADRID ATHENS SINGAPORE TOKYO
SÃO PAULO CHICAGO PORTSMOUTH (NH)
MEXICO IBADAN GABORONE JOHANNESBURG
KAMPALA NAIROBI

First published 1994

96 10 9 8 7 6 5 4

ISBN 0 435 52982 X

Designed and produced by VAP Group Ltd., Kidlington, Oxford

Illustrated by Jane Bottomley and Trevor Mason

Printed in Spain by Mateu Cromo

The authors and publishers would like to thank the following for permission to use photographs:

Cover photo: Oxford Scientific Films

p. 29 Action-Plus/Chris Barry; p. 30 Action-Plus/Mike Hewitt; p. 31 Action-Plus/Mike Hewitt; p. 114 Picturepoint Ltd; p. 137 Picturepoint Ltd; p. 72 Science Photo Library (NASA); p. 96 P.J. Bridgman & Co. Ltd; p. 106 Collections/Brian Shuel; p. 127 Robert Harding Picture Library; p. 128 Barnaby's Picture Library; p. 129 Barnaby's Picture Library and Britstock; p. 161 Allsport.

Acknowledgements:

We would also like to thank Ordnance Survey for the use of Crown Copyright material on page 49 and Aquatec, Motherwell for assistance with pages 153–160.